FINLAND IN THE TWENTIETH CENTURY

FINLAND

in the Twentieth Century

by

D. G. KIRBY

UNIVERSITY OF MINNESOTA PRESS
MINNEAPOLIS

Published in the United States of America
by the University of Minnesota Press,
2037 University Avenue Southeast,
Minneapolis, Minnesota 55455

Library of Congress Cataloging in Publication Data
Kirby, D. G.
  Finland in the twentieth century.
  Bibliography: p.
  Includes index.
  1. Finland—Politics and government—20th century
I. Title.
DK459.K57   1979   309.1'471'03   79-11651
ISBN 0-8166-0895-4

The University of Minnesota Press is an equal-opportunity educator and
employer.
Printed in Great Britain

To my father-in-law
who has lived through it all

'We are only a little country. A little new country. You must not be surprised if sometimes we do not seem to do things so well as you big countries who have been big countries for so long. You big countries do not know what it is like to be a little country. We are not used to being even a little country yet. You big countries do all the things so well that we little countries do not so well do yet.'

'Oh, but I am sure that you do. You seem to me to do everything so much better than in the big countries. That is why I enjoy being here so much.'

Anthony Powell, Venusberg (London 1932)

CONTENTS

MAP

PREFACE

Finland is a country which seldom makes the headlines in the world press. It is a relative newcomer to the ranks of independent states, situated on the northern periphery of Europe. The majority of its 4·6 million inhabitants speak a language which few foreigners ever manage to comprehend. Isolation has indeed been Finland's fate—or misfortune. As a result, its recent history is little known, even to historians, outside Finland. The present survey seeks to remedy this situation. I have sought to give not only an account of the political history of the republic, but also some idea of what it is to be a Finn in the modern world. I have also tried to present an impression of recent trends in Finnish historical research. History is a serious business for a 'new' nation, and the outsider writes his version at his peril. For my own solecisms and errors, I crave indulgence from my Finnish colleagues, without whose work this book truly could not have been written.

I am indebted to more people than I can mention here; but I would like to record a special debt of gratitude to Professors Hannu Soikkanen, Juhani Paasivirta, Ragnhild Hatton and Bill Mead for their help, advice and encouragement over many years: to Dr. Eino Lyytinen, Dr. Bill Copeland, Dr. Jorma Kalela, Dr. Martti Häikiö, Martti Turtola and Tony Upton for the stimulation generated in numerous discussions; and to Dr. George Maude, Dr. John Screen, Dr. Olga Crisp and Thomas Munch-Petersen for their valuable comments on sections of the typescript. I am also grateful to Suhrkamp Verlag for allowing me to quote the extract from Brecht's *Flüchtlingsgespräche*, and to William Heinemann Ltd. for permission to reprint the passage from Anthony Powell's novel *Venusberg*. Thanks are also due to the School of Slavonic and East European Studies for granting me study leave and to the Leverhulme Trust and Hayter Research Fund for financial assistance. The Department of Political History of the University of Turku also gave me an opportunity to pursue my research during the spring of 1977. Last but by no means least, I am forever indebted to my wife and relatives for their unfailing support and tolerance.

DAVID KIRBY

August 1978

Finland since 1944

I

THE BACKGROUND:
FINLAND IN 1900

'L'homme, de toutes les manières, a de la peine à lutter contre la nature dans ces climats glacés. On rencontre peu de villes en Finlande, et celles qui existent ne sont guère peuplées. Il ny' a pas de centre, pas d'émulation, rien à dire et bien peu à faire dans une province du nord suédois ou russe, et pendant huit mois de l'année, toute la nature vivante s'endort.'

Mme de Staël, *Dix années d'exil*
(*Oeuvres complètes*, Tome XV, Paris 1821, p. 352)

Finland in 1900 was vastly different from the republic of today. A part of the Swedish realm since the Middle Ages, the Grand Duchy of Finland had passed to Russia in 1809. Although Finland under the Russian emperors—who assumed the title of Grand Duke of Finland—enjoyed a wide degree of self-government, it did not, like Poland, have a history of independent statehood to look back on, and few people in 1900 could have predicted that Finland would become an independent state some seventeen years later. Urho Kaleva Kekkonen, who was to become President of the Finnish Republic for the first time in 1956 and who still occupies that office at the time of writing, was born on 3 September 1900 into a world still shaped by the age-old practices and traditions of an agrarian society. Most Finns were poor; most eked some sort of living out of an infertile and sparse soil; most spoke Finnish, though the small minority who were wealthy or who occupied offices of prestige for the most part still spoke Swedish. Although Finland was experiencing profound economic and social changes, the way of life in which Kekkonen grew to adolescence would have been very familiar to his ancestors in many essential features. During Kekkonen's lifetime, all this has changed for ever. The transformation of Finland from a remote and backward agrarian region on the periphery of Europe into

1

a modern, streamlined European state the citizens of which enjoy an enviably high standard of living is the major theme of this present work. What follows in this introductory chapter is an attempt to set the scene at the dawn of this present century, when the very idea of an impoverished farmer's son from remote north-eastern Finland becoming the head of an independent Finnish republic some fifty years later would have been utterly unthinkable.

Economy and society

Nature has not been kind to Finland. Lying between higher latitudes (60°–70°N.) than any other independent country, and frozen in along her Baltic coastline during the long winter months, Finland also lacks the benefits of a fertile soil or of mineral wealth. The history of the Finnish people is primarily the story of man's struggle to survive in a harsh and hostile environment, neatly summed up in a fragment of verse by the nineteenth century Finnish poet, J. L. Runeberg:

Vi Europas förpost mot naturen
Mellan isar är vår lager skuren
Och vårt bröd vi ryckt ur is och snö

We are Europe's outpost against Nature
Set down amidst the ice
And our bread have we wrested from ice and snow.[1]

During Runeberg's lifetime, a substitute bread made out of chaff and birch-bark was a staple item in the diet of many households in eastern and northern Finland, even during years of normal harvests. When the harvest failed, the effect was often catastrophic. It has been estimated that some 100,000 people, or 8 per cent of the total population, died of disease or starvation in the famine years of 1867–8. Between 1749 and 1865, the population of Finland had risen almost fourfold. This increase placed an intolerable burden on the country's backward self-sufficiency economy. By the middle of the nineteenth century, crop cultivation was unable to keep pace with the rising population. In other words, the four-fifths of the population who earned their livelihood from the land could not produce enough to feed themselves or the remaining one-fifth. Hence the bitter paradox of agricultural backwardness and growing economic overpopulation in the countryside in a sparsely inhabited land.

Table 1

POPULATION OF FINLAND, 1750–1900

Year	Total population	Living in:			
		Urban districts		Rural districts	
1750	421,500	—	—	—	—
1800	832,700	46,600	5·6%	786,100	94·4%
1820*	1,177,600	63,400	5·4%	1,114,200	94·6%
1840	1,445,600	84,600	5·8%	1,361,000	94·2%
1860	1,746,700	110,300	6·3%	1,636,400	93·7%
1880	2,060,800	174,300	8·5%	1,886,500	91·5%
1900	2,655,900	333,300	12·5%	2,322,600	87·5%

* Finland acquired some 200,000 extra inhabitants as a result of frontier changes in 1809 and 1811

Source: *Suomen tilastollinen vuosikirja, Uusi sarja. LXVII: Vuonna 1971*, Helsinki 1972, p. 5

As Table 1 demonstrates, there was no appreciable increase in the proportion of urban population in Finland until the end of the nineteenth century. Not until the first decade of the twentieth century did the number of town dwellers exceed one-tenth of the total population, a percentage that had been exceeded in neighbouring Sweden by the 1880s. Similarly, whereas the proportion of the Swedish population dependent on industry for its livelihood was 32 per cent in 1910, the corresponding Finnish figure was a mere 12·2 per cent. Not until after the Second World War did the proportion of Finns dependent on industry reach pre-First World War Swedish levels. During the second half of the nineteenth century, the problem of rural overpopulation was largely overcome in Sweden—and to a lesser degree in Norway—by the growth of industry and by emigration. Finland lagged behind in both respects. Industrial growth from the 1870s was not sufficient to absorb the pool of surplus labour, and emigration to the New World, which began at a relatively late date due to legal restrictions on movement which were not finally abolished until the 1880s, drained off a much lower percentage of the total population than in Sweden and Norway. It is true that the industrial area of St. Petersburg attracted numbers of Finns, particularly from eastern Finland, but not in sufficient numbers to alleviate significantly the pressure on land. This pressure was made even more intolerable by the sharp rise in land values from the 1870s onwards as the result of increased demand for

timber and timber products on world markets. In the long run, however, the rise in land values laid the foundation for the modern Finnish
economy, and there is good reason to take the year 1870 as a notional
starting-point of modern Finnish history.

In his recent study of traditional farming methods in Finland, Arvo
Soininen has argued that by 1870, agriculture was at the end of a blind
alley, and was only saved by the increased demand for timber, which
helped recapitalise farming. The money from the sale of timber enabled
the peasant farmer to move from the traditionalist self-sufficiency
farming of his ancestors towards modern methods of cultivation based
on extensive use of implements. He was also able to raise his standard
of living, and even to acquire the trappings of gentility by means of
purchasing an estate. The emphasis in agricultural production now
shifted away from cereals to stock-rearing and forestry, with the net
result that Finland, which had not even been able to produce enough
bread grain in previous decades to feed her growing population, was by
1910 having to import more than half her annual demand for bread
grains. On the other hand, rapid strides were made in dairy farming,
and dairy products were marketed with some success in Russia and in
Western markets. The major export commodity was however timber
and timber products. The forests of Finland had always provided
valuable export commodities such as tar and sawn timber, but exploitation was hindered by restrictive legislation from the mercantilist
era, and lack of communications and capital. The abolition of restrictions on the building of steam-driven sawmills and the cutting of
timber in the early years of the reign of Alexander II (1855–81), the
gradual lowering and final abolition of customs duties on imported
timber goods into the United Kingdom in the 1860s, and the improvement of internal and external communications in Finland simu-
lated output of timber goods and the establishment of new sawmills
on the Bothnian coast and, in particular, at the mouth of the river
Kymi in southern Finland. Between 1875 and 1914, exports of sawn
goods quadrupled: by the first decade of this century, they comprised
over two-fifths of the total value of exports, and if exports of uncut
timber, pulp and paper products are added, the share of the total value
exceeded 70 per cent by 1913. The timber industry was also the major
employer of industrial labour, providing work for 31,347 out of a total
industrial workforce of 102,751 in 1912.[2] By the outbreak of the war
in 1914, the pulp and paper industry was beginning to catch up, and
by the 1930s it had overtaken timber as the leading export industry.
Together the two branches have dominated the Finnish economy since

1870: the 'green gold' of the forests has affected the course of life in Finland as fundamentally as coal and cotton revolutionised British society in the early nineteenth century.

Remarkably, the rapid expansion of the timber processing industries was achieved within the modest framework of Finnish capitalism. There was relatively little foreign investment in Finland, and even in items of major capital expenditure such as the expansion of the state railway network, foreign loans were kept to a minimum. The timber and pulp industries were largely financed by old-established trading companies: thus Turku merchants invested capital earned from the import trade into pulpmills in the Kymi valley in the 1870s, laying the foundations for what was to become by 1904 the largest pulp and paper concern (Kymin Oy.) in Northern Europe, with a capital stock of 11·2 million marks, more than double that of its nearest Finnish rival, also a pulp and paper concern.

Although many of the obstacles to industrialisation had been removed by the 1870s, Finland remained an agrarian country in which the one raw material which grew in abundance provided the basis for the expansion of the timber processing industries and of foreign trade. Other industries showed little signs of growth. A number of textile mills had been founded in the early years of the nineteenth century, but their output remained modest and catered mainly for the small domestic market. The iron and copper smelting industries, much favoured by the mercantilist state in Swedish times, were mostly unprofitable. The metal industry was unable to compete with the rapidly expanding industries elsewhere in the Russian empire, and had to content itself with providing for increasing domestic demand. The Marxist economist Aleksandra Kollontay, while asserting in 1903 that Finland was entering a period of major capitalist growth, was unable to detect any signs of vigorous capital formation in the metal industry or any of the abrupt symptoms of the processes of capitalism encountered in the industrial countries of western Europe. More recently, the Finnish historian Eino Jutikkala has characterised the economic situation in Finland at the beginning of the twentieth century as one of gestation rather than breakthrough, although the prerequisites for industrialisation had been created.

Increased economic activity also hastened the demise of the pre-industrial social order, based upon rank, status and privilege. Jutikkala has pointed out that Gustavian legislation had to some extent helped to weaken rigid and fixed privileges. Gustav III's Act of Union and Assurance of 1789, for example, opened the way for peasants to buy estates bearing exemption from payment of land dues to the Crown, and permitted peasants to engage as many servants as they wished. In addition to strengthening the rights of the peasantry, the 1789 Act, by throwing open high offices of state to non-nobles, undermined a privilege hitherto jealously guarded by the nobility.

Gustav III was not however seeking to destroy the socio-political structure of the *ancien régime*. His main concern was to restore the power and authority of the Swedish Crown. Much of this work was undone in the Swedish revolution of 1809, but by then Finland had passed into the *de facto* possession of the Russian emperor. Russia had declared war on Sweden in 1808, and by the end of that year was in possession of most of Finland. The final severance of Finland from Sweden occurred at the Peace of Hamina, concluded on 17 September 1809. Emperor Alexander I had, however, arrived at a political settlement with his new Finnish subjects in the spring of that year, at the Diet of Porvoo. The Diet which the Emperor convened was in fact a provincial assembly (*Lantdag*), rather than a national Diet (*Riksdag*), and comprised the traditional four estates (clergy, nobility, burghers and peasants), whose rights and privileges were confirmed by the Emperor in a Charter issued on 27 March 1809. The definition of these rights and privileges was to become a matter of hot dispute in the latter half of the nineteenth century. In effect, the Diet of 1809 was a gathering of the privileged orders of society, the estates, to affirm their loyalty to the new ruler in return for his pledge to observe and respect their rights and privileges. It was a curious bargain between a representative institution (representing the estates, rather than the nation, let it be said) and an autocratic ruler of a country of which the social and political traditions were vastly different from those of Finland: but on the whole, it served remarkably well as the working basis for the relationship between the new ruler, the Emperor–Grand Duke and the Grand Duchy of Finland. It also provided the basic framework within which Finnish society could develop towards political maturity, even though it was ultimately to hinder the fulfilment of that maturity, as we shall see.

Suddenly cut off from the Swedish motherland after almost 700 years of Swedish rule, the Finns had to face up to the problem of adjusting to new circumstances, which in some respects led to the strengthening of the traditional structure of society in Finland. The aristocracy discovered a new outlet for their talents in the Russian empire. By 1850, over one-fifth of the adult male Finnish nobility was in the imperial service. During the period of Russian rule (1809–1917) the imperial Russian army attracted over 3,000 Finns, mostly but not exclusively from the aristocracy. A disproportionately high number of these recruits attained the rank of general, a clear indication of their ambition and ability to acquire rank and status in the empire. The nobility also dominated the upper echelons of the small Finnish bureaucracy until the end of the century. However, rising costs, which the impecunious Finnish aristocracy were unable to meet, and growing Russian chauvinism led to a decline in the entry of nobles into Russian service after 1860, and the dominant position of the nobility in the bureaucracy was weakened by the expansion of public services in Finland in this same period. Nevertheless, the contribution of the Finnish nobility to the relationship between Finland and the Russian empire, and towards the development of the future Finnish state, was considerable. In particular, the nobility continued the tradition of service to the state established in Swedish times, and in so doing helped to strengthen sentiments of loyalty towards the ruler. Had the emperors been faced with a factious and discontented nobility in Finland as they were in Poland, the course of Finnish history might well have been very different.

The traditions, pretensions and assumptions of the Finnish aristocracy were in any event very different from those of the Polish nobility. There were no great princes in Finland, owning vast estates and controlling the lives of thousands of servile peasants. The typical Finnish nobleman of the early nineteenth century was a former officer of the Swedish army who farmed a modest estate. For such men, service in Russia offered an opportunity for social and economic advancement, and service to the state was in any event a part of the noble tradition in Finland.

Table 2

SOCIAL GROUPINGS IN FINLAND, 1890

'Estate'	Members	%
Nobility	2,976	0·12
Clergy	6,251	0·26
Burghers	74,062	3·11
Peasants	622,312	26·15
Others	1,674,539	70·36
Total population	2,380,140	100·00

Source: *Entsiklopedicheskiy slovar*, Vol. 35, St. Petersburg 1902, p. 919

Table 2 shows how small were the first three estates, which were virtually synonymous with the ruling élite, and underlines the dangers of a constant drain of talented young men into service in the Russian empire. For much of the period of Russian rule, Finland was unable to provide adequate employment for able young men coming out of university; and since their university qualification enabled them to enter imperial Russian service at a higher point in the Table of Ranks than a Russian of comparable background, many took this course and were lost to their native land.

Imperial Russia therefore provided an attractive alternative to members of the small Finnish ruling élite during the early decades of Russian rule. There was no obvious conflict of loyalties towards the Emperor and local patriotism, and no discrimination against Finns as a distinctly separate linguistic group within the empire. Although a few bureaucrats urged the necessity of introducing the teaching of Russian into all levels of Finnish education, very little was done. Those who wished to serve the Emperor outside Finland had to learn Russian: but those wishing to enter his service in his capacity as Grand Duke of Finland needed only the command of Swedish and, from the 1870s onwards, Finnish. Swedish, which was spoken by a small minority of peasants and fishermen on the southern and western coasts, was also the language of the ruling élite and the official language of state at all levels until Finnish was given a degree of parity in 1863 and 1886. That Finnish, the language of the peasants who constituted the majority of the inhabitants of the Grand Duchy, was given official status was due to the efforts of those members of ruling élite who abandoned Swedish to champion Finnish as the only true language for a Finnish nation. In the language conflict which developed during the nineteenth century, Russian was to play little part.

Once again, the year 1870 may conveniently be taken as a turning-point in the history of modern Finland. Growing Russian chauvinism, which began to affect the career prospects of non-Russians in the empire, and the expansion of job opportunities in Finland with the quickening of commercial and industrial activity made the idea of service in Russia much less attractive. The composition of the student body at the University of Helsinki, the major channel for social advancement in Finland by virtue of its function as a training institution for the clergy and the bureaucracy, also began to change. The development of secondary education in the Finnish language and the granting of parity with Swedish for Finnish as an official language afforded opportunities hitherto unknown for a new generation of Finnish-speaking young men of peasant background. Before 1870 the proportion of peasants' sons entering university was probably no more than 7 per cent, but by the early 1880s, this proportion had doubled, and there was also a much higher influx of Finnish-speaking peasants' sons in comparison with the sons of Swedish-speaking peasants. By 1899 the number of Finnish-speaking entrants to university had begun to exceed the number of Swedish-speaking entrants, and by the spring of 1917, three-quarters of all university entrants were Finnish-speaking. The number of students enrolled at the University of Helsinki rose rapidly, from 2,400 in the autumn of 1899 to 3,659 in the autumn of 1915, giving Finland the highest proportion of students per 100,000 inhabitants in Northern Europe. Although the University's role as a training-ground for the élite had somewhat diminished with the founding of other institutions of higher education such as the Poly-technic (*Teknillinen Korkeakoulu*), it still occupied a central position in Finland's cultural and political life.

As a result of the rise in demand for timber, many freehold peasant farmers (*talolliset*) with forested land grew rich. Freed from restrictions on the disposal of their own land, and from 1864 free to buy the estates of the nobility on the open market, many peasant farmers began to aspire to the trappings of gentility. Conscious of his lack of education, the peasant farmer was eager for his sons to get on in the world, and not infrequently acquired the latest volumes of a growing Finnish literature. He invested in machinery, studied the latest farming methods, read newspapers and was active in setting up savings banks and pro-ducers' co-operatives. His wife was able to buy luxuries and to furnish her house with genteel sideboards, tables and chairs in place of the roughly-hewn benches and chests of former years.

This new-found affluence of the freehold peasant farmer served to emphasise the growing gulf between the landowning minority and the impoverished landless majority. Before the rise in land values and in the price of timber, social and economic differences in the countryside had been less marked. It had been a common practice, for example, for farmer and farm servants to live under the same roof and eat at the same table. Now the servants were increasingly housed and fed separately, and the farmer (*talollinen*) sought to identify himself with the gentlefolk (*herrasväki*) rather than with the common people (*rahvas*).

Finnish literature is rich in descriptions of the grinding poverty which was the lot of the majority who lived on the land. In *Tähtien alla* (Beneath the stars, 1910), Maila Talvio portrayed one such family as possessing only one pair of shoes which was shared by four girls: the four boys had no shoes at all. Addiction to alcohol was a particular curse and added to the burden of misery and degradation. For the poor, coffee was the height of luxury. The parsimonious tenant-farmer Jussi in Väinö Linna's novel *Täällä pohjan tähden alla* (Here under the pole star) suffers agonies every time there is a special occasion, since this means that coffee will have to be bought.[3] The glaring differences between the 'haves' and the 'have-nots' prompted a non-socialist observer to write in 1912 that 'the latent conflict of interests of the landowners and the landless has become ever more apparent as the landowners, both the gentry and the peasants, strive more and more energetically to exploit the landless . . . all of which goes to show the existence of real class differences'.[4]

Of those sections of the rural community which did not own land, the leasehold farmers (*torpparit*) were to cause the most discussion at the beginning of this century. Before the mid-nineteenth century, the pressure on land caused by a rising population had been somewhat eased by the creation of new leasehold farms (*torpat*), for which the rent was largely paid in the form of day labour on the landlord's farm. By 1860 there were some 63,000 of these farms, mostly in southern Finland, but the subsequent rise in land values and timber prices virtually put an end to the creation of new *torpat*. The leaseholder was subjected to demands for increased day labour, and since tenancy agreements were usually oral, he suffered the additional anxiety of a lack of security of tenure. In addition to these leasehold farms, many of which were of reasonable size, there were by 1912 some 95,000 scrapholdings, again mostly located in southern Finland, which were far too small to provide a decent living for the tenant (*mäkitupalainen*) and his dependants. These and the landless farmhands made up the bulk of the reserve army of rural labour. Aleksandra Kollontay, at the end of the nineteenth century, estimated that some 865,916 persons came into this category. These people were either unable to earn a living from their land or were landless, or had no trade or vocation and who supported themselves by seasonal and casual work. Recent research would suggest that of those engaged in agriculture in 1910, roughly 40 per cent were freehold farmers, 20 per cent leased their land, and 40 per cent were farmworkers with little or no land. Over three-quarters of all Finnish farms in 1910 were of less than ten hectares in size, and over half were less than five hectares, the minimum size of a holding on which a man might support himself and his family, according to the 1900 Senate commission on landholding in Finland. Furthermore, the smaller the land unit, the more likely it was to be held on lease.

Finland at the turn of the century was a country in which the great majority of its predominantly farming population cultivated smallholdings of 10 hectares or less. Given the harshness of the climate and the poverty of the soil, one can only conclude that such small farms could hardly have yielded a very good living even in good times—and it should be noted that 10 hectares was regarded as an absolute minimum for self-sufficiency by Finnish agronomists in the 1920s. It is certainly highly unlikely that the small farmer would have been able to accumulate sufficient capital to improve his efficiency. More and more, he was compelled to sell his labour to make ends meet. Kollontay observed at the turn of the century that large numbers of the landless poor and the 'middle peasantry', or small farmers, sought seasonal employment in the forests and on the log floats. On the other hand, the age-old phenomenon of the rural poor of eastern Finland having to turn to begging in the winter months virtually disappeared with the advent of regular seasonal work in the woods.

The 'green gold' brought wealth and employment, but it also aggravated the disintegration of traditional rural society. The peasant landowner who made money from the sale of his timber also sought to improve his standing in society. He bought up noble estates, and compelled his tenants to perform extra day labour services, thereby diminishing their own aspirations as farmers. He deprived the landless of their ancient rights to the forests, and he no longer fed and housed his servants in his own house, but in separate accommodation. The forests did provide work for thousands, but it was seasonal employ-ment. The rapid growth of the timber processing industry was still not enough to soak up the surplus supply of rural labour. In fact, it could be argued that the forests and the rural-based timber industry acted as a brake on migration from the countryside to the towns, providing local—if seasonal—employment. The only major industrial city in the region was St. Petersburg, which attracted large numbers of Finnish workers. Engman has estimated that there were over 24,000 Finns in the city in 1884, the third largest urban concentration of Finns in the Baltic region. Most of these immigrants were employed in industry and handicrafts, and some were sufficiently enterprising to advance their careers in Finland after receiving training in St. Petersburg. Even though the number of Finns in the metropolis had fallen to around 17,000 by 1910, St. Petersburg still attracted migrants in search of work. The opportunities for employment in the small southern Finnish towns were few by comparison. The problem of winter unemploy-ment, especially among construction workers, was particularly acute in Helsinki for example. Nevertheless, the urban population of Finland more than trebled between 1870 and 1910, even though it still con-stituted less than 15 per cent of the total national population.[5]

Foreign travellers in Finland were in fact struck by the absence of any centre or large town. The population of Turku, the administrative capital until 1827, was just over 10,000 in 1810, while that of Helsinki did not exceed 20,000 until the middle of the century. The citizens of Helsinki still drove their cattle out to graze in the nearby meadows until the end of the century, while as late as the 1840s wolves were sighted roaming the streets in the very city centre. Mme de Staël had earlier remarked that the close attendance of wolves and bears in the winter distracted the thoughts of students at the University in Turku. A German visitor in the 1830s observed of Helsinki that it presented to the world fine façades with nothing behind them, an observation substantiated by contemporary drawings: behind the beautiful neo-classical buildings designed by C. L. Engel to house the University and the administration lay a jumble of wooden houses and fishermen's shacks. By the end of the century, however, the city was beginning to spread beyond the carefully planned confines laid down in the early years of Russian rule. The wooden houses were torn down to make way for five- and six-storey brick and stone buildings, and in the words of the writer Juhani Aho, the city took on a truly 'continental' atmos-phere, with street cafés, elegant shops and ladies dressed *à la mode*. Of the city's 91,216 inhabitants in 1900, 42·5 per cent were Swedish-speaking, 50·7 per cent spoke Finnish as their mother tongue, 4·7 per cent Russian and 1·1 per cent German. The Russian element was made up mainly of soldiers, with a smattering of shopkeepers, barbers and ice-cream salesmen. Helsinki also had a small Jewish community, which held its bazaar, or *narinka*, in the poorer quarter of the city. The upper class was almost exclusively Swedish-speaking. In 1892 there were still only five secondary schools for Finnish speakers in the city as against eight for Swedish speakers. The upper class lived in the fine new houses in the city centre, the poorer classes lived in wooden houses to the west and in particular across the bridge leading north. By 1900, some 20,000 people were living in exceedingly cramped conditions in the working-class quarter 'north of the bridge'. Research carried out in 1901 showed that 68 per cent of the city's working class population lived in one-room accommodation, as compared with only 14 per cent in Stockholm. In the city as a whole, there was an average of 3·4 inhabitants per room: north of the bridge, this was as high as 4·6. The incidence of disease and infant mortality was significantly higher in working-class districts than elsewhere, as were cases of drunkenness and venereal disease. In 1915 the famous architect Eliel Saarinen saw the city as already divided into rich and poor quarters, with the upper class living in the centre and the working class on the periphery. This pattern was repeated on a more modest scale in other large towns in Finland.

By 1900, the process of economic transformation whereby the agrarian structure of society was replaced by the class society of the industrial world was under way in Finland. Nevertheless, many of the attitudes which characterised pre-industrial society still remained. Life in the countryside and provincial towns went on much as it had done for centuries. Loyalty towards the God-appointed ruler and respect towards authority was instilled in the people by the Lutheran Church, and was hardly questioned.

There were two sorts of people, the 'gentlefolk' (*säätylaiset* or *herrasväki*) and the common people (*rahvas*), divided not so much by wealth or political status as by language and culture: a small farmer might possess the right to vote for the Peasants' Estate of the Diet, but not a rural magistrate, and a cobbler might have established rights, but not a non-noble president of the High Court. Finnish was the language of the common people, and Swedish that of polite society. Despite the efforts of the Finnish nationalists—most of whom had made the conscious decision to forgo their mother tongue, Swedish—the countryman remained largely indifferent to his own language and cared little about the language conflict which went on in the nation's capital.

Nevertheless, even the most remote villages slowly became aware of change. In his novel *Rautatie* (The Railway), Juhani Aho portrays the unbelievably monotonous life of an elderly couple in northern Savo, relieved only by the passing of the seasons, the lightening and darkening of the days, and the occasional visit to the village some miles away. When the railway comes to the village, even the backwoods couple have to take a ride on it. Aho skilfully notes how the railway changes society. The wages earned by a railway worker are noticeably higher than those of a farmhand; there is a new 'aristocracy' of inspectors, conductors and stationmasters, resplendent in their uniforms and dignified by their calling. The railways, emigration to the New World or migration to the factory or town helped open up the Finnish countryside, as did the building of elementary schools from the 1880s and the establishment of shops after the abolition of restrictions on trading in country areas. Economically and socially, the Finnish countryside was in a state of transformation: its political awakening was yet to come as the nineteenth century came to a close.

The political background

The Finnish people have not only had to contend throughout their history with a hostile environment; they have also been burdened with a highly unfavourable geographical location. Finland is on the periphery of the European continent, and shares a frontier of over 800 miles with the Soviet Union. These two immutable features have played a major role in the historical development of Finland. Her peripheral position has meant that the great cultural and intellectual advances of mainland Europe have been slow to penetrate, while in the division of Europe into two widely different political and religious traditions—Roman and Catholic on the one hand, Byzantine and Orthodox on the other— Finland was placed on the northernmost border. During the Middle Ages, the Swedish Crown and the Catholic Church established control over the Finnish tribes as far east as the Karelian isthmus. The Finnish-speaking Karelians, however, came under the looser control of the Orthodox Church and the city-republic of Novgorod and, at the end of the fifteenth century, Muscovy.

The frontier was pushed eastwards beyond Lake Ladoga in 1617, and for a little less than a century the newly-acquired Karelian frontier zone, which was never absorbed into the administrative structure of Finland proper, helped to provide a land bridge for the Swedish empire between Finland and Livonia, and protected Finland. This protection failed in 1714, when Russian troops occupied Finland. Although Finland was returned to Sweden in 1721, Livonia and the Karelian border-lands, including the ancient Swedish fortress of Viipuri, remained in the possession of Peter the Great whose new capital St. Petersburg symbolised the shift in the Baltic balance from Sweden to Russia. Finland once more became a borderland, weakly defended by an enfeebled Sweden, and it lost still more territory to the Russian empire in 1743, after a brief and disastrous war. In February 1808, having failed to persuade the King of Sweden to give up his vehement opposition to Russia's erstwhile ally Napoleon, Alexander I invaded Finland. By the winter of 1808–9, his troops were in occupation of most of the country. During the course of 1808, Alexander seems to have decided against incorporating Finland into the Russian empire without more ado, and on 1 February 1809 he issued an order for the convocation of a Diet of the Finnish Estates at the town of Porvoo. In summoning this Diet, he may have been influenced by the pleadings of former Swedish army officers such as Göran Sprengtporten, who had been working for the separation of Finland from Sweden since the 1780s; and a delegation of Finnish notables who visited St. Petersburg at the end of 1808 may have persuaded the Emperor to convene a Diet. Alexander may also have seen an opportunity to put into practice in Finland some of the constitutionalist principles of his influential adviser, Mikhail Speransky. More obviously, he was well aware of the increasingly threatening European situation, and he might therefore have wished to make a rapid settlement of the Finnish question along lines similar to those followed by his ancestor Peter the Great in the Baltic lands in 1710–11. Peter had in fact guaranteed the rights and privileges of the Estonian and Livonian Estates, as Alexander was to do in Finland. In both cases, the Emperor sought to wean his new subjects away from their loyalty to the Swedish Crown, and thereby obtain security in strategically vulnerable areas. In a secret letter to his Governor-General of Finland in 1810, Alexander I explicitly stated that his intention had been to give the Finnish people a political existence 'so that they would not consider themselves conquered by Russia, but joined to it by their own self-evident interests'.[6] In an inspired phrase uttered at the conclusion of the Diet he had summoned to Porvoo in 1809, the Emperor also spoke of Finland having been elevated to the rank of nationhood. In a political sense, this was partly correct. Finland had inherited from Sweden a framework of laws and institutions which Alexander I not only confirmed, but was even prepared to extend by giving Finland its own administration, the Senate, under his ultimate control. Despite the attempts of Alexander's successors at the end of the century to curb the autonomy of the Grand Duchy, this framework remained substantially intact and was to provide the basis for the independent state which emerged out of the chaos of revolution which destroyed the old empire.

Whether the Finnish people constituted a nation in 1809 is another matter. The men who assembled at the Diet of Porvoo in 1809 were representatives of the four estates, not of the people, and their function was to ensure the transfer of loyalty from the King of Sweden to the Emperor in his capacity as Grand Duke of Finland, in return for the preservation of the *status quo*, of their rights and privileges. The ruling élite retained strong emotional, cultural and personal links with Sweden: Finnish language and culture were ignored, except by a few academics at the University. Nevertheless, the 1809 settlement was a definite parting of the ways with the old motherland. A feeling of disillusionment with the way in which Sweden had neglected Finland was already apparent before war broke out in 1808—Count Armfelt's somewhat cynical advice to his fellow-countrymen in 1802 had been to lay in a store of vodka in anticipation of a Russian invasion—and was augmented by the disastrous performance of the army during the war. Although there was much initial alarm about Alexander's intentions, this soon subsided. Among the higher officials, army officers and academics there soon developed an awareness of the necessity of accepting Russian rule, and this awareness was augmented by feelings of gratitude towards the Emperor for his noble and generous treatment of the conquered land. Loyalty towards the new ruler was strengthened in the course of time by a growing awareness of the opportunities for service within the empire, and possibly by the abrupt change of course in Sweden after the revolution of 1809. Not only was the Vasa dynasty succeeded by the Bernadotte line, but the new heir to the Swedish throne (Bernadotte succeeded in 1818 as Karl XIV Johan) implicitly renounced revanchist designs upon Finland in 1812.

The transfer of loyalty to a new ruler whose state tradition was utterly alien to Finnish concepts raised the question of a Finnish identity. A few high-ranking Finns in imperial service expressed a preference for assimilation: but Finns of all ranks showed a marked reluctance to become Russians and to be blended into the empire. Autonomy gave Finland a certain political status: it remained to find a national identity.

Although isolated from mainland Europe, Finland could not in the long run remain impervious to the momentous political, social and economic changes which were taking place in the world. On the other hand, she lacked a strong and discontented middle class which might have acted as the harbinger of revolutionary change. On the whole, the ruling élite had a vested interest in the preservation of the *status quo*. There were no revolutionary outbursts in Finland in 1830 or 1848. As Matti Klinge has observed, it was a sense of isolation which helped shape a Finnish national identity in the early decades of the nineteenth century; and this identity was developed within the framework of loyalty, and even encouraged by the St. Petersburg government.[7] Thanks in part to the slow pace of change in Finland, and in part to the connection with the very antithesis of change, the Russian autocracy, the ruling élite in Finland managed to survive and adapt to a national identity consonant with its own political interests.

The University was at the centre of the 'national awakening' which occurred in Finland during the nineteenth century. Although the student body remained small until the 1870s—around 400–450 on average—its compactness, and the students' own awareness of their future role in society made the University a forum for political debate, indeed the only one outside the closed ranks of the bureaucracy before the convention of the Diet in 1863. In this respect, the Alexander University in the capital, Helsinki, was markedly different from the older and provincial Swedish universities. Moreover, whereas Swedish intellectual life was still dominated by Romanticism and the neo-Gothic movement, Finland gravitated towards the neo-humanist and rationalist traditions of St. Petersburg. Hegelian ideas gained a footing in Finland during the 1820s, but not until the 1880s in Sweden.

The groundwork for the national awakening was performed by ethnographers, philologists and folklorists, often generously supported by the Imperial government and the Academy of Science in St. Petersburg, during the first half of the nineteenth century. On the whole, the imperial authorities were favourably disposed towards the advancement of Finnish cultural ideals—which, since the cradle of Finnish culture was commonly taken to lie in Karelia in the east, could be construed as advancing Finnish loyalty towards the Empire—as long as they remained strictly apolitical. When the neo-Hegelian philosopher Snellman began to venture into the forbidden field of politics in the reign of Nicholas I, he was quickly silenced by the authorities.

In Snellman's view, a national culture was meaningless without a conscious national spirit. The foundation for a national spirit was language, and for Snellman that language had to be Finnish. In other words, the ruling élite would have to abandon Swedish language and culture and embrace Finnish as the national tongue. This was the basic and uncompromising message spelt out by Snellman in innumerable articles for forty years. During this period, major breakthroughs for Finnish language and culture were achieved, and Snellman himself returned from provincial obscurity to a seat in the Senate: nevertheless, his views on the world situation tended to tinge his writings with gloom and foreboding. He feared that the course of history—to which as a good Hegelian he was totally addicted—was not favourable to small nations, and he constantly urged his fellow nationalists to ensure the unity of the nation on the basis of one language and culture in readiness for the *dies irae*.

There is no doubt that Snellman was aware of the growing threat of Russian nationalism, which had begun to express doubts about the wisdom of allowing Finland such freedom within the empire: but he was probably more alarmed by the persistence of liberalism, which threatened to undermine his vision of one nation, one language. Liberalism in Finland bears very little resemblance to the liberalism of Gladstonian Britain. It might loosely be defined as constitutionalist, drawing heavily upon the aristocratic traditions of the Swedish era.

Whereas Finnish nationalists stressed the importance of the national-cultural ideal and urged loyalty towards the ruler, the constitutionalist liberals saw Finland as an autonomous state with its own inalienable fundamental laws, attached to Russia by personal union alone. The liberals sought to strengthen Finland's *political* independence by emphasising the unique nature of her constitution, and by diminishing the role of the Emperor–Grand Duke—hence the arguments in favour of Finnish neutrality in conflict situations not directly involving Finland which were raised in 1863 and 1885. The nationalists wished to strengthen the *national* character of Finland through uniformity of language and culture; their principal enemies were Swedish nationalists and liberals who denied the importance of language.

Before 1863, these differences were not so noticeable, simply because of the lack of opportunity for the formulation and development of political ideas. Oppositional elements had tended towards 'Fenno-mania', an often rather vague assertion of the national character which intrigued and appealed to people as diverse as Jakob Grot, Professor of Russian History at the University, and Emil von Qvanten, an émigré poet and publicist who advocated the reunion of Sweden and Finland during the Crimean War. The summoning of the Diet in 1863—and it continued to meet at regular intervals thereafter—and the series of reforms and additions to Finland's autonomous status of the reign of Alexander II facilitated the development of party politics and political debate. The Crimean War had helped stimulate such public debate as the tight censorship would allow, since the Anglo-French assault on the Finnish coast in 1854 acted as a direct reminder to the Finns of their new position and loyalties. Although the Finnish reaction was patriotic and loyal, the possibility of further conflict with the Western powers as a result of imperial Russian policy led to arguments in favour of Finnish neutrality in *Helsingfors Dagblad*, the leading organ of liberalism throughout the reign of Alexander II. Liberalism was always concerned to protect the interests of the Finnish state from excessive involvement with—or subjugation by—the empire. By the 1890s Finnish liberalism, having failed as a separate party political creed, had become fused with the Swedish party. Since that party had been created in response to Finnish nationalism, the more positive political approach of aristocratic and urban constitutional liberalism, which had in fact drawn its support almost exclusively from the Swedish-speaking upper class, was able to survive and flourish. Finnish nationalism, politically organised in the Finnish party, was becoming increasingly conservative, and the older generation's obsession with the language question was such that a number of younger party members broke away in the 1890s to form the Young Finnish party, which expressed concern about social problems and sympathy with constitutionalist arguments in defence of Finnish autonomy.

Though Finnish nationalism was beginning to appeal to the wealthier peasantry, neither nationalism nor liberalism had deep roots in the country as a whole, since both strands of thought had evolved in the narrow milieu of the political and cultural élite. The great mass of the peasantry, smallholders, workers and landless remained outside the pale of political debate, indifferent to the arguments of the 'gentry' in Helsinki. The deep gulf between the centre of Finnish political life and the periphery was to become suddenly apparent in the early years of this century, when the élite sought to rally the country in defence of Finnish liberties. In his novel *Hurskas kurjuus* (Meek heritage) Sillanpää observed that the rural poor were completely at a loss to understand why the position of the 'Finnish people' had suddenly become so gloomy: young students from the capital were shocked by the indifference of the peasantry to their efforts to rally national support in protest against Russian attempts to curb autonomy. A pamphlet printed in remote Kajaani in 1899, which was intended to combat this indifference, noted that comments such as 'now the gentry are in a sweat' and 'these here new laws don't concern us peasants, they're only taking the power off the gentry' were to be heard in the countryside and even in the towns.[8]

The idyllic image of the Finnish countryside and the peasantry portrayed by the poet Runeberg was to be rudely shaken in the last years of imperial Russian rule. The main beneficiary of the political awakening of the rural proletariat was to be the socialist movement, which was beginning to emerge from bourgeois tutelage. In 1899, the year in which the Finnish Labour Party (*Suomen työväenpuolue*) was founded, the labour movement was still small, drawing its support mainly from artisans and craftsmen, and reformist in character. By 1906, the party (the Finnish Social Democratic Party from 1903) had reached a peak membership of 100,000, mainly new recruits from the countryside, and was markedly more revolutionary-Marxist in its outward appearance, if not in practice. The idealised 'Finnish people' of romantic nationalism suddenly became an ugly reality in the changed political arena.

Finland on the eve of the twentieth century

Finland in 1900 was markedly different from the countries of western and central Europe. A traveller in 1833 described it as 'terre primitive, dont la nature a fidèlement gardé, parmi les révolutions humaines, son charactère, pour ainsi dire, antédiluvien, et dont les peuples n'ont pas d'origine connue'[9]—a sentiment echoed by later travellers, such as the intrepid Mrs. Tweedie, whose account of her travels in carts through wildest Finland enjoyed a wide readership in late-Victorian England. Mrs. Tweedie described Finland as a 'vast continent about which strangers hardly know anything'. Although enchanted by the wild countryside and simple peasants, this formidable lady was less enthusiastic about the cockroaches and bugs which shared the simple peasant's dwelling—a subject upon which she delivered several lengthy homilies in her book.[10]

Even allowing for the romantic imagination of the traveller, Finland was a far cry from late-Victorian England—and from Wilhelmine Germany, for that matter. The most obvious contrast was that whereas in every western European country north of the Pyrenees there was a large urban population, the vast majority of Finns still lived on the land. In Finland the middle class, which provided the backbone of British liberalism, was small and politically unimportant. The Finnish Diet with its four Estates and restricted franchise was a survival from the Swedish era. Governments were appointed by and were responsible to the ruler. Political activity was circumscribed by proscriptive legislation and censorship. There were no major extra-parliamentary pressure groups such as the Anti-Corn Law League or the Swedish franchise reform movement of the 1890s. Indeed, there were no political parties in the modern sense of the world. National organisations were virtually non-existent. Communications were poor, in spite of railway construction. Thousands lived much as they had always done in remote settlements, oblivious to the changing world. The patriarchal values of the society of rank (*sääty-yhteiskunta*) were still strong. If they were challenged, it was by the pressure of economic change, and not by an articulate organised radicalism. Liberalism and nationalism were essentially concerned to preserve the social order, though it is true that there was a growing awareness of the need for social change among members of the younger generation.

Unlike Britain and Germany, Finland also lacked a coherent and articulate working-class tradition; indeed, it would be premature to speak of a working class before 1900. There was, to be sure, an ancient and well-documented tradition of hostility and resentment towards the 'gentry' (*herrasviha*), which found expression in the revivalist movements within the Lutheran Church, but there was no clearly expressed class consciousness. Despite the fact that the social values of the society of rank were crumbling away, Jutikkala is undoubtedly right in maintaining that nineteenth-century Finland was still dominated by such values. Loyalty to Church and ruler were real and enduring features of Finnish life, but when these loyalties were subjected to intense pressure in the first decade of this century, the final remnants of patriarchal society collapsed, intensifying the degree of frustration and despair experienced by a rural proletariat which had no solid working-class tradition to fall back on, as had the factory workers of Victorian England.

If Finland did not fit into the same category as the industrial nations of the West, neither did it resemble the more backward societies within the Russian empire. The rigid caste mentality of the Baltic barons hardly existed in Finland. The upper class may have spoken Swedish, but they regarded themselves as Finnish. There was no brutal oppression of the peasantry, which did indeed have political representation. Serfdom was unknown in Finland. The institutions and laws of Swedish rule remained intact, and had even been developed in an appropriate manner. Above all else, the Grand Duchy retained its autonomy, its special status within the Russian empire, which had enabled the 'embryonic state' created by Alexander I in 1809 to develop into a more or less fully-fledged entity.[11] This special status had come under attack from Russian nationalists, but Finland had not been subjected to russification as had the Baltic provinces in the 1880s. In 1900, however, it seemed as if the *dies irae* of pitiless assimilation foreseen by Snellman was at hand.

2

OPPRESSION AND RESISTANCE: THE LAST YEARS OF AUTONOMY

1900–1917

'I fear there are evil days ahead for Finland; but she has won through worse, and she is now a distinct national entity conscious of herself, and prepared. Surely she will be no mean factor in the great Eastern struggle for liberty that some of us foresee? ... though many may fall by the way, Finland's people are made of the stuff that endures, and their cause will triumph in the end.'

Rosalind Travers, *Letters from Finland,*
August 1908–March 1909, (London 1911, p. 376)

The pattern of government established for Finland by the Emperor Alexander I was tripartite in nature. In St. Petersburg there was the Minister State-Secretary for Finland, who was usually of Finnish birth, while the Emperor's representative in Helsinki was the Governor-General. The latter, invariably a high-ranking Russian Military officer, had his own Chancery, was in overall command of the troops stationed in Finland, and as chairman of the Senate was the formal head of the civil administration. However, as the Emperor also chose to establish a native government—the Senate, confusion of roles and functions inevitably ensued. Much of the Russian opposition to Finland's special status was founded on the belief that the Governor-General, as the representative of imperial state interests, lacked any effective status or powers.[1] Nevertheless, it was the Governor-General in practice who recommended candidates for appointment to the fourteen-man Senate by the Emperor, and not infrequently a majority opinion could be ignored by the ruler if the Governor-General chose to side with the minority in his report attached to the Senate's memorandum. The Senate comprised two departments: a juridical department, which

22

functioned as the highest court of appeal in the land, and the 'economic department', or government proper, which dealt with matters pertaining to the 'public economy' of Finland. Since the Senate was nominated by the ruler, it retained a heavily bureaucratic composition, although from the 1860s onwards, recognised political figures such as Snellman and the liberal Leo Mechelin were appointed. The Senate was also responsible to the ruler, not the Diet. It had no right to initiate new taxation or provide for extraordinary expenditure, and its legislative powers were severely circumscribed.

The Gustavian fundamental laws of 1772 and 1789 had swung the balance of power decidedly towards the ruler: hence the Emperor, who inherited these laws, was within his rights in not summoning a Diet between 1809 and 1863, since the 1772 Form of Government decreed that the right to summon a Diet belonged exclusively to the ruler. In 1869 this situation was amended so that the Diet was henceforth to be called at least once every five years, but the ruler still retained the right to end the session when he chose and to dismiss the Diet. According to the Gustavian constitution, the ruler could not pass laws without the consent of the Diet, but until 1886 he alone had the right to initiate legislation. He also possessed the right of absolute veto on any piece of legislation approved by the Diet. The Diet determined internal revenues and fixed standing taxes in consultation with the ruler; but although the Diet did obtain a greater say in the raising of state loans and the disposal of revenues in the reign of Alexander II, its fiscal and financial powers were still strictly circumscribed.

The structure and composition of the Diet in 1900 was little different from what it had been in 1809. The three-class system of the House of Nobility had been abolished in 1869, but the nobility still continued to sit by right as did the archbishop and bishops in the Estate of Clergy. The franchise was widened slightly in 1869 to accommodate those 'persons of rank' who did not fit into any one particular estate, such as industrialists and university teachers, and ten years later the old franchise of burgherage was replaced by an income threshold for the Burghers' Estate. In spite of these changes, the Finnish Diet was a distinctly antiquated and unrepresentative institution, some forty years after the sister institution of the Swedish Diet had been replaced by a bicameral legislature. Only in the Peasants' Estate was there anything like a sizeable electorate; even then, more than two thirds of the Finnish people were without the vote at national or local level (see Table 2).

Such was the system of government in the Grand Duchy on the eve of the present century. Although antiquated by western European standards, it did nevertheless allow the Finns a large measure of control over their own affairs. In addition, Finland had its own distinct legal system and civil and criminal law codes, its own school system, railway administration and even its own army, created in 1878. The language of administration, the courts, schools and army was Swedish and/or Finnish. Citizens of the empire resident in Finland did not enjoy the same rights as Finnish citizens, though as we have seen, many Finns were able to advance their careers and fortunes in the empire. Before the 'astonished eyes' of the Russians, Finland did indeed appear to be 'a well-organised, self-governing society with thousands of schools, where, *horribile dictu*, the language of the empire is not taught, with its own industry, which in part competes with their own markets, and with its own firmly secured finances and credit system in the world markets, which many richer countries might even envy . . .'[2]

Before 1863, there had been little objection to Finland's status within the empire (although the Decembrist Pestel voiced criticisms). However, after the Polish revolt of 1863, slavophil sentiments tended to become more nationalistic, and a much more critical tone began to appear in the Russian press treatment of Finland. The Crimean War raised the bogey of 'Finnish separatism', which the demands of Finnish liberals for a Finnish neutrality in the event of war did little to assuage. The growing confidence of the Finns, with their relatively free press, regular Diet and enhanced sense of national identity angered Russian nationalists such as Katkov and alarmed military men who could not understand why a strategically vulnerable frontier area had been allowed its own army in 1878.

Much of the polemical debate of the 1880s centred on what sort of status had been granted to Finland by Alexander I in 1809. Russian nationalists such as K. F. Ordin maintained that Alexander as Autocrat would have been denying the very basis of his legitimacy as ruler if he had embraced an 'alien' constitution. He merely bestowed upon Finland a gracious gift, which he or his successors could just as easily revoke. The Finns based their case on Alexander's assertion of their political existence and the inheritance of fundamental laws which he had confirmed, and were further emboldened to claim some sort of *de jure* recognition of a Finnish constitution by the Emperor as a consequence of the 'constitutional era' of Alexander II's reign. However, as Schweitzer has pointed out, Finland's separate status ran contrary to the interests of the overall unity of the empire, and could only be preserved if the risk of conflict were minimised by the willingness of both sides to preserve a *modus vivendi*. By the 1890s, the ground of consensus had begun to shrink. Finland's separate status was seen in imperial government circles as posing a problem for the unity and security of the empire. It was widely felt that matters of general state interest should not be left to the Finns to decide for themselves. In 1890 the Finnish postal service was brought under imperial control by decree, a measure which provoked Finnish protests of an infringement of the constitution. The appointment of General Nikolay Ivanovich Bobrikov as Governor-General in 1898 was a further step towards bringing Finland into line with the rest of the empire.[3]

Much of Bobrikov's military career had been spent in the St. Petersburg military district, and it is clear that preoccupation with the problems of defending the capital was the keystone of his Finnish policy. He was not an advocate of russification in a cultural sense and did not wish to deprive the Finns of their national heritage. In his programme for Finland, sanctioned by the Emperor in August 1898, Bobrikov claimed that although Finland had been conquered by Russia in 1809, the purpose of that conquest had to date not been fulfilled. Finland, a vital frontier region, still remained a foreign area in which the authority of the imperial state was weak. To remedy this, Bobrikov proposed a thorough investigation of Finland's position, similar to that undertaken in the Baltic provinces in the 1880s, and he outlined a number of immediate steps which could be taken to curb 'Finnish separatism' before the results of the investigation were revealed. These steps included merging the Finnish army into the imperial army, the introduction of the Russian language into the Senate, civil service and schools, permitting Russians to enter freely into the Finnish civil service, and a general strengthening of the powers of the Governor-General.[4]

The first indication of a new policy towards Finland came in January 1899, when Bobrikov introduced proposals, which had been drawn up and discussed at the highest levels in St. Petersburg, concerning military service. If implemented, these would have had the effect of increasing recruitment in Finland and of permitting Russian troops and officers to serve in Finnish units and Finnish troops to serve elsewhere in the empire. As such, the proposals were bound to meet with resistance from the Diet, which had been specially convened to debate them. A further Russian broadside was delivered on 15 February when Nicholas II issued a 'manifesto', or decree, outlining the steps to be taken towards curbing Finnish autonomy for the sake of state interests. This decree had to be promulgated by the Finnish Senate, which at first seemed to find no alternative course of action; after a number of leading political figures had spoken at a meeting on 17 February, however, opinion began to change. The final vote for or against immediate promulgation was a tie, and promulgation was only carried by the vice-chairman's casting vote. All the Senators were agreed on the necessity of a petition to the Emperor, urging him to reconsider the contents of the manifesto.

The split in the Senate foreshadowed a much deeper gulf which was to emerge between conservative Finnish nationalists, who urged loyalty, and compliance, and liberal constitutionalists who proposed passive resistance to the new measures. In the spring of 1899, however, these deep divisions were not yet evident. It was widely believed that the Emperor had been misled by his advisers: once his loyal Finnish subjects had revealed the truth to him, all would return to normal. It was in this spirit that a Grand Address of over half a million signatures was collected throughout the country and presented to the Emperor (he refused to see the delegation bearing the Address, or representatives of the Senate and the Speakers of the four Estates, or an international delegation bearing an international Address, signed by over 1,000 distinguished supporters of the Finnish cause). The international Address had been devised by a number of Finnish expatriates, who for the next six years worked assiduously to present their country's case in the Western nations. They were undoubtedly helped by the fact that Russia was widely regarded as a reactionary and despotic country all too ready to trample on the rights of small nations, but as George Maude has shown in his study of British attitudes towards Finland, the desire of the British government to seek better relations with Russia in the end precluded effective official action on Finland's behalf.

The assault on Finland's position within the Russian empire, known in Finnish history as the first period of oppression (*ensimmäinen sorto-kausi*), had three major consequences. In the first place, it brought Finland to the attention of political circles in the West at a time of increasing international tension, not least in Northern Europe, where the Union between Sweden and Norway was entering upon its final phase. In the second place, it made the Finns more aware of the politics of the Russian empire, of which they had been largely ignorant for most of the nineteenth century. Similarly, the Russian revolutionary movement began to take a keen interest in Finland, where the prospect of a potentially hostile population on the doorstep of the capital and of new routes for the smuggling of revolutionary literature and arms was particularly promising. Finally, the struggle against Russian oppression led to a genuine political awakening of the Finnish people as a whole, although the consequences of this awakening were to prove divisive.

The first major split occurred in the ranks of the narrow political élite. In June 1900, a decree ordering the gradual introduction of Russian as the principal language of state in the Finnish administration was placed before the Senate. Seeking to avoid conflict, the Senate petitioned the Emperor to withdraw the decree. Nicholas II's negative response left the Senate little option but to promulgate the decree. The eight Senators who voted against promulgation thereupon resigned, to be replaced by men more amenable to imperial demands. In August the first steps were taken towards the formation of a co-ordinated national committee of resistance, which came into existence the following year with a central committee in Helsinki, and which was given the derisive name of 'Kagal' by the Russian administration.[5] The moving spirits behind the Kagal were liberal constitutionalists, although a number of the more radical Finnish nationalists were involved. The passive resistance campaign was nevertheless run almost entirely by members of the ruling class, and predominantly by Swedish-speaking liberals. At first, the main task was to create an awareness in the country as a whole of the dangers which threatened and to stress the lofty patriotic duty of passive resistance, but the promulgation of the Military Service Law in 1901 was to reveal the strength and expose the weakness of passive resistance in Finland.

The 1901 Military Service Law was to be the real test of Bobrikov's policy. Conscripted Finns were henceforth liable to serve in any part of the empire. Only one battalion of guards and one regiment of dragoons of the old Finnish army were to remain: the rest was to be disbanded and incorporated into the imperial army. This measure had not been without its opponents in high circles in Russia, who feared it would only provoke new unrest in Finland. Bobrikov was thus left in the unenviable position of having to implement a measure central to his policy which was viewed with misgiving by leading members of the Imperial Council of State. The disaster of the conscription levy in the spring of 1902, at which, according to Bobrikov's own figures, less than half of those called up appeared, meant that the Imperial government had either to abandon or to modify the plan, or bail the Governor-General out. Bobrikov had already suffered a defeat over the extension of the railway from Oulu to the Swedish frontier, which he had vigorously opposed, and his position was constantly being undermined by his rival V. K. Pleve, the Minister Secretary of State for Finland since 1898, and Minister of the Interior from 1902. In April 1903, he was granted wide-ranging extraordinary powers to banish dissidents, prohibit meetings, and dismiss and appoint local officials at will, but the granting of these powers was more in the nature of a salvage operation than a conscious tightening of the screws of the Bobrikov policy.

Since the 1901 Law explicitly stated that it was the sacred duty of all Finns, irrespective of social rank, to serve in the Emperor's armies, its implementation was bound to affect even those who had hitherto remained largely indifferent to the struggle against the new measures. It also compelled many clergymen and doctors to take a stand, for the former were required to read the Law to the congregations in their churches, and the latter were required to serve on committees administering the call-up. On the whole, the traditional obedience of the Lutheran church towards authority asserted itself, although a few clergymen were prepared to refuse to read out the Law. The civil servants who engaged in acts of disloyalty were liable to be dismissed, as were the members of provincial courts of appeal who refused to comply with the new laws.

By the summer of 1903, the situation in Finland appeared critical. Bobrikov had already suppressed a number of Finnish newspapers for voicing protest, and he now used his powers to banish leaders of the resistance. Only 32 per cent of those called up in the spring failed to appear, and the percentage fell to 25 per cent the following year. Finns who continued to occupy high office or who replaced those dismissed incurred the opprobrium of the passive resistance, and after the death in 1903 of Y. S. Yrjö-Koskinen, the most outspoken advocate of compliance with Russian demands, his followers became increasingly unhappy and confused about their position. Passive resistance also seemed to have reached an impasse. The cautious and conservative leadership was unwilling to depart from the narrow path of 'lawful' disobedience of 'illegal' decrees, or to commit the movement to an alliance with the Russian revolutionary movement. By the autumn of 1903, a small group of young activists were beginning to hatch plans to engage in a campaign of direct action against the Bobrikov regime.

There are however good reasons for maintaining that Bobrikov's policy had reached the end of the road. He lacked effective support in St. Petersburg, and had to contend not only with the opposition of influential figures such as the former minister Count S. Y. Witte, but with the tortuous dealings of his rival V. K. Pleve. In 1904, however, both Pleve and Bobrikov were removed from the scene by assassins. With their deaths, any hopes for an immediate coherent policy on Finland vanished. Caught up in war against Japan, the imperial government availed itself of the links which Danielson-Kalmari, a leading Finnish 'appeaser', had kept open to St. Petersburg and sought conciliation by convening the Diet, and suspending the Military Service Law (in March 1905) in anticipation of recommendations to be made by a joint committee set up to examine matters of state interest. In lieu of military service, Finland had to pay an annual sum of 10 million marks for the next three years. In the event, Finns were never again called upon to perform military service in the ranks of the imperial army.

The year 1903 marks a critical turning-point in the sense that the Finnish resistance began to turn towards violent means, and became more involved in the Russian revolutionary movement. Violence had already occurred in April 1902, when the Cossacks had to be called out to disperse demonstrators at the call-up ceremony in Helsinki, and there had also been rowdy demonstrations outside the houses of leading 'appeasers'. Acts of terror, the most striking being the assassination of Bobrikov by a young Finnish patriot in June 1904, were amateurish and modest by Russian standards, but they provoked a great deal of anguished debate in a country which prided itself on law-abiding loyalty. In January 1905, at a time of high tension in the empire following the Bloody Sunday massacre, there were demonstrations in Helsinki, and again in April as the Diet debated proposals for electoral reform drafted by the Senate. The proposals were shelved, but the very fact that they had been made is an indication of the extent to which political life in Finland had been transformed within a few short years.

The unrest which had been fermenting throughout the Russian empire in 1905 finally erupted on 25 October. After five days of revolution, the badly shaken autocracy was compelled to issue a manifesto guaranteeing individual rights and promising reform. The revolution did not immediately affect Finland, since the revolutionaries in St. Petersburg had asked Finnish railwaymen on the line between the capital and Viipuri to keep the line operative in order to maintain a link to the West. Not until Sunday (29 October) did traffic on the Viipuri–St. Petersburg line come to a halt. That evening, at a meeting of leaders of the passive resistance in Helsinki, resolutions were passed calling for the dismissal of all officials 'illegally' appointed during the past five years, including the Senate and the Minister Secretary of State for Finland, and the immediate convention of the Diet. An eight-man delegation to co-ordinate action was also set up after the representative of the labour movement present at the meeting spoke of the desirability of such a step. This was cautiously endorsed by a meeting of labour representatives on the Monday evening. The same meeting also proclaimed a general strike and elected a strike committee, which was to co-operate with the constitutionalist passive resistance. On the Tuesday morning, the newspapers appeared for the last time, with the news of the imperial manifesto. By the afternoon, much of the country was in the grip of a national and patriotic strike.

Collaboration between the constitutionalists and the labour movement soon foundered as the divergencies of their aims became apparent. Whereas the socialists and the small activist party which had been founded in 1904 demanded the election of a national constituent assembly on the basis of universal suffrage, the constitutionalists wanted the convention of the Diet, which would then consider parliamentary reform. After a meeting at the Governor-General's residence on Tuesday evening (31 October), at which the Senate announced its resignation and the Governor-General accepted the constitutionalists' proposals to be forwarded to the Emperor, a delegation of constitutionalists went by sea to the capital to assess the situation there.

As the strike spread, the question of maintaining order became acute. The Russian gendarmerie was either arrested or relieved of authority, and the Finnish police joined the strike. A national guard was set up in Helsinki on the Tuesday, and similar militia groups were formed elsewhere. By the end of the strike week, however, the Helsinki national guards had split into Red and White guards. Russian troops in Helsinki maintained a low profile—an unsuccessful attempt at gunrunning in the Gulf of Bothnia on the eve of the revolution seems to have created in Russian circles the myth of a hostile Finnish population armed to the teeth—but their presence induced caution. Thus, although the central strike committee in Helsinki endorsed the demand put forward on 1 November by the Tampere strike committee for the election of a provisional government by all the inhabitants of Helsinki over the age of twenty-one, the arrival of a fleet detachment from Tallinn and the warnings of the Governor-General effectively nullified the whole idea. The elections were held, with the proviso that the results be submitted to the Emperor for confirmation, but by then (Saturday, 4 November) it had become obvious that, with the restoration of order in Russia, it was only a matter of time before the strike would come to an end in Finland. The constitutionalists' proposals were approved by the Emperor, and the Helsinki central strike committee had no option but to call off the strike on 6 November. The near-clash between White and Red guards in the streets of Helsinki on that Monday morning is some indication of the bitterness and confusion with which the strike ended.[6]

The victors of the strike action seemed to be the liberal constitutionalists. The manifesto signed by the Emperor on 4 November embodied their programme of a return to the *status quo ante* Bobrikov. On 1 December, Nicholas II confirmed the appointment of a new Senate, headed by Leo Mechelin and composed of liberal constitutionalists, with one socialist as Minister without Portfolio. The Diet was convened at the end of the year to debate a wide range of reforms prepared by the Senate. On 20 July 1906 the Emperor confirmed the most important reform of all: the replacement of the old Diet by a unicameral assembly (*Eduskunta*) of 200 members elected by all Finns over the age of twenty-four on the basis of proportional representation. This long-overdue, yet major transformation—with which all parties in Finland were in basic agreement—and the accompanying legislation guaranteeing freedom of speech, assembly and association had, on the surface, catapulted Finland into the ranks of the advanced democracies of the world. But Trotsky's warning to the Russians applied in Finland as well. A constitution might have been granted, but the autocracy remained. In the first ten years of its existence, the new *Eduskunta*—which the Emperor could still convene, suspend and dismiss—failed to function as a real legislative body. Such reforms as it managed to pass were vetoed by the Emperor, who by 1910 had managed to reduce the Senate to a subservient body of time-serving nonentities. The liberals' hope of a return to the golden era of the reign of Alexander II were dashed in an even more ferocious and effective onslaught on Finland's autonomy, this time conducted by the imperial government under the powerful figure of P. A. Stolypin.

The Soviet historian V. V. Pohlebkin has stressed how alarmed Russian bureaucrats, soldiers, businessmen and nationalists were by the creation of a virtual 'republic' in Finland, and how the question of what was to be done with Finland was widely debated. The policy which evolved was aimed much more at breaking down Finland's economic privileges and allowing the extension of Russian business activities into the Grand Duchy. As early as 1908 Stolypin managed to establish the Council of Ministers as the arbiter of whether or not matters raised by the Finns were or were not of general state interest, and two years later the Duma passed Stolypin's bill which decreed that all legislation concerning Finland which could be construed as having 'general state interest' could only be made by the Russian state apparatus. The Finnish *Eduskunta* was entitled to legislate only on purely local matters and merely to voice an opinion on matters of state interest. When the *Eduskunta* protested, it was summarily dissolved. Imperial decrees

placed the Finnish pilot system under Russian control, encroached upon
the administration of the Finnish railway system, and in 1912 gave
Russian citizens the same rights as Finns in the Grand Duchy. These
measures were supported by a much wider section of the Russian
public, from the crude nationalist Black Hundreds to the Octobrists
who had hitherto been inclined towards sympathy for Finland, which
Lenin and the Finnish Marxist socialists interpreted as clear evidence
that the mask of liberalism had been replaced by naked class interests,
in which the Russian bourgeoisie fought the Finnish bourgeoisie, and
both oppressed the proletariat.[7]

The revival of oppression, now conducted by a much more effective
force, was one reason why a return to constitutional legality was impossible in Finland. The amazing growth of the Finnish labour movement as a consequence of the revolution of 1905 also meant that a return
to the pre-1899 era was no longer feasible, since the ruling élite now
faced a powerful political challenge from a socialist party which could
claim nearly 100,000 members, with a national organisation, its own
press, and eighty seats in the first *Eduskunta*, elected in 1907. Before
1905, the small Social Democratic Party had been dominated by re-
formists, mainly concerned with obtaining the vote, and a section of
the party had also supported co-operation with the passive resistance.
The strike experience of 1905 gave the labour movement a sense of its
revolutionary power, which the disappointments of not having
demands fulfilled only intensified. There was considerable unrest in
1906, culminating in Red Guard support for a mutiny of Russian troops
on the fortress of Sveaborg off Helsinki, which the party leadership
privately feared but publicly did little to discourage.

After 1905, the Social Democratic Party adopted a rigidly class-
conscious Marxist ideology which took its inspiration from the ideas
propounded by Karl Kautsky, the leading theoretician of German
social democracy. The Finnish Social Democratic Party expelled the
veteran socialist J. K. Kari in 1906, after he had taken office in the
Mechelin Senate, and it used the *Eduskunta* as a forum for pursuing the
class struggle rather than for constructive reform. Social democracy in
Finland between 1907 and 1917 had in fact no opportunity to engage in
constructive democratic activities, since the legislature did not work,
the government was in the hands of imperial nominees, and local
government remained unreformed. On the other hand, unlike Russian
social democracy, it was never forced underground. In an atmosphere
of political frustration and stagnation, the Social Democratic Party
became ideologically entrenched behind a barrier of revolutionary

class consciousness, waiting for the historically inevitable collapse of the bourgeois order, when it would then supposedly inherit power. A more positive course of action was never seriously envisaged by the party's leadership.

The main strength of the Social Democratic Party lay in its rural support. After 1905, at least three-fifths of the party membership was made up of members of rural workers' associations, even in 1911 when party membership sank to less than 50,000. The proportion of votes cast for socialist candidates was also consistently higher in the rural 'red belt' stretching across the southern hinterland from Satakunta to Lake Ladoga than it was in the towns. In spite of declining membership —although there was a recovery during the war years—the Social Democratic Party's mandate increased with every national election, and in 1916 the party became the first and only Marxist party in the world to obtain an absolute majority (103 seats) in a parliamentary election before the Russian revolution.

The reasons why the Social Democratic Party was able to win such support in the countryside are difficult to pinpoint. The land policy of the party was shaped by practical considerations rather than along strictly Marxist lines, and tended to favour the claims of the leasehold farmers to own their own land. The party succeeded in winning the support of the leaseholders after 1905 because of its ability to organise and channel the frustrations and desires of a socially insecure group. Similarly it attracted the support of the landless poor and the scrap-holders with the demand for the compulsory cultivation of the land which might meet the landowning aspirations of the rural poor. Socialism also provided an alternative culture of class consciousness, and held out the prospect of radical change to the impoverished rural masses, galvanised into political awareness in revolutionary circum-stances. It was to be the party's misfortune that its leaders failed to understand the underlying strength of this revolutionary dynamic force which propelled the labour movement to the forefront of post-1905 Finnish politics.

The growth of a strong, politically organised labour movement committed to the class struggle shattered the sentimental image of the Finnish 'people' portrayed in the writings of Runeberg and the popular historian Zachris Topelius. The Finnish people had shown their pre-ference for a party whose leaders regarded the struggle against Russian oppression as being inspired by the Finnish bourgeoisie, intent on preserving their own interests. The politics of class conflict weakened hopes for national unity in the face of renewed Russian oppression.

Numerous Finns continued a stubborn resistance to the measures of the imperial government, enduring imprisonment and Siberian exile for their cause, but there was no nationally organised campaign of passive resistance after 1905. Activism also lapsed into quiescence.

The first period of Russian oppression has received much attention from historians; yet the second period, which began around 1907 and which was incomparably more dangerous for Finnish constitutional liberties, has been somewhat neglected. Stolypin was a far more formidable adversary than Bobrikov, whose position in St. Petersburg was by no means secure, and whose attempt to conscript Finns into the imperial army ended in disaster. Not only was Stolypin able to engineer support for his policies within the State Duma, but he also went to the heart of the matter by denying the right of the *Eduskunta* to legislate on matters of general state interest. This complex issue had been discussed by numerous committees since 1884. Stolypin's 1910 legislation decreed that all laws of general state interest appertaining to Finland were to be made by imperial Russian institutions, with the Senate and the *Eduskunta* merely having the right to voice an opinion.

Stolypin undoubtedly enjoyed wide support for his policy. Russian businessmen were angered by the way in which Finnish laws prevented Russians from setting up businesses in the Grand Duchy and were alarmed by the penetration of Russian markets by certain Finnish commodities such as paper, which had captured one-third of the Russian market by 1913. There was also some alarm felt at the growing dominance of Germany in Finland's import trade, and the tariffs imposed by decree in 1914 were largely designed to stem the flow of cheap German grain into the country. Finland still retained its own legal code and courts, which could defy the efforts of the imperial police to bring fugitive revolutionaries to book. After 1905 Finland became something of a haven of refuge for the Russian revolutionary movement, much to the disgust of the right-wing press in Russia. Fear of German military might and the apparent untrustworthiness of the Finns as a whole strengthened the determination of the government and army command to deal with Finland as a borderland, and no longer as a special case. Furthermore, Finnish unwillingness to participate in the State Duma prompted many former foreign sympathisers to accuse the Finns of unreasonable conduct.

The growing inability of the ruling circle in St. Petersburg to regard the Finns as loyal undermined the efforts of those Finns who sought to preserve autonomy by a policy of compliance. Very few Finns had been prepared to go along with the ageing nationalist leader Y. Z. Yrjö-

Koskinen in denouncing the passive resistance as a Swedish clique wagging a Finnish tail, but many shared his basic conviction that Finland was the weaker party in a conflict in which legalistic arguments carried little weight. The pessimistic historical determinism of Snellman and Yrjö-Koskinen, the belief in the Finnish language as the cornerstone of national identity, a respect for authority and a pragmatic approach to the realities of politics formed the substance of the 'appeasement policy' of the Old Finn party. After Yrjö-Koskinen's death in 1903, a more sophisticated 'bridge-building' policy was pursued by J. R. Danielson-Kalmari, who maintained close connections with leading Russians such as Pleve and who sought to meet Russian demands half-way. By 1912 however, Danielson-Kalmari had come to the conclusion that the trend of thought in Russia which had been willing to leave the basic institutions of the Grand Duchy intact in return for acknowledgement of the broader interests of state was no longer a force. He then gradually aligned himself with the opposition, taking much although not all of the Old Finn party with him.

The constitutionalist opposition's principal argument was that to give way before Russian demands would inevitably lead to the whittling away of Finland's constitutional liberties and the destruction of the Finnish state and its institutions. The constitutionalists also hoped for a change of government in Russia, believing that the autocracy would sooner or later give way to a liberal, constitutional state. The crisis of the last years of Russian rule revived once more the old debate about Finland's relationship with Russia. Whereas the Finnish 'appeasers' tended to stress loyalty towards the ruler and an appreciation of the interests of an empire of which Finland was an inseparable part, the constitutionalists tended to present Finland's fight as a defence not only of constitutional liberties but also of Western culture and values against the forces of darkness.

The passive resistance of 1900–5 is a fascinating example of the ability of a small and oppressed nation to organise an effective protest movement, but in retrospect, its limitations were perhaps more striking than its successes. Conservatives on the one hand argued that civil disobedience would inevitably weaken respect for the law, while many young radicals felt that the passive resistance did not go far enough. In their view, the violence of the oppressor had to be met by violence. By 1904, an active resistance movement had come into being. Although activism was never a major political movement, the ideas it generated were to be of some importance in the shaping of Finnish independence. The early activists—mostly Swedish-speaking students and intellectuals

—were committed to the revolution in Russia and the destruction of the autocracy, and it was this commitment which enabled them to see a future role for an independent Finland which neither the Finnish nationalists nor the liberal constitutionalists of the older generation were able to visualise. Activism was above all a youth movement and a revolt against the cautious conservatism of the older generation. Many of the early student activists were shocked by the indifference of the rural population they encountered while they were collecting signatures for the Grand Address of 1899, and they advanced the necessity of close co-operation with the labour movement to further radical social and political reforms in subsequent years. The programme adopted by the Finnish Active Resistance Party in 1904 advocated undermining the loyalty of the people towards the Emperor by the dissemination of revolutionary literature and arms. Activists smuggled weapons into Finland and across the border into Russia, gave refuge to fleeing Russian revolutionaries, and provided accommodation for their meetings. The *enfant terrible* of the movement, Konni Zilliacus, worked tirelessly all over Europe to further the revolutionary cause. He sought to persuade the Japanese to finance his activities, which ranged from persuading Polish soldiers to desert the imperial army in Manchuria to diverting a consignment of second-hand weapons destined for the King of Siam to the revolutionaries. In addition, he wrote scores of articles excoriating the authorities in Finland and advancing the cause of Finnish independence.[8]

The activist commitment to the cause of revolution in Russia was severely pragmatic: revolution in Russia was seen as advancing the cause of Finnish independence. In the same way, a military victory for Germany over Russia in the First World War was deemed to be to Finland's advantage, and it was on Germany that the revived activist movement now pinned its hopes. Early in 1915, agreement was reached in Berlin between the Finnish activists and the German high command for a number of Finnish volunteers to receive military training in Germany. Some 2,000 Finns in all received such training after a hazardous underground exit from Finland. Although the volunteers came from all walks of life, a disproportionate number were Swedish-speaking university students. Activism was in general the response of the Swedish-speaking student youth to Russian oppression. The rapid expansion of the student body during the first decade and a half of the twentieth century had occurred at a time when the measures of the imperial government seemed to threaten employment prospects in the Finnish administration and judiciary: patriotic sentiment, not to speak of Russian chauvinism, virtually precluded a career in the empire. Two of the traditional career openings for the Swedish-speaking student were thus significantly threatened, and this diminution of career prospects may well account for the growing sense of alienation and pessimism of the Swedish student body.

Activism did not attract many Finnish-speaking students, especially in its early days. On the other hand, a number of students who joined the socialist movement came from the ranks of Finnish nationalism. There was indeed a degree of similarity between Finnish nationalism and the deterministic socialism of Karl Kautsky, embraced by the Finnish Social Democratic Party. Both doctrines stressed the importance of preserving a distinct identity and an ideological purity in the face of the enemy; both attached great significance to the workings of historical determinism. It may be that this similarity provided a bridge across which Old Finn students such as O. V. Kuusinen could cross into the socialist camp. In any event, many of the students who joined the labour movement just before its rapid expansion soon secured prominent positions within the party. The old guard of craftsmen and artisans gave way to a younger generation, who gave the party a distinctly more Marxist outlook. One disgruntled socialist remarked in 1907 that 'the party has been swamped by gentlemen in search of a meal ticket, and in order to get this, they try and make themselves out to be as radical as possible so that they aren't accused of being bourgeois.'[9] The revolutionary rhetoric of the party leaders concealed an unwillingness to put slogans into practice, as the Red Guard insurgents discovered during the Sveaborg mutiny of 1906. The leadership of the labour movement was unwilling to commit the entire organisation to the vicissitudes of an underground revolutionary struggle: but the stifling of political life in Finland meant that the movement was unable to maximise its strength in an effective and productive manner. The ineffectiveness of Finland's political institutions only helped reinforce the laager mentality of revolutionary passivity which characterised the Finnish Social Democratic Party.

The party dominated the labour movement. Although the Finnish trade unions came together in 1907 to form a central organisation, *Suomen Ammattijärjestö* (S.A.J.), the trade union movement was still very much in its infancy. Many labour conflicts after 1905 began as a result of the workers' impatience and unrealistic expectations, and failed miserably because of a lack of strike funds. Employers were increasingly reluctant from 1907 onwards to enter into collective bargaining agreements, and showed an aggressiveness in their use of lockouts, blackleg labour and blacklists which underline the basic weakness of the unions. Workers were frequently subjected to victimisation and arbitrary treatment by foremen and employers. Many factories were situated in the countryside, and the employers were therefore in a better position to isolate the workers from outside political influences. The chronic problem of rural economic overpopulation brought large numbers of itinerant and unemployed workers to the outskirts of the larger towns. These areas acquired a reputation for harbouring violent and criminal elements. The potentially dangerous problem of unemployment was highlighted in a letter from a committee on unemployment to the Helsinki town council in the disturbed year of 1906: 'Destitution, which is growing day by day, offers a fertile ground for anarchism and is an ideal source for agitation in the hands of the revolutionary elements in society.'[10]

The land question continued to pose problems. The Social Democratic Party had gained a great deal of political capital from the strikes for a reduction in day labour service and the widely publicised evictions of leaseholders on the Laukko estate in 1907. Attempts to solve the leasehold question by legislation ran into difficulties, and the moratorium on leases of 1909 was due to expire in March 1916, when up to 62,000 tenants faced the possibility of eviction. The Emperor's manifesto of October 1915 prolonged all leases *sine die* until a solution to the problem could be found, but with the Diet seemingly suspended for the duration of the war, such a solution looked unlikely.

The war years if anything exacerbated the social and economic problems of Finland. From the turn of the century the timber industry had begun to direct its exports to Western markets, which became virtually inaccessible with the outbreak of war. By 1917 nearly half the prewar labour force in the timber industry—which employed nearly one-third of the total industrial workforce—had been laid off. The pulp and paper industry suffered less, since it was able to develop its trade with Russia, but smaller industries dependent on Western markets suffered on a scale comparable to that of the timber industry. On the other hand, the metal industry profited from Russian war orders. The gross value of output quadrupled in three years and the number of men employed in the industry almost doubled in two years. There were similar striking increases in output and employment in the textile, leather and chemical industries. This boom did not last; when the demand for war orders ceased in 1917, large numbers of men were laid off. The war also provided employment for able-bodied men as labourers on fortification works. One estimate puts the numbers as high as 100,000 in 1916. The presence of large numbers of these men, often single, and of Russian troops (100,000 by the autumn of 1917) in southern Finland caused considerable social and economic disruption. Fights over girls, drunkenness and outbreaks of hooliganism were frequently recorded in the local press. The army's demands for food supplies, animal fodder and equipment also placed a great strain on the local economy.

The war years seemed to highlight the sense of impotence and lack of purpose which had developed in Finnish society. Political activity had been suspended for the duration. The Senate was in the hands of nonentities supervised by Bobrikov's protégé, Governor-General Seyn. Plans revealed in November 1914 for a comprehensive assimilation of Finland into the empire offered patriotic Finns little incentive to support the Russian or even the Allied war effort. Finland suffered many of the civilian hardships of war without the outlet of military involvement, since she continued to pay the 'war millions' contribution in lieu of conscription. Finland had no soldier heroes, save perhaps the clandestine *Jäger* volunteers. All she had were the speculators, the profiteers, the hoarders and the hooligans.

The malaise of Finnish society during the war years was brilliantly captured by the novelist Joel Lehtonen in his novels *Sorron lapset* (The children of violence) and *Punainen mies* (The red man). In these works, the war profiteers guzzle and think of nothing but amassing more wealth. Farmers, getting rich on the inflated prices of their produce, seek to ape the gentry. The cynical *jeunesse dorée* indulge in a profligate, immoral life, heedless of the future. The 'grey masses', oppressed by rising prices, food shortages and at the mercy of the hoarder and the speculator, are easy prey for the fanatic, the 'red man' who haunts the drifting, disillusioned protagonist of the two novels. The atmosphere of the war years 'was like the period before a thunderstorm, stifling, suffocating, making one restless, almost as if longing for some sort of explosion . . . Finland, once full of hope and youthful vigour, slumped into a heap and began to rot like a mushroom.'[11]

The thunderstorm was to break in 1917.

3

A HARD-WON INDEPENDENCE
1917–1920

'A revolution is generally followed by a reaction. A revolution may be powerful enough to overthrow an existing régime which is already enfeebled, but it is rarely so powerful as to be able to create a new one. In other words, it does not represent the force of right; it becomes a state of oppression lacking legitimacy and therefore will not last . . . It is in vain to talk of the supposed new spirit created by revolutions: history teaches us that they belong to periods of decadence in nations and states to a far greater extent than to periods of development.'

J. V. Snellman, in *Litteraturbladet*, 1881

Revolution and civil war (1917–1918)

During the revolutionary days of March 1917, the pillars of imperial authority in Finland collapsed amid a great deal of confusion. The Finnish political parties, initially taken by surprise by the rapid course of events in Petrograd, were able to secure from the Russian Provisional Government a manifesto on 20 March which rescinded the decrees of the previous decade directed against Finnish rights, promised a new constitutional settlement, and convened the *Eduskunta* elected in 1916. A new Governor-General, known for his support of Finland in earlier days, and a Finnish-born Minister State-Secretary were appointed, while the Senate was taken over by a coalition of six socialists and six non-socialists. Throughout the country the old and hated servants of the fallen régime were arrested and driven from office. Finns could once more feel in control of their own destiny, or at least in control of the institutions guaranteed by the former rulers of the Grand Duchy.

However, the collapse of the autocracy posed a question which was evaded in the scramble for a restoration of rights in March: who should

40

inherit the prerogatives of the former ruler? The more conservative Finnish jurists and politicians argued that plenary powers during the interregnum passed from the deposed ruler to the Provisional Government, while the socialists and activists held that the Provisional Government had no claim to exercise authority in Finland; with the demise of the ruler, the right to exercise his prerogatives passed to the *Eduskunta*. This latter argument was weakened by the fact that the Provisional Government had exercised one of these prerogatives by convening the *Eduskunta*, and by choosing to negotiate with that government, the Finns only strengthened its claims to authority in Finland. For its part, the Provisional Government consistently maintained that it was merely holding the ring until the National Constituent Assembly could meet to decide finally what the future relationship of Finland and Russia was to be.

The relationship between the Provisional Government and the Finnish Senate and *Eduskunta* was overshadowed by the war, which in 1917 spread into the eastern Baltic. The Russians were aware of the presence of Finnish volunteers in the German Army, and were anxious to minimise German influence in Finland, although the conciliatory tone of Kerensky and others, who in March promised an amnesty to all Finns under arms in Germany, soon changed. The advance of the German armies in the summer of 1917 led to a build-up of troop units in Finland, at a time of increasing food shortages in the country and of widespread indiscipline among the soldiers and sailors. Serious mutinies had occurred in units of the Baltic Fleet on 16–17 March, and discipline was further undermined by political agitation. Soviets were set up in fleet and army units stationed in Finland; although largely non-political in composition at first, by the autumn they were mostly dominated by the Bolsheviks and left-wing Socialist revolutionaries, both hostile to the Provisional Government. The presence of a politicised soldiery in Finland undoubtedly added to the problems faced by a harassed Senate, grappling not only with the problems of inflation, food shortages and social unrest but also trying to sort out Finland's relations with the new Russia.

During the spring and early summer, the Social Democratic Party played the leading role in efforts to advance the cause of Finnish independence. The party held an absolute majority in the *Eduskunta*, and half the seats in the Senate. In a memorandum handed to Kerensky on 29 March and later presented to representatives of Russian socialist parties, the socialists argued for complete and internationally guaranteed internal independence for Finland within the framework of union with

Russia. Even in the dying moments of post-revolutionary euphoria and goodwill, Kerensky voiced his misgivings, and as April drew on it became clear that the Provisional Government was unwilling to countenance even minor amendments to the Russo-Finnish relationship. By the end of April deadlock had been reached and attitudes had begun to harden. On 20 April, in a speech to the *Eduskunta* which aroused considerable alarm in the circles supporting the L'vov government in Russia, the socialist deputy chairman of the Senate, Oskari Tokoi, appealed to the Russian people and government to allow Finland the right of national self-determination. A month later Tokoi and Yrjö Mäkelin, a socialist with close activist connections and an old campaigner for Finnish national independence, presented a new set of proposals to Prince L'vov, calling for the transfer of all the prerogatives of the former ruler to the Senate, with the exception of matters which affected the constitutional relationship between the two countries and the rights of Russian citizens and institutions in Finland. This surprise move annoyed the non-socialist members of the delegation which had gone to meet L'vov, and caused deep resentment in government circles in Petrograd. At the same time Kerensky, in a speech to Russian units in Helsinki, made it plain that his government did not intend to give way to Finnish separatist demands.[1]

The Finnish Social Democratic Party, which had been extremely isolated from the developments of international and Russian socialism during the war years, now began to turn to their fellow-socialists for support. A delegation sent to Petrograd at the end of April found the Mensheviks distinctly unsympathetic, but the Bolsheviks were prepared to support Finnish independence and urged the Finnish socialists to drop the idea of international guarantees and come out openly against the Provisional Government. A Finnish socialist delegation was also sent to canvass support among the Western socialist parties which had sent delegates to the Stockholm conference, convened by a Dutch-Scandinavian committee to prepare a socialist peace initiative.

On 8 June the Senate laid before the *Eduskunta* a bill which sought to provide a temporary arrangement of Finnish affairs which might be acceptable to the Provisional Government. The bill could be construed as conferring certain important prerogatives, such as the convening of the *Eduskunta*, upon the Provisional Government; but since it refrained from naming that government and employed the vague formula of 'supreme government authority', the bill merely opened the door for further debate on the very nature of that authority. During the committee stage, the bill was radically transformed. The *Eduskunta* was given the right to convene and dissolve itself, and the Senate was to be made responsible to it. These changes were the work of the socialist majority, which had now abandoned the policy of compromise it had hitherto followed in its dealings with the Provisional Government. At the Social Democratic Party conference in mid-June, a resolution demanding full national independence was passed and was presented to delegates attending the first All-Russian Congress of Soviets at the beginning of July. Although the Bolshevik minority at the congress urged support for full Finnish independence, the majority resolution on the Finnish question, although conceding the right of national self-determination, insisted that final settlement of the Finnish question could only be achieved in the All-Russian National Constituent Assembly. The Finnish socialists chose to ignore this vital rider. Instead, the three main clauses of the resolution passed by the Congress of Soviets, which shifted most of the prerogatives of the former ruler to the competence of the *Eduskunta*, became the basis for a new bill which replaced that originally introduced by the Senate on 8 June. This was passed by a large majority of socialist and non-socialist supporters of independence at its final reading on 17-18 July. The debate on the final reading occurred at the height of the July uprising in Petrograd, when the fate of the Provisional Government seemed to hang in the balance. The suppression of the uprising strengthened the hand of the Provisional Government. A number of leading Bolsheviks were arrested. Others, including Lenin, took refuge in Finland. The rebellious sailors of the Baltic Fleet were cowed into submission, and when Finnish socialists tried to enlist support for the law of 18 July among the representatives of the soldiers and sailors, they were rebuffed. Kerensky, now Prime Minister, responded to the Finnish action by ordering the dissolution of the *Eduskunta* on 31 July. Although the socialist majority protested, it was powerless to offer any opposition.

The dissolution of the *Eduskunta* marked the apogee of the Provisional Government's influence upon events in Finland. During the autumn its authority waned rapidly as the Soviets in Finland came under the control of its opponents, who virtually refused to obey the orders of the Kerensky government. The constitutional deadlock remained until the Bolshevik seizure of power in Petrograd created a new power vacuum in Finland. By this time, the political initiative had passed decisively from the socialists to the non-socialist parties, who managed to achieve a total of 108 seats in the *Eduskunta* elections of 3-4 October. During the spring, the non-socialist parties had lacked a cohesive and united policy on the question of Finland's future. Conservative opinion tended to favour a cautious and conciliatory policy, and the advocates of independence were even denied space in official party newspapers. The activists were isolated from the traditional mainstream of Finnish politics, and were regarded with suspicion by those with pro-Entente sympathies. By the late summer, however, the faction pressing for independence had made considerable headway in the non-socialist parties, thanks in part to the intransigence of the Provisional Government which revived old fears and suspicions about Russian chauvinism and weakened the conservative view of the Provisional Government as the legitimate inheritor of the Emperor's prerogatives.

It is difficult nevertheless to view the evolution of the idea of Finnish independence during 1917 as anything other than an exploitation of the opportunities which war and revolution had suddenly opened up. This is not to deny the existence of the idea of an independent Finland—which had been discussed, albeit in a desultory fashion, from the late eighteenth century onwards. But on the whole the preservation of Finnish autonomy had been the objective of the established political groups right up to the 1917 revolution. The experience of 1917 showed that this was no longer enough. The final demise of the autocracy suddenly opened up a debate on the future of Finland in which independence came to be accepted by all sides as the only solution.

What sort of independence this was to be, and how it was to be achieved, provoked various responses. Revolutionary solidarity inclined the social democrats to demand a peaceful settlement with the Russian people and government, yet they were unwilling for Finland to enter into any sort of democratic federation and they displayed great suspicion of the intentions of the Provisional Government. Although the resolution on independence passed at the party conference in June 1917 resembled Lenin's advocacy of the right to national self-determination, i.e. that this would enable the proletariat to pursue the class struggle more freely and effectively, there is little evidence to show that the Finnish socialists regarded this as a necessary prelude to the creation of a brotherhood of socialist republics. The Finnish socialists also shared the view of the activists of the necessity of international guarantees for an independent Finland, which the Bolsheviks condemned as a futile exercise. The tone, if not the substance of the memorandum presented to the preparatory committee for the Stockholm conference by the Finnish socialist delegation was markedly different from that employed in dealings with the Russian revolutionaries. One of the socialist delegates to Stockholm later admitted privately to a fellow-delegate that the party flirted with the activists at the same time as it played games with the Russian revolutionaries, and detailed examination would indeed suggest that the socialists were opportunists rather than men of principle on the question of Finnish independence.[2]

The socialists' principal achievement, the law of 18 July, was more a challenge to the Provisional Government than a serious attempt to solve the problem of who exercised supreme authority in Finland. It transferred fundamental powers to the competence of the *Eduskunta*, but since foreign affairs and the control of the armed forces were specifically excluded from that competence, the question of sovereignty still remained an open one.[3]

The Social Democratic Party in 1917 was faced with the dilemma of exercising power in a bourgeois state, and although the argument that exceptional circumstances might justify entry into government prevailed in the party council, the party never gave wholehearted support to its luckless right-wingers who entered government. It remained unwilling to take up the challenge of participation in government in a bourgeois state, and it was incapable of planning a revolutionary seizure of power in the Leninist manner. Unlike the Bolsheviks, the Finnish socialist party had never been proscribed: it was a mass party with all the paraphernalia of a large modern political party, responsive to developments in Western social democracy rather than to the Russian revolutionary movement. On the other hand, however, the paralysis of Finnish political institutions during the last decade of Russian rule meant that the labour movement was given virtually no opportunity to accustom itself to the running of the affairs of the state, at any level. In such circumstances, the Social Democratic Party was able to maintain its ideological hostility towards any idea of participating in the government of the bourgeois state: hence the highly ambivalent attitude adopted by the party leadership towards socialist participation in government in 1917. It is also important to remember the 'revolutionary inheritance' of the party, which had become a major political force as a result of the revolution of 1905. In 1917 the party leadership was subjected once more to pressure from its masses, who demanded radical solutions in revolutionary times.

The stresses and strains in Finnish society were particularly acute in 1917. The shift from arable to dairy farming in previous decades meant that by 1914 Finland was only able to satisfy about 40 per cent of domestic consumer demand for bread grain. During the war, it had had to rely on imports of Russian grain, but in the chaos of revolution, these supplies could no longer be guaranteed. The Senate had failed to maintain stocks, and Väinö Tanner as minister in charge of food supplies discovered in spring 1917 that grain stocks were virtually non-existent. Food shortages were accompanied by rising prices. In the summer of 1917, prices of certain comestibles shot up to as much as six times the level of 1913 prices. The cost of living index (1913=100) was 200 at the end of 1916, and 400 at the end of 1917, while the internal purchasing power of the mark (1913=100) fell to 22 points. As the exchange rate for the rouble had been fixed by imperial decree in 1913, the Bank of Finland accumulated millions of all but worthless Russian notes and was forced to increase the normal mark issue almost sixfold. Goods, such as dairy produce, which fetched high prices in Petrograd almost vanished from Finnish markets as farmers and speculators cashed in on the fixed exchange rate. The wartime industrial boom collapsed as war orders dried up; the digging of fortification lines, which had employed many thousands, came to an end, not only exacerbating rising unemployment but releasing rough and unstable elements into the heady atmosphere of revolution.

Strike action had been forbidden during the war, but the revolution also unleashed a huge wave of labour conflicts, especially in the countryside. Whereas industrial workers struck principally for higher wages, farmworkers were more concerned with reduction of working hours. Striking farmworkers were often ill-organised and poorly co-ordinated, and as farmers banded together to defend their interests and recruited strike-breakers, violence frequently flared up. The demands put forward by the strikers were often hopelessly unrealistic, indicative of the revolutionary atmosphere in which the strikes were conducted and the weakness of trade union discipline. There were also a number of attempted takeovers of local councils, and food riots occurred in the towns, where the socialist-dominated militia which had replaced the police forces often proved incapable of maintaining order. As the summer lengthened, there were growing calls in the non-socialist press for firm measures to end the lawlessness. The restoration of law and order was a major issue in the October elections, and it served to bring together the two Finnish parties into an electoral bloc. The major victor of the elections was the Agrarian Party, which contested the eastern and northern electoral circles, increased its 1916 vote by 70 per cent and won seven new seats. The 1917 election in fact reflected the growing conflict between urban consumer and rural producer as much as anything else. The success of the Agrarians, who had supported the law of 18 July and were committed to independence for Finland, placed them in a key position when the *Eduskunta* met in November.

Growing social unrest and the loss of its absolute parliamentary majority in the elections caused the Social Democratic Party to adopt a more openly militant line. The party and union leadership sanctioned the creation of workers' guards, which soon adopted the more emotive title of Red Guards, partly in response to the growing *Suojeluskunta* (civil guards) movement, which brought together those seeking to win national liberation and the anti-labour vigilante groups set up by farmers in strike-ridden southern Finland during the summer. A wide-ranging programme of political and social demands was laid before the *Eduskunta* by the socialists on 8 November. On the same day, as the Bolsheviks were seizing power in Petrograd, a central revolutionary council of trade unionists, members of the party executive and the *Eduskunta* group, was set up to exercise temporary direction of the whole labour movement. Although there is some evidence to suggest that a plan to seize power had been sketched out by O. V. Kuusinen, the leading party theoretician, subsequent events were to show that the revolutionary council was in no way committed to this course of action. On 9 November the socialist programme of reforms and an Agrarian motion calling for the promulgation of the law of 18 July by the *Eduskunta* were both defeated as a result of tactical voting by the bourgeois bloc, and the non-socialist majority approved the Speaker's motion calling for the election of a regency council, in accordance with the terms of the Gustavian Act of Government of 1772, to exercise temporary supreme authority.

From the outset there was strong opposition from the sizeable minority of moderate advocates of a parliamentary tactic on the revolutionary council to any form of revolutionary action. On the other hand, the parliamentary way now seemed closed. Further attempts to push through the demands of the labour movement were rebuffed in the *Eduskunta*, and on 13 November the threatened general strike began.

The strike was sufficient to persuade the moderates of the necessity of pushing reforms through the *Eduskunta*, and on 15 November the socialist and Agrarian groups made common cause to vote through a new motion, transferring supreme authority temporarily to the *Eduskunta*. The socialists then took the opportunity to force through two bills of the previous session dealing with the eight-hour working day and local government franchise reform. The moderates who dominated the socialist parliamentary group were clearly prepared to compromise in order to achieve legislated reforms, and by 16 November they had virtually withdrawn from the revolutionary council, which was also under pressure from militant workers to implement an effective seizure of power. Early in the morning of 16 November, the revolutionary council voted by a narrow majority to seize power, but hastily reversed this decision after the trade unionists had declined the honour of sharing the task of carrying out the seizure of power. Three days later the strike was called off. The workers were told of the reforms forced out of the *Eduskunta*, and were promised a socialist government. The strike ended in considerable disorder. Dissident groups of Red Guards threatened to break with the party and carry on the struggle. In an atmosphere of mutual recrimination, an extraordinary party conference on 25–7 November finally resolved to leave the question of future tactics to the joint decision of the parliamentary group and the party council. In the meantime, on 26 November, the non-socialist majority in the *Eduskunta* approved the government programme of P. E. Svinhufvud, and this veteran opponent of Russian oppression immediately acted on his government's declared intention of proclaiming Finnish independence. On 4 December the new government gave notice of its intention to the *Eduskunta*, and two days later the bourgeois majority voted approval for the government to embark on measures essential for the recognition of Finnish independence. The socialists declared their support of independence, but proposed negotiated agreement with Russia as the best means of achieving this. The failure of foreign powers to recognise the independence of Finland vindicated the socialists' position, and after three weeks of hesitation, a delegation headed by Svinhufvud received formal recognition of Finnish independence from the Soviet government at the end of the year.

Independence was the only alternative open to Finland in the chaos of a new revolution in Russia, but it did not settle who exercised sovereign authority. The resolution of this problem was the major task of the Svinhufvud government, but in seeking to establish its own authority it clashed with the organised labour movement, which was being driven by pressure from below to adopt a revolutionary stance. The majority vote in the *Eduskunta* on 12 January granting the government full powers to create a police force and army to restore order was interpreted by the labour movement as a whole as directed against the working class, and it undoubtedly helped to bring the moderates and radicals closer together. The dissident Red Guards, with whom the socialist party leadership had concluded an uneasy truce in January, were busily engaged in gun-running activities on the Viipuri-Petrograd line. White Guard attempts to disrupt this traffic brought about full-

scale fighting in the Karelian isthmus on 19 January. General Mannerheim, a former imperial Russian officer of thirty years' service, arrived
in Ostrobothnia on the same day, three days after his appointment as
commander of the government's forces. His brief was to organise
and train a force to restore order. On 25 January, the day on which the
Suojeluskunta White Guards were officially proclaimed the troops of the
Finnish government, a special five-man directive committee set up by
the action of the Social Democratic Party council took the decision to
seize power.

At the same time as the Reds staged their seizure of power in Helsinki
on 27–8 January, White forces in Ostrobothnia were moving into
action to disarm the Russian garrisons stationed there. Although the
Reds managed to occupy key public buildings without much incident,
they were unable to prevent the escape of three government ministers
who managed to reach Mannerheim's forces and set up a rump government in Vaasa. Other leading politicians, including Svinhufvud,
managed to evade capture. Having mopped up the Russian troops
without much resistance by the beginning of February, the White army
turned to the second stage of its war of liberation: the suppression of
the Red rebellion in the south. The civil war front stretched from
Ostrobothnia to Karelia, with the Reds in control of much of the industry and most of the major towns in the country. The Whites held
northern Finland, Ostrobothnia and most of Karelia, with the railway
line between Vaasa on the coast and Käkisalmi on Lake Ladoga linking
the forces of the White army. The Red Guards, although probably
numerically superior (estimates vary between 75,000 and 100,000 men,
although the combat strength was probably no more than 50,000),
were poorly equipped and lacked trained and effective leadership, and
they failed to break the vital line of communication between Ostrobothnia and Karelia in a series of offensives in February. The White
army (about 70,000 men by the end of the war), professionally led by
Swedish volunteers and former Russian army officers of Finnish birth
such as Mannerheim, and further stiffened by the return of the German-
trained *Jäger* troops, took up the offensive against the key industrial
town of Tampere in March. Tampere fell as a German expeditionary
force was landing in southern Finland, having been sent in response to
pleas for aid from White Finnish representatives in Berlin. Red
resistance collapsed in April, and hundreds of refugees fled with the Red
government to Russia. Thousands more were interned in prison
camps.[4]

The Finnish civil war lasted some three months. Unlike the civil disorders which erupted elsewhere in Europe in 1918–19 it was a full-blooded national war, fought on fronts and not on streets. Moreover, unlike other European socialist parties, the Finnish Social Democratic Party preserved formal unity throughout the war. The split in the Finnish labour movement did not occur until August 1918, when left-wing exiles founded the Finnish Communist Party in Moscow. The programme adopted by the new party reflected the 'infantile disease' of left-wing communism, later castigated by Lenin and symptomatic of the bitterness of defeat, rather than a continuation of the line followed by the old Social Democratic Party. Although one Finnish historian has recently made some interesting comparisons between the Finnish Red government and the Council of People's Commissars, it must be said that in all important respects they were widely different, in particular with regard to the motives for seizing power. The Finnish socialists saw their principal task to be the preservation of democracy from the threat of a reactionary bourgeois coup, and shrank from pursuing a full-blooded social revolution. The men who staged the ineffectual seizure of power in January 1918 were kinsmen of the German Independent Socialists rather than of the Russian Bolsheviks.

In spite of emotional bonds of revolutionary solidarity, the Finnish Red government found itself gravely embarrassed by the White accusation that it relied on foreign bayonets, and was anxious to settle affairs with the Russians as soon as possible. In the negotiations leading to the 1 March treaty settling outstanding issues between the two countries, the Finnish delegates sought to emphasise the national independence of Finland and even to acquire further territory. Russian troops who did fight on the Red side were ill-disciplined and more of a liability than an asset. The major Russian contribution to the Red effort was the supply of arms and equipment.

The Whites regarded the civil war as one of liberation, a fight to rid the country of Russian troops, and the evil influences of Bolshevism, in order to establish Finland's independence. Reformist socialists saw the war as a tragedy, provoked by bourgeois intransigence and the machinations of the revolutionary element in the Social Democratic camp. Communists accounted for the failure of the revolution by criticising the lack of revolutionary awareness and ruthlessness of the old party leadership. More recently, the neutral term 'civil war' has tended to replace emotive labels, just as dispassionate and objective detailed studies have replaced the tendentious literature of earlier decades. Nevertheless, Finnish historians still tend to see the war as caused primarily by events in Russia in 1917. Rasila has for instance concluded that 'the social shortcomings in Finland would apparently not have been enough to cause a civil war without the impetus provided by the events in Russia and the presence of Russian troops in the country', and Puntila has asserted that 'the events in Finland at the beginning of 1918 were a war of liberation, in which an alien army was expelled from the country'; this alien army hindered the establishment of authority, and encouraged rebellion against any attempts to establish authority by its continued presence.[5] Given that Finland had been linked to Russia for more than a century, it is highly unlikely that she could have escaped the civil unrest which attended the collapse of the empire. The implicit belief of most modern Finnish historians of the civil war, that Finland was somehow temporarily afflicted by the disease of revolution which had broken out in Russia, ignores the fact that civil unrest and conflict were endemic throughout Europe in the period 1917–20 at the end of a traumatic and revolutionising war. It also tends to underestimate the social and political problems within Finland itself, or rather the way in which contemporary Finns thought they should solve these problems. In the decade or so before 1917 social and cultural restraints upon violence had been seriously weakened in Finland. Russian political oppression had divided society, and encouraged more extreme elements. Activism saw force as the only way of combating autocratic oppression. The 1905 strike left a myth of the efficacy of spontaneous mass action which the failure of the *Eduskunta* to provide vital reforms did nothing to diminish. The revolution of 1917 seemed to offer a new opportunity for radical reform borne forward by revolutionary mass action. The frustrations of past years welled up in demands for immediate redress and change, and the aggrieved were not averse to using desperate means to secure their objectives. The social shortcomings of Finland were by no means exceptional, but they were made worse by the distortions of the political situation. Politics in Finland lacked the normal restraints and limits of everyday democracy. Parliamentary democracy had never functioned properly, and Finnish politicians lacked experience of the responsibilities which appertain to working democracy. Their perspectives were therefore often hopelessly unreal and their actions were sometimes taken without much regard to the consequences. The lack of power was as damaging as a surfeit of power, for it made the short-cut and the big gesture that much more attractive.

The Svinhufvud government voted into office by the non-socialist majority of the *Eduskunta* in November 1917 was committed to independence and the restoration of law and order. In seeking to establish its authority this government clashed with the labour movement. The leaders of the labour movement were driven to attempt a seizure of power in January 1918 more by fear of being left high and dry by insurrectionary mass action than through conviction of the necessity of social revolution. They believed they were fighting to preserve democracy against a vicious bourgeois counter-revolution. The initial White version of a civil war provoked by 'a number of power-hungry individuals' who had incited a section of the Finnish populace to rise up in rebellion against legitimate authority 'aided by foreign bayonets' soon gave way to the notion that the Whites were fighting a war of liberation to create a strong national state. The dynamic element of White ideology undoubtedly came from wartime activism and the *Jäger* movement. The *Jäger* officers were strongly pro-German, and distrusted the older ex-imperial Russian army officers such as Mannerheim who commanded the White forces. A number of wartime activists were also influential in the forging of Finnish foreign policy in 1918. For these men, Russia was the principal enemy, and russophobia came to be the moving force of the Finnish nationalism forged during the war years. Hence the term 'War of Liberation' (*Vapaussota*) had a political significance for the inter-war nationalists who sought to replace class antagonism by a sense of national solidarity.[6]

The recognition of Finnish independence (1918–1920)

The concept of a war to liberate the Finnish people from the Russian yoke acquired a new dimension even before the Reds were finally defeated. In his Order of the Day issued on 23 February 1918, Mannerheim swore not to sheathe his sword until the last soldier of Lenin had been driven not only from Finland, but from Karelia as well. Karelia had long been cherished by Finnish nationalists as the heartland of Finnish culture, but only the western fringes had ever been a part of the Grand Duchy. In the chaos of war and revolution the idea of 'liberating' the area bounded by Ladoga in the south, Lake Onega in the east and with a White Sea coastline stretching north to the Kola peninsula and placing it under Finnish control gained new impetus. In 1917, Finnish activists had been working on a programme of autonomy for Karelia. In January 1918, a meeting of Karelians in the Kem district called for a Karelian republic and sought the aid of the Finnish *Eduskunta* to achieve this end. During the civil war, the Finnish Reds sought to acquire Karelian territory in their negotiations with the Soviet government, while on 15 March Mannerheim ordered expeditionary units across the frontier into the Kem district. With its vast tracts of forest and mineral resources, Karelia was a rich prize, and it seems that the Karelians themselves were reluctant to cede away these resources without some guarantee of local economic autonomy from the Finns. In the event, however, the vast majority of Karelians were either indifferent or openly hostile to Finnish intervention, and Karelian nationalism itself was very much a Finnish-inspired creation.

Not only the Finns were interested in the fate of Karelia. British commercial interests were well aware of the potential of the northern Russian forests, and these played an important part in the development of British intervention in Russia during the years 1918–19. On 4 March 1918, the War Cabinet in London decided to send naval reinforcements to Murmansk to strengthen the garrison defending a valuable supply depot which it was feared might fall into German hands as a result of the Russo-German peace, or of German aggression via Finland. The German landing on the Åland islands on 5 March, and on the Finnish mainland in April served to strengthen fears of a German thrust towards the Murmansk base, and the White Finnish attack across the Karelian frontier was interpreted as part of a sinister German design. The Finnish representative in London was given to understand in April that Britain would regard a Finnish seizure of the Murmansk railway as a *casus belli*. On 10 May, a small unit of Finnish Whites sent to occupy the ice-free port of Petsamo on the Arctic coast, to which the Finnish government laid claim, was beaten off by a detachment of British Marines and Russian Red Guards sent to protect the port. This incident further inflamed relations between London and the new Finnish régime, especially as a protest note drafted by the Finnish government seemed to imply some sort of ultimatum.

The Petsamo incident revived Allied fears of German influence over Finland, and revealed the inexperience of the new Finnish government in the complex arena of international affairs. The conduct of foreign policy was in the hands of men totally lacking in diplomatic experience; moreover, those in key positions still pursued the political aims of activism. For this reason, White Finland found itself enmeshed in the final phase of great power politics before the collapse of the Central Powers. The political and commercial treaties concluded with Germany in March 1918 virtually reduced Finland to the status of a vassal. The Senate's decision in May to allow the German troops to stay in Finland and even move north into Lapland, and the hectic attempts to secure a German prince as king of the new state, placed Finland firmly in the German camp as far as the Allies were concerned. The Finnish representative in London, Rudolf Holsti, was distrusted and kept in the dark by the Senate. Relations with Sweden, the one Baltic state which might have offered diplomatic aid to Finland, were extremely bad as a result of an ill-conceived Swedish attempt to establish a kind of protectorate over the Åland islands in February.

By July 1918 the Finnish government was caught between Germany and the Allies. The latter demanded that Finland show her good faith by desisting from any further aggression against Karelia, while Germany wished to involve Finland in an attack against Murmansk in conjunction with Red Russian troops. All that the Germans could offer as bait was a vague promise of territorial adjustment in Karelia with the Soviet government. The Finns were unwilling to fall in with the German plans, but since the failure of the expeditionary force to conquer and occupy Karelia in the spring and the evident rejection by the Allies of the Finnish plea that they merely wished to protect their Karelian kinsmen from Bolshevik rule, they had little option but to continue negotiations with Germany. A projected military alliance drafted in July contained no explicit mention of Finland's claims to East Karelia, and it obliged Finland to introduce a constitutional settlement—namely a German king—as a prerequisite of future friendly relations. The Finnish government was already committed to this kind of settlement, and had indeed made the election of a German prince to a Finnish throne a necessary condition for German support for Finnish claims to East Karelia. However, the Germans rebuffed Finnish attempts to persuade the Kaiser to allow his son, Prince Oskar, to be proposed as a future king of Finland, and they also failed to back Finnish demands for East Karelia in the abortive peace negotiations between Finland and Soviet Russia held in Berlin in August. These negotiations were held as a result of an offer of co-operation between Finnish and Russian troops made by the Soviet government, alarmed at the build-up of Allied troops in Archangel, and their failure illustrated the profound mistrust and double-dealing which existed on all three sides. The Bolsheviks needed aid in their fight against intervention, but suspected German designs against Petrograd. These fears the Germans sought to dispel in the supplementary treaty with Soviet Russia of 27 August in which the sphere of operations against the Allies was kept well clear of the Petrograd area. Germany undertook to respect Russian territorial integrity in the area of operations and ensure the withdrawal of Finnish troops once the Allied forces had been driven out. This was not what the Finns wanted, as a new draft military treaty, calling for German aid in conquering Karelia, clearly showed.[7] This Finnish draft was never taken up by the Germans, and although officials of the *Auswärtiges Amt* intimated to the members of the Finnish peace delegation in Berlin that the annexation of Karelia might be linked with an assault on the Allies in northern Russia, it seems clear that this was a deception rather than an actual German intention. The indignant characterisation of the policy of the German government as a 'brutal exploitation of the patriotic idealism' of the Finns by Carl Enckell, one of the delegates sent to Berlin in August 1918, is a sad but apt comment.[8]

Although Finland found herself enmeshed in great power politics, her position was made worse by the rather ingenuous pro-German policy of the Svinhufvud and Paasikivi governments (the latter taking office in May after the elevation of Svinhufvud to the office of Regent). The activists had been agitating throughout 1917 for some form of German intervention on Finland's behalf, and they were given active encouragement by Svinhufvud when he assumed office in November 1917. The treaties concluded with Germany in March 1918 not only effectively established German patronage over the independent state, but offered scope for German economic penetration which would have turned Finland into a virtual German colony. The government's decision to model the new Finnish army on German lines, with German advisers supervising training, caused the resignation of General Mannerheim, and the attempt to have a German prince elected as king of Finland not only divided the country, but was seen in the West as further proof of Finnish subservience to Berlin. The German collapse in November therefore placed the Finnish government in an exceedingly difficult situation.

Of the Allied powers only France had recognised Finland, on 4 January, but the pro-German policy of the Finnish government caused a rupture in diplomatic relations. Britain too had been on the verge of recognising Finland's independence, but the outbreak of civil war and the subsequent conflict in northern Russia prevented this step being taken. In his study of Anglo-Finnish relations at this time, Eino Lyytinen has argued that by August 1918 the British Foreign Office was beginning to see the value of Finland as a potential ally in the growing conflict in Russia. After the crisis in Anglo-Finnish relations as a result of the Petsamo incident, the British began to adopt a conciliatory policy towards Finland, assuring the government of their sympathy with Finland's right to national self-determination and even with the Finnish claim on Petsamo. British troops in the Murmansk area were ordered not to violate Finnish territory, and the British government disclaimed any intention of supporting an attack on Finland by the Murmansk Legion, which was largely composed of Finnish Red refugees and which had concluded a form of alliance with the British command in northern Russia in May to repel German and white Finnish attacks.

The reason for the policy of conciliation was the growing awareness of the British Foreign Office that a German collapse was imminent, and a desire to use Finland in the fight for a 'reconstituted' Russia. The Finnish government welcomed this new approach, but remained sceptical about the Allies' intentions. Germany was committed by treaty to gain recognition for Finnish independence at a peace conference, and the Finns still believed that a negotiated peace was possible. They also cherished hopes of obtaining East Karelia. Although certain junior officials in the Foreign Office suggested that Britain secure Finnish loyalty by according recognition of independence and even supporting territorial demands, official policy was one of reserve.

The first Finnish approach to the Allies in November was made via General Mannerheim, who was commonly regarded as having escaped the general opprobrium now attached to the Finnish régime by his resignation in protest at the Senate's policies. Mannerheim visited London and Paris, and was presented with six demands as a precondition for the resumption of diplomatic relations by the French government. These included the formation of a new government friendly to the Allied victors, which would repudiate the pro-German policies of its predecessors, the evacuation of German troops still in Finland, and the holding of elections for a new *Eduskunta*. Although Mannerheim assured the British government that a number of these conditions had already been fulfilled, Britain was by no means satisfied and continued to withhold recognition, although the embargo on food supplies was lifted.

The future of Finnish independence was once more linked to the future of Russia. In the end, this was to be determined by the collapse of foreign intervention in Russia and the retention of power by the Bolshevik regime, but at the end of 1918 it was a central issue in the post-war politics of the victorious Allies. The dominant theme of the complex web of negotiations was whether or not the future Russia should occupy the territory it had held in 1914. In spite of the fierce anti-Bolshevism of leading advocates of intervention such as Winston Churchill and General Mannerheim, the crux of the matter was territorial rather than ideological. This is the view of most Western historians. For example, Richard Ullman has argued that the separation of peripheral areas from the former Russian empire would have corresponded to the imperial interests of Britain in Asia, and Lyytinen has developed this thesis with regard to Finland. Kalervo Hovi has characterised French policy as moulded by fear more of Germany than of Bolshevism. The *cordon sanitaire* was, in his view, a short-term attempt to contain Bolshevism, and its possible deleterious effects in Germany, and it was subordinate to the main aim of French diplomacy, the creation of a *barrière de l'est* directed against Germany. France was also concerned about British involvement in the Baltic, and sought to counter this by supporting Finnish and Estonian demands for recognition. Unfortunately for France, her ambitions were not matched by her resources. Germany was replaced by Britain in the Baltic sphere of military operations, although significantly the British were unable to match German economic penetration of the Baltic area, and their military and naval presence in the Baltic was to be a temporary phase.[9]

The arguments advanced by Lyytinen and Hovi are very persuasive, but they do tend to assume a continuity of aims in a period of fundamental change. The old order in central and eastern Europe collapsed in 1917–18. Out of the ruins emerged a new Communist régime, dedicated to world revolution. In 1919, it seemed as if the 'Red peril' would spread across Europe, and this menace added an ideological dimension to intervention in Russia which had been lacking in 1918, when economic interests were mingled with hopes of containing German influence in the East. The emergence of small states clamouring for recognition out of the husks of former empires also posed problems for the statesmen of the great powers. Would these states prove viable, or would they be reduced to economic or political dependence upon larger and potentially hostile powers? The example of Finland in 1918 was not an encouraging one for the Allied powers: even if Finland could be won over to the Allied interventionist cause by recognition of its independence, the problem of keeping Finland in the Allied camp would still remain. Given that British foreign policy traditionally regarded the Baltic as a German-Russian preserve, the likelihood of any future direct British aid to a beleaguered Finland was remote. It may well be that Britain desired to weaken Russia in Asia by erecting a barrier of Caucasian and Transcaucasian states—and this was defined as the British sphere of influence in agreement with the French at the end of 1917—but it does not follow that she wished to weaken Russia still more by supporting the independence of small states on her European borders. Indeed, the evidence suggests that Britain adopted a very reserved attitude even to the creation of an independent Poland; and although willing to support the small Baltic states in their struggle to drive back the Bolsheviks, Britain was not prepared to grant recognition until all hopes of a reconstituted Russia had faded away. France was noticeably more willing to recognise Finnish independence at the end of 1918 than Britain. On 19 January 1919, the French proposed joint and final recognition of Finland by the Allied powers, and on 1 February resumed diplomatic relations without waiting for the reply of the other powers. The British and American governments refused to modify their conditions, insisting that a thorough change of policy would have to be made in Finland before any recognition could be countenanced.

In Hovi's view, France's unilateral and somewhat precipitate action was designed to counter German influence and steal a march on Britain. Both Britain and the United States were disposed to accept Finnish independence as a *de facto* reality, but were in no hurry to provide *de jure* recognition. The Finns appeared slow to comply with the conditions laid down by the Allies—the Ingman government established in November 1918 still contained a number of compromised pro-German monarchists, prompting the French envoy to Stockholm to comment sarcastically: 'À la place d'un cheval aveugle, nous avons maintenant un cheval borgne: c'est un progrès.'[10] As a result of the *Eduskunta* elections at the beginning of March, however, the pro-German right suffered defeat, and was eliminated from the new government appointed on 17 April by Mannerheim, who had replaced Svinhufvud as Regent in December. The way now seemed open for the final Allied recognition of Finland. The only obstacle remaining was the U.S. President Woodrow Wilson who, in spite of his affirmation of the rights of nations to self-determination, had consistently refused to discuss territorial changes with regard to Russia, and on 27 January he had supported an Italian proposal at the Paris peace conference that the Finnish question could only be settled in connection with a general settlement of Russian affairs. Wilson was finally persuaded to accept Finnish *de jure* independence by a memorandum drafted by Herbert Hoover, who had spent some time in Finland administering a relief programme, and who had been pressed to intervene with the President by the new Finnish Foreign Minister Rudolf Holsti. The decision to grant recognition was taken at the meeting of the Council of Foreign Ministers in Paris on 3 May, in the absence of the Italians. No provisos were attached to the decision, although it was agreed that the Finnish government should be urged to accept the decision of the peace conference regarding Finland's frontiers and to grant an amnesty to the members of the Murmansk Legion.

The decision to recognise Finnish independence provoked immediate protest from the 'Conférence politique russe', set up in Paris in January 1919 to monitor the peace conference. The reluctance of the White Russians to concede full national independence to Finland was to be a major stumbling-block in the protracted efforts to involve Finland in plans for intervention on Russia's northern frontiers. The Japanese ambassador had in fact proposed that in return for recognition Finland should allow General Yudenich to use Finnish territory for his operations against Petrograd at the meeting of the Council of Foreign Ministers on 3 May. This appears to have been a personal initiative rather than one inspired by the White Russians, but it was welcomed by the French, who were prepared to act on the proposal. Britain and the United States rejected the idea, and it went no further. Yudenich had shifted his headquarters to Helsinki in January, and was in close contact with Mannerheim, who had peddled his ideas on intervention during his visit to London and Paris in late 1918. The Finnish government proved unresponsive to Yudenich's appeals for aid, and in February Professor Struve was sent to London to persuade the White Russian organisations to agree to Finnish independence. The White Russian envoy in London, K. Nabokov, agreed with this view, and recommended that the Omsk government of Admiral Kolchak recognise Finnish independence, which the Allies were in any case bound to do at the peace conference. Such a step the Kolchak government refused to take. Kolchak himself declared categorically that the Finnish question could only be resolved by the All-Russian National Assembly when it finally met. He was equally adamant in his reply to the Allied note of 26 May, proposing that he recognise, amongst other things, the independence of Finland and Poland.

In spite of Kolchak's obduracy on the Finnish question, Yudenich continued negotiations with Mannerheim and, without the knowledge of the Finnish government, a draft treaty was produced on 19 June. This was to form the basis of a future settlement between Finland and Russia, and included categorical recognition of Finnish independence, recognition of complete rights of self-determination for the people of East Karelia, protection of religious and linguistic rights for the people of Ingria (who were Finnish-speaking Lutherans) and settlement by the peace conference or the League of Nations of Finland's demand for Petsamo. In return, Mannerheim was to lead a Russo-Finnish army against Petrograd. This draft treaty was rejected as 'fantastic' by

Kolchak, and the British were only prepared to support it if Kolchak consented and the *Eduskunta* approved the venture; in other words, Britain was lukewarm towards the whole idea. The Finnish government was also sceptical of Yudenich's intentions, and clearly disagreed with the activities of the Regent Mannerheim. Nevertheless, before hearing of the draft treaty, Kolchak had appealed for Finnish support for an attack on Petrograd, and Mannerheim seems to have entertained the notion that prompt action by Finland was necessary. He endorsed a plan concocted by a group of former activists in which he was to dissolve the *Eduskunta* after confirming the Constitution Act, then in its final stages; in the ensuing political hiatus, operations against Petrograd would be launched. Such a move, if successful, would also strengthen Mannerheim's chances in the forthcoming presidential elections. This plan was put to representatives of the right-wing National Coalition Party, but they declined to give it their full support. Mannerheim thereupon informed Kolchak that without White Russian recognition of Finnish independence, the *Eduskunta* would not support Finnish participation in the assault on Petrograd. On 17 July, he signed the Constitution Act; eight days later, he was defeated in the first presidential election under the new constitution by the republican liberal K. J. Ståhlberg.

Mannerheim's defeat was a blow to the hopes of those wishing to involve Finland in the intervention, but these hopes still persisted. There was considerable right-wing pressure for Finnish participation during the successful early days of the Yudenich offensive, launched from Estonian territory in October, and the sudden revival of the fortunes of White Russian forces undoubtedly caused the majority of the *Eduskunta* to reject Soviet peace overtures on 16 October. However the Finnish government also rejected White Russian overtures, and Mannerheim's 'Open Letter' published in the Finnish press on 2 November, which spoke of Finland's last chance to help overthrow Bolshevism, was coolly received even by right-wing nationalists.

By the end of 1919, the Allies were ready to negotiate with the Soviet government. Estonia concluded an armistice, and made peace with the Soviet government in February 1920. On 25 May, the Finnish government accepted a Soviet proposal, probably occasioned by fear of Finland joining the then advancing Polish forces in an attack on Russia, and suggested that peace negotiations should begin on 10 June in the Estonian town of Tartu.

The main bone of contention between Finland and Soviet Russia was the future of East Karelia. In April 1919, a volunteer force with the moral and material backing of the Finnish government had invaded the province of Olonets on the northern shores of Lake Ladoga. The southern detachment was thrown back by Red Russian troops, but in the north the Finnish volunteers came into contact with the advancing British forces. Although General Maynard was prepared to accept Finnish assistance in capturing the town of Petrozavodsk, he insisted that they accept his command and hand over any conquered territory to the White Russian administration. The Allied Baltic Commission in Paris also declared that any Finnish occupation of East Karelia would be regarded as a breach of Russian territorial integrity. Forced to retreat from East Karelia, the Finnish volunteers were able to hold on to the border commune of Porajärvi, which the Finnish government annexed, just as it had annexed another commune, Repola, the previous year.

Although political opinion was divided over the question of intervention in association with Yudenich, even the socialists supported Finland's claim to East Karelia, though they disapproved of the means whereby the government sought to obtain it. On the other hand, the Allies were resolutely opposed to Finnish plans for annexation, and representations made in Paris by the Finns and Karelians proved in vain. Furthermore, a provisional Karelian régime set up in Uhtua in February 1919 opted for an independent Karelia, which did not correspond to the plans of the Finnish government, and which was in fact inspired by former Red Finns and Karelian volunteers in the Murmansk Legion. This régime survived the withdrawal of Allied troops in the autumn of 1919, and summoned a congress at the end of March 1920 as Red Army units occupied the area in the wake of White Russian evacuation. This congress affirmed the desire for separation from Russia and requested the withdrawal of Soviet troops. After negotiations, this last request was agreed to, though the Soviet negotiators in armistice talks with Finland later in April insisted on the right of Soviet Russia to occupy East Karelia. These talks were broken off on 24 April, and the Sixth Finnish Regiment of the Red Army moved into the Kem area, driving the Uhtua provisional government and its supporters into Finland. Five days before peace talks were due to begin in Tartu, the Finnish Communist-inspired Karelian Workers' Commune was created by Soviet decree. The Soviet negotiators were thereby given a pretext for rejecting Finnish demands for national self-determination in Karelia, since they could claim that the new Commune was an expression of the Karelians' wishes.[11]

The Tartu negotiations took place against the background of the Russo-Polish war. At the opening session on 12 June, the Finnish delegation put forward the demand for the right of national self-determination for the Karelian people, which was promptly rejected as interference in Russian internal affairs by the Soviet side. The Karelian question was still unresolved when the conference was suspended for a fortnight on 14 July. Four days earlier, the beleaguered Poles had sought Allied aid, and the Soviet government rejected an Allied proposal for a general conference, to which all the Baltic states would be invited, on 17 July. In the light of events, the Finnish peace delegation was given instructions to delay negotiations until the diplomatic situation had clarified. A minimal programme was also adopted. The demand for Karelian self-determination could be dropped if the people of Repola and Porajärvi were allowed to vote on their future, and Petsamo were ceded to Finland. When it became clear that the Allies' proposed conference would not take place, the Finnish delegation signed an armistice with Russia, on the basis of the *status quo*, and began final negotiations on territorial issues. Polish successes encouraged the Finns to press for concessions, but in the end they had to settle for Petsamo only; Repola and Porajärvi were to be reunited with the autonomous region of East Karelia, although their inhabitants were to be allowed to leave with their possessions. Finland also agreed to neutralise the islands in the Gulf of Finland and destroy the batteries at Ino and Puumala on the Karelian isthmus. The Soviet delegation refused to accept an article guaranteeing the Karelians' right to self-government, although a statement to this effect was appended to the protocol.

The peace treaty between Finland and Soviet Russia was signed in Tartu on 14 October 1920. It was essentially a settlement of frontiers and in no way established a basis for future friendly relations between the two countries. The right-wing in Finland attacked the treaty as 'shameful', while the Communists regarded it as a temporary stage on the road to revolution in Finland. The establishment of the Karelian Workers' Commune settled the Karelian question as far as Soviet Russia was concerned, but in Finland it remained a burning issue. The presence of what was to become virtually an autonomous Finnish Soviet state on Finland's eastern frontier only added fuel to the flames.

The signing of the treaty set the final seal on Finnish independence. Seen in a European perspective, the upheavals of 1917–20 in Finland were part of a general crisis in which many accepted values and concepts were seriously challenged. The war accelerated this crisis, but its root causes had existed long before August 1914. In the case of Finland, the inability of industry to absorb excess rural population and the insecurity and poverty of the rural proletariat caused discontent which could not be palliated by reforms since the legislature was unable to function properly. Economic change helped to weaken accepted social values, but lacked the dynamic force needed to create a new order of society. Political conflict also undermined values. Violence became an acceptable means of enforcing change, especially as peaceful political alternatives appeared not to exist. Political leaders in Finland were denied the opportunity to exercise real power in the last years of Russian rule; they were accustomed to assume attitudes rather than responsibility. Many of the errors committed nationally and internationally during the first years of independence can be attributed to the sheer lack of experience in political responsibility of those who had suddenly been called to guide the fortunes of the new state.

Finland achieved independence at the end of 1917 because no other course was open, and because independence was acceptable not only to all the parties in Finland, but to the Soviet régime as well. Independence in itself was not in the end an issue; the real question was what sort of state Finland would be. Lenin was prepared to concede its right to become separate from Russia in order to deprive the Finnish bourgeoisie of the opportunity of 'deceiving' the Finnish proletariat by claiming that Great Russian chauvinism threatened Finnish liberties. In this way he hoped to strengthen the resolve and ability of the Finnish working class in its struggle against the bourgeoisie. But he was to be disappointed: the socialist seizure of power failed, and a hostile White Finnish state was established. For the White victors, Finland's independence had been won in a war against Bolshevist Russia and its Finnish cohorts. For many, the war remained unfinished.

4

THE FIRST DECADE OF INDEPENDENCE 1918-1928

'We have only one political slogan: I believe in the great future of Finland. Secondary issues must give way to that article of faith. But it embraces a broad programme: the restoration of unity of the divided Finnish people, the bringing together of divided Finnish territory: the complete elevation to power of Finnishness in everything—in the university and in the student body—the gathering of the Finnish tribes for the great work of culture.'

Martti Haavio, 'Nuoriso ja politiikka', *Ylioppilaslehti*, 12 October 1923

Problems and divisions of the new nation

It has been estimated that the number who fought on the Red side during the civil war was around 100,000, against 70,000 who fought on the White side. Some 6,794 men were killed in battle. More than 1,500 were murdered during the 'Red terror' of the winter of 1917-18; 8,380 were executed in the aftermath of war, and more than 9,000 died in the prison camps, into which the Whites herded as many as 80,000 men during the summer of 1918.[1] The brutal trauma of these events was to affect Finnish society deeply, and it exercised decisive influence over the development of the newly independent state.

Recent analyses of the social background of the participants in the civil war have shown that 'workers' comprised the largest social group on the Red side, and independent farmers the dominant group on the White side. It has also been shown that leasehold farmers, who had long formed something of a rural backbone for the Social Democratic Party, were less than enthusiastic in their support for the Red cause, especially in the vicinity of the front. The more militant Red Guards were frequently young, unmarried workers, who had drifted to the

64

towns of the south during the war and who were newcomers to the labour movement. The unrest of 1917 had thrown up a new type of popular leader in the shanty suburbs of the major towns, and it was the commitment to direct action of these men and their bands of followers which had forced the party leadership into an attempted seizure of power in January 1918. The Whites drew their inspiration and much support from the landowning peasantry of Ostrobothnia, an area where traditional patriarchal values still survived in the absence of major new industries. White propaganda, and a considerable number of leading figures in the country's cultural life, made a great deal of the contrast between the vigorous, honest and patriotic peasant and the corrupted, degenerate, bolshevised workers of the industrial cities. Swedish-speaking Whites also hinted at the Finnish workers' propensity to make common cause with their barbarous eastern neighbours. A barrage of ugly racist invective against the Russian people was to continue for the next quarter of a century.

There can be little doubt that a sense of insecurity inspired the russo-phobia of the inter-war years. As Matti Klinge has shown, anti-Russian sentiment in the nineteenth century was peculiar to Sweden, which felt threatened by imperial Russian ambitions in the Baltic, whereas Finland enjoyed the privileges bestowed by Alexander I. Such anti-Russian sentiment as did occur in Finland was confined largely to the ranks of the Swedish speakers, who had identified more closely with the former Swedish motherland. The events of 1899–1918, however, helped to foster the notion of a traditional Russian enemy among the Finnish nationalists, in particular the younger generation which made common cause with the Finnish Swedes in defending Finland's con-stitutional rights. Independence was followed by civil war—a struggle for national liberation in the Whites' view—and unsuccessful attempts to wrest East Karelia away from Russia. Finland was now alone. The demands of Finnish nationalism caused friction with Sweden and made any sort of accommodation with Soviet Russia impossible. In this sort of situation, hatred of all things Russian served to bolster national self-esteem; and it provided a means of healing the wounds of the civil war. The idyllic myth of the sturdy, honest Finnish 'people' had received a severe blow when thousands of Finns joined the ranks of socialism, but the civil war in some way restored the image of the sturdy peasant-Finn, driving out the Russian and chastising the misguided Finnish worker. National unity could be purchased by ascribing all evil to the Russians. Finland would henceforth defend the frontiers of western civilisation against the barbarians.

In 1922, the Academic Karelia Society (A.K.S.) was formed. The original intention—of providing aid to Karelian refugees—soon gave way to an openly nationalistic political programme. Russophobia was the dominant theme of the society's early years, and an inner group *Vihan veljet* ('brothers of hate') was set up for the very purpose of disseminating anti-Russian propaganda. In 1924, however, the idea of national unity along purely Finnish lines began to gain ground in the movement, and a number of leading russophobes left the society to form the League of Independence. This new direction within the A.K.S. was much influenced by Yrjö Ruutu's book *Uusi Suunta* (A new course), which appeared in 1920. In it Ruutu advocated a form of state socialism, with direct state interference aimed at erasing social defects and strengthening the dominance of the Finnish-speaking people. In Ruutu's view, the *Mittelstand* would play a vital role in the future state. This was taken up by the theoreticians of the A.K.S. who saw student youth fulfilling that role. The A.K.S. began to demand the finnicisation of the University, and the breaking down of the old barriers between the intellectual and cultural élite and the people, which had been largely responsible for the civil war. However, by stressing cultural rather than social reformist integration, the A.K.S. failed to win support from the socialists, and its nearest potential ally the Agrarian Party was more interested in pursuing rural socio-economic interests than in recreating a new cultural élite. This failure to win support in the political arena probably strengthened anti-parliamentarian sentiment in the A.K.S., which devoted much of its energy in the 1930s to the language issue at home and the threat of Russian Communism on the frontier.

Nearly three-quarters of the membership of the A.K.S. between 1922 and 1940 were registered at Helsinki University, by far the largest institute of higher education in the country, although the society had a strong footing in other centres of learning. The social background of the members was predominantly middle-class, with sons of the clergy particularly in evidence. The A.K.S. tended to appeal more to the student up from the country. Although the majority of its members came from southern and western Finland, in relative terms the best recruiting areas were the provinces of Ostrobothnia. Alapuro has seen this rural bias as the response of the periphery to the somewhat alien and superior cultural dominance of the centre. The Finnish-speaking student from the country found himself in an 'alien landscape' in the half-Swedish University of Helsinki, but in the A.K.S. he could find an outlet for his sense of national pride. It was an élitist organisation, whose members had to swear a sacred oath to devote their lives and work to the cause of the fatherland and Finnish people. Its influence upon the intellectual, cultural and political life of Finland was immense. It was more than a society—it was a philosophy of life.[2]

Intense nationalism and a vague yearning for some kind of *Volksgemeinschaft* which might bind up the wounds of civil war were the characteristic features of intellectual life in Finland in the 1920s. The *avant-garde* art and literature of central Europe found no echo in Finland. The younger generation rejected many of the values and beliefs of their seniors. Liberal values in particular came under fire. Cosmopolitan liberalism had played a worthy role in the era of Russian oppression, wrote the young Urho Kekkonen in 1927, but it had no place in independent Finland, where the defence of the fatherland was of first importance.

The nationalism of the student generation was not content to accept the *status quo*, and in this it differed from the conservative values of the older generation of nationalists who were to play a leading role in the affairs of state. The first few years of independence also showed that there were deep-seated differences among the White victors as to how the state should be constituted. Finland had been proclaimed an independent republic on 6 December 1917, but the experience of civil war was a powerful impetus to right-wing and pro-German circles favouring the installation of a monarchy. A campaign for a monarchy began in the last days of the war. On 14 May 1918, a group of leading politicians issued a statement calling for a monarchy and the introduction of a number of delegates of certain social and economic interests groups into the *Eduskunta* to counter the 'onesidedness' of universal suffrage. The government of P. E. Svinhufvud, on whom the rump *Eduskunta* had conferred the title of Regent or 'possessor of supreme authority' on 18 May, was wholly monarchist. On 11 June it presented its proposal for the institution of a constitutional and hereditary monarchy, in which the king would have extensive powers. The monarchists were well-organised in the country, and commanded a narrow majority in the *Eduskunta*, from which the socialists had been almost completely excluded. The future king was to be of German stock, and thus the whole campaign would stand or fall on the success or failure of the German war effort. Although the *Eduskunta* accepted the bill and invoked the terms of the 1772 Swedish constitution by urging the government to proceed with the election of a king, the Germans were reluctant to offer the Kaiser's son and were in any event somewhat inclined to regard the matter as a dubious venture. Prince Friedrich Karl of Hesse was eventually elected king of Finland by 64 votes to 41 in the *Eduskunta* on 9 October. On 14 December 1918 the prince declined the offer as the monarchy collapsed in Germany. The victorious Allies demanded a new government and fresh elections in Finland as conditions for recognition, and the leading figures of 1918 withdrew from public office.

The conflict between monarchists and republicans was extremely bitter, and destroyed the temporary White bourgeois unity of the civil war. The Finnish-speaking monarchists from the Old and Young Finn parties came together in the aftermath of the war to form the conservative *Kansallinen Kokoomus*, or National Coalition, while the Finnish-speaking republicans formed *Kansallinen Edistyspuolue*, the National Progressives. The Agrarian Party (*Maalaisliitto*), which had increased its representation from nineteen to twenty-six seats in the 1917 elections and was on the way to becoming a national rather than a peripheral (Karelia-Ostrobothnia) party, had also promoted the republican cause, although more out of suspicion of the Swedish-speaking upper class than through liberal convictions. Liberals in the Swedish People's Party had also supported the republican cause. The demise of the pro-German policy of the right, and the withdrawal of Svinhufvud and Paasikivi from public life, laid the way open for the parties of the centre and offered the Social Democratic Party a means of political rehabilitation. Less than a year after the end of the civil war, the socialists obtained eight seats in the *Eduskunta* elections, with the Agrarians jumping to forty-two seats. Although the Social Democrats persisted in their principled opposition to participation in government in a bourgeois state, they could not be ignored, and their tacit support was an important consideration for the centrist bourgeois governments of the early 1920s.

The constitution of the independent republic of Finland was finally approved by the *Eduskunta* and the new head of state or Regent, General Mannerheim, in July 1919. It was largely based on the work begun in committee in 1917, but it was also influenced by the experience of civil war and the constitutional debates of 1918. The most evident contrast with the constitutions of a number of other newly-independent states such as Latvia and Estonia was the emphasis laid upon strong executive power in the person of the president. However, all the Presidents of the inter-war years had great difficulties in establishing themselves as authoritative heads of state. Ståhlberg, elected first President of the republic in 1919, had to contend with slurs and insults from the Right, and his decision not to stand for re-election in 1925 was probably as much the result of the rough treatment he had been subjected to as of his own convictions about the need to involve the right more actively in the affairs of state. His successor, L. Kr. Relander, was not even a candidate in the elections, but he emerged as a compromise candidate in the balloting of the electoral college; his eventual victory was unkindly ascribed to his Swedish-speaking wife, who was thought to have tipped the scales with the Swedish party bloc in the electoral college. P. E. Svinhufvud's narrow victory in 1931 was a triumph for the right, but even the fatherly image of this doughty if limited fighter for Finnish independence failed to win general national acceptance. None of the interwar presidents played a decisive role in the shaping of foreign policy, in marked contrast to their post-war successors.

The language question caused a second major split in the ranks of the White victors of the civil war. During the last years of Russian rule there had been a revival of Swedish nationalism in Finland. The Swedish-speaking upper class had lost its political hegemony with the abolition of the four-estate Diet in 1906, and a new generation of university-educated Finnish speakers had begun to compete for jobs hitherto dominated by the Swedish-speaking élite. Although the experience of the civil war fostered a sense of national unity, the notion that the Finnish-speaking working class was somehow prone to 'Asiatic' Bolshevism was prevalent in certain Finnish-Swedish circles. The qualities of leadership and cultural superiority of the Swedish race were also underlined.

During the early years of independence, a vigorous separatist movement developed in the wholly Swedish-speaking Åland islands. The Swedish People's Party officially opposed this movement, fearing that it would cause Finnish resentment and would weaken the Swedish minority's position in Finland should the islands secede to Sweden, but it supported the campaign for regional self-government for the enclaves of the Swedish minority on the mainland. These demands led to a good deal of political recrimination at the time, but did not become a major lasting issue. The 1919 constitution guaranteed the position of Swedish as an official language, and further measures such as the 1922 law on the languages of state and the creation of a separate Swedish department within the national education board caused the agitation for regional autonomy to die down. The Åland islands were granted self-government in 1920.

The demands of the Swedish minority for some sort of regional autonomy can be interpreted as a last attempt by the old ruling élite to safeguard some sort of special political status for themselves within the new republic. The creation of a three-tier voting system for local assemblies in Ostrobothnia, Uusimaa and the archipelago would have ensured Swedish dominance, but had these proposals been carried through, they would have confined Swedish influence to a regional level. The demand for regional autonomy was virtually a tacit acceptance of minority status by Swedish speakers in Finland, but it did help establish the Swedish People's Party as a broad-based 'interest' party for the minority. The party contained right-wing conservatives and social-reformist liberals, bankers and farmers, reflecting the widely divergent social background of its electorate.

A third cleavage occurred in the ranks of the Finnish army. Even during the civil war, conflict had arisen between the young *Jäger* officers and the ex-Russian imperial army generals. Mannerheim had in fact resigned as commander-in-chief at the end of the war in protest at the government's decision to invite the German general von der Goltz to supervise the training of the new Finnish army. The young men who had gone secretly to Germany during the war to receive military training had been moulded in the spirit of Prussian militarism and had formed a strong sense of comradeship in the *Jäger* battalion. Those who chose to follow a military career on their return to Finland were deeply resentful of the dominance of former Russian army generals in the upper echelons of the new Finnish army. They were also prepared to engage in politics to get their way, though the reluctance of Ståhlberg and the centrist governments to become involved in intervention in Russia tended to draw the two elements together in a temporary pressure group. In 1924, nearly 90 per cent of the Finnish Officer corps threatened resignation unless the government acceded to the demand for the removal from the army of 'all such elements whose patriotism is questionable or in whom Russian concepts, spirit and habits have taken hold'.[3] Ståhlberg, aware that the majority of the *Eduskunta* favoured some kind of purge, was forced to give way, although the demands of the officers were not fully met. The army chief, General K. Wilkama, was given sabbatical leave, and a number of other former Russian army officers resigned or were moved to lesser posts. Ståhlberg's successor was openly sympathetic to the *Jäger* officers and their allies in the *Suojeluskunta*, the paramilitary civilian organisation which carried the spirit of White Finland, and dismissed Wilkama on his return from leave. Aarne Sihvo, his replacement, was a former *Jäger* officer, and under his leadership the *Jäger* generation began to occupy the upper echelons of the Finnish army.

The problems of running an independent state brought these conflicts and differences to the fore and soon dispelled the hopes and idealism of the ardent Finnish nationalists. Some felt that the Peace of Tartu was a shameful surrender of the Karelians and a betrayal of Finland's historic mission. Some expressed contempt for the parliamentary system and attacked the weakness of liberalism in having given amnesty to Red prisoners. Nevertheless, Finland was not Weimar Germany. There were no bastions of anti-republican sentiment, and no parties openly hostile to the republican form of government. Although the army officers demonstrated their hostility to Ståhlberg, there is no evidence to suggest that they would have contemplated open disloyalty towards the constitutional system. The political divisions in White Finland allowed the socialists to play a political role; but it must be said that the memory of 1918 still clouded relations between socialists and non-socialists, and the possibility of collaboration between the two sides in government was remote indeed.

In the last days of the civil war, a group of moderates who had played no active part in events began to sketch out the basis for a new, reformist Social Democratic Party. In spite of harassment, the moderates managed to re-create some sort of organisation and to convene an extraordinary party conference in December 1918, at which the party committed itself to a parliamentary tactic and rejected the revolutionary doctrine of the Finnish Communist Party, founded in Moscow in August 1918. During the course of 1919, however, radical elements made deep inroads into a number of Social Democratic organisations, and the party conference held in December 1919 witnessed a head-on clash between left and right. The left, in alliance with the centre, managed to drive through a noticeably more radical resolution on tactics which was in the spirit of the old party's principled opposition to participation in government in a bourgeois state. In other respects the left failed to push the party towards acceptance of revolutionary methods, and in May 1920 the radicals completed their plans for a new party, *Suomen Sosialistinen Työväenpuolue*, the Finnish Socialist Labour Party.

The new party's programme was masterminded by O. V. Kuusinen, who was at loggerheads with the leadership of the Communist Party at that time. Kuusinen appears to have recognised that the total rejection of parliamentary and trade unionist tactics contained in the Communist Party programme was hopelessly unrealistic, and he was to have his views vindicated at the third Comintern congress in 1921, which urged Communist workers to join and capture trade union and other labour organisations. The programme of the Socialist Labour Party was openly Communist, but markedly more cautious with regard to the question of how the dictatorship of the proletariat was to be achieved. This was in part necessary to avoid immediate suppression, but it is clear that certain leaders of the new party did not consider it to be simply a legal front for the banned Communist Party. In the first elections contested by the new party, it obtained twenty-seven seats and 14·8 per cent of the vote, as against the Social Democrats' fifty-three seats and 25 per cent of the vote. Large numbers of suspected Communists were arrested and imprisoned throughout the 1920s, and the Socialist Labour Party was banned in 1923 after the arrest of its entire parliamentary group. Thereafter the Communist Left operated as an electoral organisation, obtaining between 10–13 per cent of the vote in subsequent national elections. It was also dominant in the trade unions, where the Communists' emphasis upon political struggle did little to advance the cause of collective bargaining or to strengthen organised labour in its fight with the employers.

The emergence of a radical rival and the subsequent split in the labour movement tended to strengthen the old Kautskyite centrism which still prevailed in Finnish social democracy. Reformism had never gained a strong hold in the Social Democratic Party before 1918, largely because the necessary preconditions simply did not exist. The impotence of the legislature, the lack of a strong social-liberal party with which the socialists might ally themselves, and the nature of the social problems to be dealt with all helped to strengthen the Social Democratic Party's attitude of revolutionary determinism. This attitude did not disappear with the creation of an independent republic. Although the party moderated its attitude towards participation in government, and permitted Väinö Tanner to form a minority socialist government in 1926, it still remained fundamentally a party of opposition. The party programme adopted in 1903, which was largely based on the 1891 Erfurt programme of the German Social Democratic Party, was a clear reminder of the party's Marxist centrism. The Tanner government has been described by a recent commentator as a 'curiosity', a deviation from the general norm of Finnish political life in the inter-war years; the party viewed the experiment with grave misgivings and a further ten years were to pass before participation in government was again seriously discussed in socialist circles. The party's inability to shake off the legacy of Kautskyite economic determinism has also been seen as one of the main reasons why Finnish socialism failed to come up with an effective programme to combat the effects of the depression.[4] The Finnish Social Democratic Party in the 1920s was in many respects the direct heir of the old party and its way of thinking.

If the Social Democratic Party represented the continuity of old traditions, the Finnish Communist Party showed all the symptoms of confusion brought about by revolutionary turmoil. The programme adopted in August 1918 in Moscow was a classic example of 'infantile communism', with its rejection of all that the old party had stood for and insistence on the worker's duty to prepare for the forthcoming armed revolution. Agents were sent to Finland to foment and direct revolutionary activity, and a party school was set up in Stockholm. The Stockholm group, led by Kuusinen and Sirola, did not discount the value of parliamentary and trade union activity, and clashed with the party leadership in Russia. Unity was only restored after Lenin's personal intervention, and the party conference of July 1921 was a vindication of Kuusinen's policy of creating a broad workers' and peasants' front under Communist leadership. The Communist Party was to be henceforth 'a strong underground organisation, effectively and skilfully exploiting both legal and illegal tactics in order to win over and maintain the support of the majority of the Finnish working class and to lead it to certain victory in the revolutionary class struggle'.[5]

However, the Communist Party suffered from a number of serious disadvantages. The unity of the 1921 party conference was precarious. Disgruntled ultra-leftists were probably responsible for a raid into Lapland in 1922, and continued to cause trouble within the central committee of the party until their expulsion in 1927. The party could not operate legally in Finland. Many of its agents were rounded up by the police, and in 1928 the entire underground organisation was discovered. Within the Finnish Socialist Labour Party, a group of left-radicals critical of the policies and role of the Communist Party emerged. In 1925, a number of imprisoned left-wingers issued a manifesto, calling for closer links with left-wing social democrats and condemning the overwhelming influence of the émigré Communists in the direction of the radical socialist movement. These dissidents were to continue their opposition on the trade union front, the one area in which the Communists did exercise considerable influence. By 1920, the Communists had captured control of many of the large unions, and dominated the central trade union organisation, *Suomen Ammattijär-jestö* (S.A.J.).

The Social Democratic minority considered breaking with the Communist-dominated unions on several occasions. In 1926, the socialists planned to bring the S.A.J. out of the Communist trade union international, Profintern, and to separate trade unionist activities from the highly political line hitherto pursued by the Communists. If this could not be achieved, the socialists were ready to form their own central trade union organisation. The S.A.J. congress ended in an uneasy compromise, with the Communists making a few concessions in order to preserve a united front. Nevertheless, the constant friction between the two political parties of the left did little to strengthen an already feeble trade union movement in Finland. The Communists' emphasis on the unions as training grounds for revolutionary activity, and their rejection of collective bargaining as a worthwhile trade union aim meant in many cases the loss of even the modest amount of ground gained in previous decades. Strikes in the 1920s, especially in northern Finland, where communism found eager recruits in the hitherto virtually unpoliticised camps of the lumberjacks, were often bitter and hopeless clashes. The employers were easily able to resist them. A strike-breaking organisation called *Vientirauha* was set up in 1920, and was called in to deal with a large number of strikes of unskilled labour. *Vientirauha* recruited mainly from the Ostrobothnian area, and it had good contacts with the police and the *Suojeluskunta*. It certainly regarded itself as an instrument to fight communism, and its chief agent Martti Pihkala was to play a leading role in the development of the Lapua movement. By the end of 1928, *Vientirauha* had over 20,000 men on its books. Trade union membership in that year was just over 90,000.

The conflict between organised labour and organised employers was indelibly tinged with Red and White ideology. The radical and Communist leaders of the strikes looked forward to the day of reckoning when White bourgeois Finland would be overthrown; the employers, bourgeois newspapers and politicians, on the other hand, were determined not to give way to Communist coercion. In such a situation, any moves towards the creation of proper industrial relations were obviously foredoomed. Labour conflicts were bitter and often politically coloured in other countries, but in the advanced industrial nations of Europe the beginnings of modern industrial relations were taking shape. Trade unionism in Finland was to remain decidedly the weaker element, not even recognised as worthy of equal negotiating rights by the employers until 1944. The inferior status of the unions can be attributed to the political nature of the labour movement in Finland, which had stymied the development of trade unionism; but the ever-present menace of Communist Russia and a 'Red Finland' in the shape of the Autonomous Karelian Soviet Socialist Republic undoubtedly prevented employers and much of the public from seeing the unions as anything other than fronts for communism. The 'Red scare' tactic used at different times in most non-communist states was that much more effective in a country with an eight-hundred mile frontier with Soviet Russia.

Society and politics

In the first ten years of independence Finland underwent fifteen changes of government, including one minority socialist cabinet and two purely non-political caretaker cabinets. The parliamentary dominance of the left and centre was given political significance in the fight to obtain a republican and democratic form of government in 1918–19. The socialists' willingness to tolerate a centrist government which was ready to carry out reforms, and the recent bitterness which had separated right and centre meant that there was a bias towards coalitions of Progressives and Agrarians, the two parties of the centre. The Agrarians continued to increase their mandate in national elections, and by the end of the decade were threatening to overtake the socialists, from whom they had undoubtedly taken voters as the leasehold farmers became independent. The Progressives, like many other European centre-liberal parties, declined in support and influence. The Agrarians cannot be classed as 'liberal' in ideology; although the party declared itself to be opposed both to capitalism and socialism and in favour of the rural interest, it was very much a party for the independent farmer. It surrounded itself with an aura of mawkish populism, and liked to stress the virtues of unsullied rural life, although in fact the party leadership of the 1920s had very little time for the sentimentalities of the movement's spiritual father, Santeri Alkio. It was also the first non-socialist party with firm and deep roots in the Finnish-speaking populace, as opposed to the finnicised élite. It was the party of the rural agricultural interest, hostile not only to the banking, industrial and bureaucratic interests of the capital but also to the old Swedish-speaking élite. It represented an alternative to the conservative nationalism of the older 'language' parties, and a number of its leaders were to flirt with the Lapua movement at the end of the decade. On the other hand, capitalism had made great inroads into agriculture in Finland by 1930, with the result that hard economic interests determined the party's political position and attitudes, rather than the authoritarian and backward-looking nationalism which tended to prevail in the peasant parties of the less advanced eastern European countries.

The vexed problem of the leasehold farmer was finally resolved in 1918 by a law enabling tenants to purchase their holdings at 1914 prices. Inflation and the provision of cheap loans with which to buy out the landlord meant that by 1930, nearly 90 per cent of all rented farms and plots had been purchased by the tenants. On the other hand, the average size of the newly-independent holdings was very small, a problem not alleviated by further reforms aimed at encouraging the creation of new farms. In 1929, 75 per cent of all holdings were of less than 10 hectares, an even greater proportion than in 1901. The chief success of the land reforms lay in the fact that the leaseholder and scrapholder came into possession of his own land. The small farmer was able to take advantage of interest-free loans to bring hitherto uncultivated land under the plough—some 600,000 hectares were gained in this way—and through the medium of producers' co-operatives was even able to share some of the benefits of a market for his produce. However, he was still gravely hampered by the inadequacy of his holding; many small farmers were compelled to sell their labour in the forests and on the log floats, and their main concern was still to feed themselves and their families rather than to concentrate on one or two commercial crops. The freeing of the scrapholders simply meant that 'most western Finnish farmworkers obtained their own plot of land and a potato patch, but they remained workers'.[6]

Although many of the structural problems which had made for social discontent in the countryside before 1918 still remained, they no longer had the same revolutionary political potential. The former tenant farmer certainly had credit problems and struggled even to maintain a minimum level of efficiency, but he was his own master. Leasehold farmer support of the Social Democratic Party had shown signs of waning during the war years; in the 1920s many newly-independent farmers left the party, and not a few joined the ranks of the Agrarians—although the majority probably still continued to vote socialist. The efforts of the state to encourage small farming, and the image of a healthy 'peasant republic' which was constantly put across by the Agrarians and the many rural interest pressure groups, may also have helped foster a sense of belonging to an independent producing class rather than to a downtrodden and exploited section of the rural populace. The Social Democratic Party supported reforms aimed at creating an independent class of small farmers, but it failed to come up with a programme which might have protected these farmers from credit squeezes and shortages. When the economic crisis hit Finland at the end of the decade, the harassed small farmers banded together rather than rallied to the Social Democratic Party.

It is hard to assess living standards in the small farmer class, but it is probable that supplementary earnings and smaller families did allow for a modest rise in standards. The growth of the industrial labour market and the tertiary sector also stimulated migration from the land to the cities and industrial centres. The rapid development of a road network brought the town nearer to the countryside. The lorry helped the farmer to get his produce to market, and the bus took his wife to the shops in the village centre or the town; but it also took his sons and daughters to the cities, often never to return. Whereas the rural population remained at around 2½ million through the inter-war years, the urban population nearly doubled. In 1920, the proportion of Finns who lived in a town was one in six; in 1940, it was one in four.

The development of communications, and the quickening pace of economic development in southern Finland tended to widen the gulf between north and south. It is interesting to note that the Communists enjoyed their greatest successes in northern and eastern Finland among the poor and backward farmers and lumberjacks, hitherto politically passive. The flame of economic advancement and social progress, which to some extent relieved the lot of the rural poor in southern and western Finland, burned very weakly in the remote forests of Kainuu and Lapland.

The ideological image of the sturdy peasant-farmer, devoted to his country and to hard work, was very characteristic of all eastern European countries which had gained their independence at the end of the war. Finland was no exception, but social and economic circumstances contrived to give Finnish peasant politics a rather different character. Thanks to the 'green gold' of the forests, even the small farmer was able to improve his efficiency by the purchase of implements and mechanised equipment; co-operative marketing organisations flourished, and the demands of the domestic consumer allowed the farmer to branch out into new areas of cultivation. His interests were vigorously pursued by various pressure groups, such as the Central Association of Agricultural Producers—*Maataloustuottajainkeskusliitto* (M.T.K.)—and by the Agrarian Party itself.

The Agrarian Party (*Maalaisliitto*) was founded in 1906. Before 1917, its main areas of support had been in Ostrobothnia and Karelia, but in the 1920s the party began to make inroads into the southern Finnish constituencies. It was very much a party of and for the middle peasantry, although as it grew it did manage to attract the support of the smallholder and the large farmer. In many respects, it was the political party with the greatest potential in the early years of independence. It stood for rural interests against those of the town, and was thus attractive to all who disliked city bureaucrats, tax-collectors and interfering central government. It adopted a hard line on the language question, thereby appealing to the ardent Finnish nationalist. It claimed to be neither capitalist nor socialist, but radical and reformist and for the rural interest. The strong *Gemeinschaft* elements of the party's 'peasantist' philosophy struck the right note with those seeking to establish national unity after the civil war.

In spite of the misgivings of many of the party's old guard about participation in government, the Agrarian Party sat in eleven out of thirteen party political governments formed between 1918 and 1928. Of necessity it was forced to compromise and tacitly to abandon a number of its stated aims. The emergence of oppositional small farmer parties in 1926 and 1929 was an indication of dissatisfaction with the Agrarian Party, which seemed unable or unwilling to offer greater protection for the small farmer. Although the Agrarians adopted a noticeably more intransigent attitude on the language question in 1926, they failed to push through reforms which would have completely finnicised the University of Helsinki, and this weakened their standing in the eyes of many nationalist students.

In his sympathetic study of the growth of the Agrarian Party, David Arter has shown how the party was able to establish a dominant position in Finnish political life, in spite of the severe natural and economic limits which ultimately made the party's vision of a prosperous nation of small farmers impossible to achieve. The necessity of having to come to terms with the problems of building a modern state and a viable economy probably saved the Agrarian Party from becoming a reactionary and authoritarian movement like other east European peasant parties; but the party's peasantist ideals nevertheless contributed to the paradoxical image of 'a *kantele* [an ancient stringed instrument used by the singers of folk poems] hanging on the wall of a Functionalist building', an apt if exaggerated summary of Finland in the inter-war years.[7]

In common with other newly independent countries of the post-war era, Finland faced serious financial and economic problems. The volume and value of her foreign trade fell sharply in 1918. Industrial output was less than half what it had been in 1913. There was a crippling shortage of goods and foodstuffs, which tended to force prices even higher. The wholesale price index (1913=100) rose from 432 in the last quarter of 1917 to 658 in the last quarter of 1918, while the cost of living index in 1918 increased by 105 per cent, largely because of food shortages. The value of the mark fell against foreign currencies, and foreign exchange controls had to be introduced. There was a general lack of confidence abroad in the economic viability of the new state, especially as the inexperience of the men called upon to formulate policy led to dubious and often contradictory remedies. The state treasury continued to resort to the Bank of Finland for short-term credit, 'the oldest and surest road to inflation'.[8] State expenditure rose by 149 per cent between 1918 and 1921, and the budget had to be balanced by resort to short-term credits, since revenue from taxes was delayed because legislation had first to be passed. The introduction of a progressive income tax in 1920 slowly began to bite, and together with a stabilisation of the currency and the policy of fiscal retrenchment pursued by successive governments, the state treasury was able to amass a large cash balance by 1925, which enabled it to pay off short-term debts and thereby reduce its dependence on the Bank of Finland. The 1925 monetary law adopted the recommendations of the Swedish economist Eli Hecksher in returning to the gold standard, although not at pre-war parity. At the end of 1920 the Bank of Finland had attempted to restore the mark to something like pre-war parity levels, but the end result was a rapid fall of the mark against the dollar. This unwitting devaluation, coming at the onset of a world trade slump, made Finnish exports more competitive and helped reduce the volume of imports. By 1925, the volume of exports exceeded 1913 levels for the first time, and in 1928 was some 56 per cent up on the pre-war levels. Industrial output increased at a rapid rate, providing Finland with a hitherto unknown degree of economic buoyancy. In the golden years of 1925–8, the number of industrial undertakings rose by one-fifth, the industrial labour force by 20 per cent and the gross value of output by 33 per cent. A peak export volume of 1·3 million standards of sawn timber was attained in 1927. The cellulose and pulp industry was making even more rapid strides, and was to overtake timber as the major export industry in the early 1930s. The loss of the Russian market was compensated for by increased trade with the Western countries, especially Britain, which took on average 38 per cent of the total value of Finnish exports in the 1920s, and 46 per cent in the 1930s. The great economic upsurge after 1925 brought with it more or less full employment in industry, and stimulated the consumer market. It also prompted the state to take action to preserve the stocks of timber on which the Finnish economy so much depended.

The stabilisation of the currency and strengthening of the national economy enabled the state to introduce a number of cautious but necessary social reforms, including the creation of an administrative structure to deal with public health and social welfare. Some labour legislation was also passed, although progress in this field was hindered by the factious nature of labour relations. The proportion of the budget devoted to defence costs remained around 15 per cent, and the *Eduskunta* invariably trimmed the estimates presented to it. The Tulenheimo government felt itself compelled to resign in 1925 when the *Eduskunta* refused to accept its reduced estimate for a four-year shore defence programme, and it was not until the late 1930s that all parties came to accept the need for extra funding for military and naval defence. In the 1920s, despite its paramilitary *Suojeluskunta* and the occasional martial utterances of the right, Finland was far from being a militarist's paradise.

The first decade of Finland's independence coincided with a rapid development in communications throughout the world. The cinema and radio enabled the Finn to learn more of the world at large, and the opening up of new sea and air routes allowed him to travel abroad. But more importantly, they enabled him to know more of his fellow-countrymen; the motor bus and the radio have probably done more to create a sense of national identity than the entire output of Finnish literature and the arts. Moreover, although Finnish writers such as the Nobel prize-winner Frans Sillanpää, and architects and composers began in the 1920s to win international recognition, incomparably the most popular national hero was the middle-distance runner Paavo Nurmi.

The civil war cast a grim shadow over the first decade of independence, making the task of building national unity wellnigh impossible, since the defeated Red leadership had found a home in Russia where they proceded to build something of a Red Finnish state in the Autonomous Republic of Karelia. Finland's status as a nation was brought into sudden and sharp focus by the break with Russia in 1917–18, but Russia's geographical proximity still largely determined what the future of the new nation was to be. The national independence of the new state was much bolstered by a fierce russophobia. 'I am only now beginning to realise that we are the frontier-post of Western civilisation in the East', wrote the novelist Juhani Aho during the civil war, a sentiment echoed countless times in future years.[9] Matti Klinge has shown how russophobia, which had not been a very noticeable feature of Finnish political or cultural life during the years of autonomy, became virtually synonymous with patriotism in the 1920s and '30s. The countervailing view of Russia as the socialist fatherland has not been so well charted, but it clearly existed. In the years of the depression, many Finns crossed the frontier to seek a better life in Karelia, like the rootless and pathetic Pate Teikka of Pentti Haanpää's novel *Noitaympyrä* (1931). The fate of some of those who were tempted by 'Karelian fever' to seek their fortune in the workers' paradise has been movingly described in the memoirs of Aino Kuusinen.[10]

Although Communist Russia provided an ideal for the Left in Finland, it was not necessarily a model which native Communists strove to imitate. Slavish imitation of the 'Moscow line' was not really a feature of any Communist party in the 1920s, if only because of the confusion and continuing power struggles within the Communist Party of the Soviet Union itself, which were reflected within other parties. There was a prolonged struggle between various factions of the Russian-based Finnish Communist Party, which did not end until the purges; and this in turn weakened the party's authority in Finland. Resentment against the policies urged upon Communist cover organisations in Finland came to a head in the late 1920s, although the dissident left-wing elements were unable to make common cause with the Social Democrats. The Social Democrats held the middle ground, a position which was to become increasingly untenable as the militant right began its campaign against communism. The Social Democratic Party rejected the communist road to power, but was ideologically and emotionally unable to accept the 'White' bourgeois state. Prime Minister Tanner's decision to take the salute at the traditional parade of the *Suojeluskunta*, in the absence of the sick President, caused enormous embarrassment in the Social Democratic Party, and epitomised the dilemma of participating in the running of a state the institutions of which were still regarded with great suspicion by many on the left.

These underlying political tensions had little opportunity to break to the surface during the 1920s. In spite of structural problems, the Finnish economy was remarkably buoyant. Having survived the stormy seas of the immediate post-war years, the new state was able to settle into the calmer waters of fiscal orthodoxy and balanced budgets. Relations with Soviet Russia were on the whole cool but correct, while Finland began gradually to repair the breach caused in her relations with Sweden during the Åland islands dispute. Many of the issues which occupied the attention of the government and *Eduskunta* were relatively mundane and non-controversial in nature, such as the question of civil servants' pay, the defence estimates and the grain tariff. Prohibition, introduced in 1919, proved a disastrous social experiment, but was hardly likely to lead to serious social unrest.

Although the left continued to regard the new state and its institutions with some suspicion, independent Finland was a different political arena to that circumscribed by Russian autocracy prior to 1917. Local government reform allowed socialists for the first time to participate in local decision-making. In a number of industrial towns and communes, socialists established majority control over the councils. At a national level, the *Eduskunta* might still be regarded as a 'class institution' by left-wingers, but it did work, and could produce reforms. Rapid strides were made in other fields of labour activity such as the consumers' co-operative movement, in which Väinö Tanner played a leading role. The one area in which little or no progress was made was industrial relations. The trade union movement was weak and divided, and under Communist control it sought to provoke conflict rather than work for collective bargaining and the integration of the trade unions into the framework of industrial relations. The civil war continued in the factories and in the forests of northern Finland. The protracted conflict in the metal industry in 1927 was followed in the following year by the dockworkers' strike, a conflict of classic proportions and the culmination of the ideological struggle between employers and the unions. On 14 May 1928, the union presented its demands to the employers: a wage increase of two marks an hour, increases in piece-work rates and a national wages agreement. The employers asked for time to consider, in order to discover if the *Vientirauha* organisation could provide enough strike-breakers. Norrmén, speaking for the employers, voiced a commonly held view in rejecting the idea of a national wages agreement, which in his view would give the unions equal bargaining status with the employers, thereby increasing their power, and consequently the power of the Communists. For the sake of the 'health of society and the morals of the non-Communist work-force', it was essential for the employers to stand fast.[11]

The strike began on 2 June. *Vientirauha* recruited, in all, some 15,600 strike-breakers, mostly from southern Ostrobothnia. The strikers managed to obtain nearly 15½ million marks in support from foreign unions, mostly in Scandinavia, but attempts to black ships going to or from Finnish ports were not very successful. The strike ended in April 1929 with the intervention of the Minister for Social Affairs, on terms which represented a defeat for the strikers.

The dockworkers' strike of 1928–9 was seen at the time as a major ideological conflict: for the Left it was a test of strength against the bosses and the strike-breakers' organisation; for the right it was a fight against a Communist-inspired attempt to ruin Finland's export trade (the Soviet Union re-entered world timber markets at this time). It was, in a way, the overture for the troubles to come.

5

CRISIS AND RECOVERY

1929–1939

Se ajanhenki lentänyt tänne kait
on, mustasiipi, etelän tuulten myötä,
jos kohta hahmon ottikin täällä tutun,
hyvän hartioilleen löys talonpoikaisnutun.
Jos vallan sais se, nyrkki jos laatis lait,
ois aika laulaa: Kansani, hyvää yötä!

(That black-winged spirit of the times/ has flown here, borne on southern winds,/ and clad itself in more familiar guise,/ a peasant's jacket on its shoulders lies./ If power should come its way, or laws fall to its fist,/ it would be time to sing: my countrymen, good night!)

Uuno Kailas, *Kylmän kevään maa* (1932)

From Blue-Black to 'Red Earth'

On 27 November 1929, the President of Finland made the following entry in his diary:

The newspapers contain an item of news from Lapua. The local White population, angered by the red-shirted and red-scarfed Communist youth—they were even sporting Soviet Russian emblems—who had poured into the town last Sunday to celebrate a Communist festival, administered physical punishment and tore off their red shirts. That such a thing has happened in a law-abiding society is of course regrettable, but on the other hand it is fully understandable— the people of Lapua by their actions were following the intentions of the dead, to use le Bon's phrase.[1]

President Relander's comment on the incident is very revealing of White sentiment in general. The Lapua incident, in itself rather

83

insignificant, inaugurated what might be termed the second phase of the civil war, the final settling of accounts with the Red threat which plagued White Finland. It occurred at a time of deepening political and economic crisis in Finland, and the movement to which the incident gave birth undoubtedly flourished on this discontent, even if it did not capitalise upon it. The Lapua movement was a symptom of the ills of the young Finnish republic rather than a cure.

The declared task of the 'men of Lapua' was the eradication of Communism in Finland. Although the methods they used were 'regrettable' in a law-abiding society, their aim was widely supported in all non-socialist parties. The Communist Party was a banned organisation in Finland. Large numbers of Communists and left-wingers had been arrested and imprisoned in the 1920s, although constant police action and prosecutions had failed to kill the spectre which haunted the White public. In 1928, the Communist International ordered its member-parties into an all-out attack in anticipation of the forthcoming collapse of capitalism. In Finland, as elsewhere, this proved a disastrous mistake, but it did help to strengthen the resolve of many Whites, such as Relander, to crush communism once and for all.

The Finnish Communist movement in 1929 was probably less of a threat to the established order than it had been at any time during the previous decade. The exiled party leadership had still not settled its differences, while the leadership in Finland was young, inexperienced and ill-equipped to cope with the sudden twists and turns imposed by the exiled leaders and the Finnish police alike. The latter had by 1928 managed to penetrate the underground organisation, and had also dealt several body-blows to the movement's legitimate organisations. A number of the Finnish-based leaders began to turn against the *émigrés*, and were in a state of open conflict with them in 1929. Although the protracted labour conflicts in the metal industry and the docks in 1927–9 failed to bring victory and exhausted the unions' funds, the Communist-dominated Confederation of Trade Unions (S.A.J.) sought to follow the swing to the left decreed by Moscow and spelt out in the Strassburg theses. The socialist minority, which had threatened to leave the confederation in 1926, refused to accept an agreement made in Copenhagen in 1928 between delegates of Finnish, Norwegian and Soviet trade unions, which the Finnish socialists feared would bind the S.A.J. closer to Profintern, the Communist trade union international; although this agreement was not ratified at the May 1929 congress of the S.A.J., the Communist majority behaved in such an uncompromising way that the socialists felt compelled to withdraw from the confederation. The S.A.J. was eventually banned as a result of police prosecution in July 1930. Although the socialists managed to set up a new reformist central trade union organisation, *Suomen Ammattiyhdistysten Keskusliitto* (S.A.K.), its membership at the end of 1930 was a mere 15,000, compared with 90,000 members of the S.A.J. at the end of 1929. A few workers were persuaded to join anti-Communist 'yellow' unions, but the great majority simply turned their backs on trade unionism.

The inability of the Communists to push through ratification of the Copenhagen agreement at the S.A.J. congress, and the fiascos of the 'Red day' demonstrations called on 1 August and the general strike called in November 1929 in support of hunger-strikers at the Tammisaari penitentiary, were clear indications of the weakness of the movement in 1929. Nevertheless, it was still vociferous. The spring elections to the *Eduskunta* had returned twenty-three Communists, who took every opportunity to harass the government. On 3 December, the Kallio government struck back. A Communist interpellation on the Lapua incident was turned into a demonstration of anti-Communist solidarity by the bourgeois majority, which approved the government's measure which gave the Minister of the Interior the right to suspend temporarily any organisation directed against the established order. This was not in fact the first anti-Communist measure put forward by the Kallio government, which had sought to introduce curbs on the Communist press in the autumn. There can be little doubt that the dock strike had helped to draw up the lines of confrontation. A number of new anti-Communist organisations had been set up, while the Safeguard Finland Association (*Suomen Suojelusliitto*), founded by leading civil war heroes in 1923 to combat the internal threat of communism, began organising anti-Communist rallies before the incident at Lapua.

Lapua was a rather unfortunate place for the Communist youth movement to choose for their rally. It was in the Pietist heartland of Ostrobothnia, where the Whites had begun their war of liberation, and it was a centre for the recruiting activities of the *Vientirauha* strikebreaker organisation, some of the leaders of which became deeply involved in the Lapua movement. The flaunting of red shirts and banners in a deeply religious small town on a Sunday was not only a singularly stupid act of provocation; it was also a serious political mistake. The picture of an exasperated, honest and God-fearing loyal peasantry venting their wrath upon the godless and disloyal Red youth who had dared to venture into sacred White territory provided excellent propaganda for the anti-Communist movement. The 'Law of Lapua', a vague and essentially crude concept designed to preserve Finland from the Red peril by all possible means, was the slogan of the day at numerous rallies and meetings throughout the winter of 1929–30. Although these rallies were given the appearance of spontaneous popular movements, they were in fact carefully staged by right-wing elements, although it seems as though internal jealousies and rivalries prevented the emergence of a really strong central directing committee for the Lapua movement.

The response of the Finnish government to the Lapua movement was vacillating and weak. President Relander was openly sympathetic with its aims, and Prime Minister Kallio, although more concerned with observing the letter of the law than the President, had already set in motion legislation aimed at throttling legal Communist activity in Finland before the Lapua incident. When the government's proposals for stiffer controls over the press were held up by socialist, Communist and Swedish People's Party opposition in March 1930, the Lapua movement replied by smashing the presses of a Communist newspaper in the town of Vaasa. Members of the local *Suojeluskunta* and the police force were involved in the planning and execution of this act. The trial of its perpetrators, who had ostentatiously given themselves up to the police, marked the beginning of a new phase of violence. The Communist lawyer for the printing press was seized by a mob, beaten up and driven out of the province with a warning never to set foot in it again. The Lapua movement declared that it would not tolerate the reappearance of the Communist newspaper in question; on 15 June, the government banned the publication of all Communist newspapers, an action for which it had no legal authority. President Relander also gave his Prime Minister to understand that he should resign at the first suitable moment to allow a more broad-based government to be formed. P. E. Svinhufvud, the White hero of 1918 who had virtually withdrawn from public life during the first decade of the republic, visited Lapua in June, where he praised the patriotic spirit of the movement and promised its leaders that he would form a government. While Kallio was still in office, Svinhufvud began publicly to choose his cabinet, even though he was not a member of the *Eduskunta* and had received no presidential invitation. On 1 July, the Kallio government laid before the *Eduskunta* a series of laws designed to outlaw communism; and in spite of receiving a vote of confidence on this issue, Kallio resigned the next day, leaving the way open for Svinhufvud. Svinhufvud had offered two places in the government to Kosola and

Kares, leading members of the Lapua movement, but they withdrew at the last minute, leaving a government composed of members of all the non-socialist parties.

Although the Lapua movement had managed to achieve a government committed to the elimination of legal Communist activities in Finland, it did not cease its policy of violence. On 3 June, two Communist members of the *Eduskunta* constitutional committee were seized in committee session and dragged out of the building by Lapua supporters. The government responded by having all the Communist members of the *Eduskunta* arrested for plotting treason. This action did not prevent the Lapua movement staging a massive 'peasants' march' in Helsinki—for which the Minister of Transport arranged cheap excursion rail fares—or kidnapping the Social Democratic Speaker of the *Eduskunta* in an attempt to persuade the government to order a complete ban on Communist participation in the forthcoming national elections. These elections were decreed by the government after it had failed to obtain the five-sixths majority necessary for the immediate promulgation of the anti-Communist laws, which necessitated constitutional amendments.

The wave of violence continued throughout the summer. Socialist as well as Communist politicians, functionaries and supporters were beaten up and, in several instances, murdered. A favourite Lapua method was the dumping of unfortunate kidnapped victims over the Soviet frontier. On 14 October, the former President of the Republic, K. J. Ståhlberg, and his wife were seized outside their home and driven towards the frontier, where they were abandoned at the eastern Finnish town of Joensuu. Ståhlberg had aroused the ire of the Lapua movement by his public condemnation of its illegal violence, and the order for his seizure had been given by the chief of the general staff of the Finnish army, Major-General Wallenius. This outrage was a serious blow to the Lapua movement. Many earlier adherents, members of the National Coalition and Agrarian Parties, had already begun to dissociate themselves from it, since it seemed ever more intent on the overthrow of the whole parliamentary system in Finland. The government had managed to obtain a two-thirds majority in the October elections, and was thus able to push through the anti-Communist laws in November. With communism effectively crushed, there seemed no reason for further agitation for the great majority of bourgeois politicians. Although the government had toyed with proposals aimed at reducing the power of the *Eduskunta* in the summer of 1930, and in spite of dissatisfaction and disillusionment provoked by constant government crises in the late

1920s, there is no evidence to suggest that the major political parties—with the possible exception of an element within the National Coalition Party—favoured any sort of radical surgery upon the body politic in Finland. As Rintala has pointed out, most of the leading political figures in Finland had been intimately involved with the fortunes of the democratic *Eduskunta*. Svinhufvud, for example, had endured imprisonment and exile for his defence of parliamentary privilege. It was the abuse of the democratic system by the Communists, rather than the system itself, which the bourgeois politicians sought to curb.

Rintala has suggested that the younger generation which reached political maturity during the last phases of Russian rule were less attached than their elders to parliamentary institutions and procedure. The formative experience for those of the 'activist' generation was the Great War, the *Jäger* movement and the fight for Finnish independence, during which a strong bond of comradeship had been forged and a national ethos created. The first decade of independence was one of disillusionment for those who had been active in the fight for Finnish independence, much as the era of transformism alienated the heroes of the *Risorgimento* in Italy.[2] Failure by the government to defend the rights of the Karelians at the Tartu peace negotiations, continued Communist agitation and what the right wing saw as government 'softness' over political amnesty and treatment of the Reds helped to foster discontent; and the failure of the centrist Vennola government to give active Finnish support to an uprising in Soviet Karelia in 1921 was widely condemned by the nationalists.

In February 1922 the Minister of the Interior, Heikki Ritavuori, who had aroused anger by his firm treatment of Karelian refugees, was assassinated by a right-wing fanatic. Ritavuori's murder was the culmination of a period of intense internal conflict, in which there were rumours of a planned *coup d'état* by the *Suojeluskunta*.[3] The position of this 100,000-strong paramilitary organisation within the republic had not been satisfactorily defined, and when President Ståhlberg sought to compel the resignation of the chief of the Helsinki district *Suojeluskunta*, after the latter had written a newspaper article critical of the government's foreign policy, he provoked a crisis. A meeting of *Suojeluskunta* leaders demanded the reinstatement of the commander of the organisation (whom Ståhlberg had also compelled to resign) or his replacement by Mannerheim; Ståhlberg stood his ground and refused to accept Mannerheim. Legislation also placed the *Suojeluskunta* under the President's direct control, but in spite of this, it remained a potentially dangerous force, especially as Ståhlberg's successor was a patron of the organisation, and unlikely to take the same strong action should further trouble arise. Although members of the *Suojeluskunta* were involved in numerous Lapua-inspired incidents during 1930, Relander took no steps to purge the organisation. Its commander from 1921 to 1944, the former *Jäger* Lauri Malmberg, played a crucial role in the presidential election of 1931, which took place amid rumours of an impending coup. It seemed as if the Agrarian supporters of Kallio would switch their votes to Ståhlberg on the third ballot, thus assuring him of victory over Svinhufvud. Malmberg phoned Niukkanen, the leader of the Agrarian bloc in the electoral college, warning him that he could not guarantee to maintain order if Ståhlberg were elected. The right-wing *Aktivisti* newspaper had already published a scarcely veiled incitement to assassination if Ståhlberg should win the day, and the last pro-Ståhlberg Agrarian in the electoral college later revealed that he had changed his mind when he was told that armed Lapua men were in the capital ready to unleash a bloodbath if Svinhufvud were not elected.

Svinhufvud's electoral bloc only managed to take 21·6 per cent of the total poll: 30·2 per cent voted for the Social Democratic bloc, 17·7 per cent for Ståhlberg (a far higher poll than his own National Progressive Party had managed to achieve in the 1930 parliamentary elections), and 20 per cent for Kallio, whom the Agrarians had chosen in preference to Relander, whom they regarded as too lenient towards the Lapua movement. In other words, the great majority of the Finnish electorate voted for candidates or a party clearly opposed to the excesses of the Lapua movement.

Although Svinhufvud's narrow victory was a triumph for the forces of the right and of anti-communism, it was also a victory for the conservative forces of law and order. Having achieved the suppression of communism, the bourgeois parties began to turn against the excesses of the Lapua movement, which finally shot its bolt in March 1932. In its Tampere programme in November 1931, it had broadened the scope of its demands, calling for the replacement of proportional parliamentary representation by one-man constituencies, high protective tariffs, curbs on trade union activity and the banning of the Social Democratic Party, against which its activities were now directed. At the end of February 1932, a mob tried to prevent a socialist member of the *Eduskunta* from addressing a meeting at Mäntsälä, a small town some thirty miles north of Helsinki. The mob refused to obey police orders to disperse, and shots were fired. On the following day, aid and reinforcements were promised from Lapua bases throughout the country, and on 29 February the movement's leadership decided to back the rebels. On 2 March the rebels demanded a new government under General Walden, a close friend of Mannerheim. The government had meanwhile invoked emergency regulations and isolated Mäntsälä with troops. Svinhufvud addressed the rebels over the radio, appealing to them to return home and forbidding *Suojeluskunta* units to place themselves under the command of Major-General Wallenius, who had taken over the leadership of the rebellion. Although a number of *Suojeluskunta* men joined the rebels, the leadership did not, and the army remained loyal to the government throughout. Isolated and without hope, the rebels surrendered on 5–6 March.

The punishment meted out to the rebels was surprisingly light. Only ten leaders received light prison sentences; the rank and file initiators of the revolt were pardoned. There was no major purge of the *Suojeluskunta*, although it had been heavily compromised in the revolt, and Malmberg was allowed to remain in office as commander, although his own attitude towards the revolt was somewhat ambiguous. The provincial governor and the Minister of the Interior, whose firm actions had undoubtedly prevented the spread of the revolt, were relieved of their offices in the summer. Although the Lapua organisation was banned, it reappeared almost immediately under a new guise. Three weeks after the Mäntsälä revolt, a group of diverse right-wing figures, including Svinhufvud himself, met to discuss the continuation of Lapua's aims by legal means. On 10 April, the new 'White front' party, *Isänmaallinen Kansanliike* (I.K.L.), the People's Patriotic Movement, was founded in the spirit of Lapua.

The I.K.L. was soon to assume the trappings of fascism. In so doing, it lost not only the support of right-wing politicians, but also much of the popular support which the Lapua movement undeniably enjoyed. It was the party of the educated classes, and enjoyed much support in the Academic Karelia Society, but it failed to win over working-class support or to make much headway among independent farmers. Fascist movements thrive on discontent, and apart from the fear of communism, there was very little in Finland on which fascism could feed. Its anti-Swedish stance appealed only to the Finnish-speaking nationalist élite, and the Swedish-speaking minority was not really a suitable subject for racial vilification. Anti-semitism was a non-starter in a country with few Jews. There were economically depressed groups, such as the small farmers, but the I.K.L. failed to cash in on their grievances. It had no charismatic leader, and its anti-Swedish attitude alienated the one figure who might have provided strong leadership, the remote and aloof Mannerheim. Vihtori Kosola, the self-projected strong man of Lapua, was a pathetic and increasingly embarrassing drunkard: and the leaders of the I.K.L. were little more than younger and more right-wing versions of the National Coalition Party leadership.

The Lapua movement was in the end little more than the forceful expression of widely-held bourgeois sentiments, and as such it was able to exercise considerable political influence. When it began to move beyond the bounds of anti-communism, bourgeois political opinion began to rally behind the system. The role of the Agrarian Party was perhaps crucial. In the first months of the Lapua movement, Agrarians were openly sympathetic, and several played leading roles in it, but by 1932 the party had linked up with the centre and left in defence of the parliamentary system. Kalela has sought to explain the shifting Agrarian policy in economic terms, suggesting that the Agrarians co-operated with the right in order to push through an agricultural policy aimed at self-sufficiency, but found themselves having to reassess their position in the light of the credit crisis in agriculture. More and more farmers were unable to repay debts or raise credit, with the resulting compulsory sale of their farms or distraint of their property. In the winter of 1931, 'crisis' protest movements sprang up among the small farmers, threatening to erode the basis of rural support enjoyed by the Agrarian Party which, as a partner in government, bore responsibility for its tight monetary policy. The net result was Agrarian withdrawal from government at the end of 1932 into political isolation, since the other bourgeois parties would not agree to support the policy of credit reflation advocated by the protest movements and adopted by the Agrarians.

Although he is right to draw attention to the economic background to the political crisis of 1929–32, Kalela has tended to ignore the purely political aspects, such as the factionalism within the Agrarian Party (well chronicled in Relander's diary) and the strong respect for law and order which eventually drove many Lapua sympathisers away from the movement. Kalela also sees the Lapua movement as a carefully organised 'spontaneous popular movement', controlled by powerful capitalist interests which, having achieved the suppression of communism and the weakening of the trade unions with a right-wing government committed to the 'right' sort of economic policies, then withdrew gradually from Lapua. J. Hampden Jackson, writing in the late 1930s, also saw the movement as essentially 'a conspiracy of certain capitalist interests to establish a form of Fascist dictatorship in Finland', financed by the bourgeois co-operative movement, timber exporters and private banks.[4] This contemporary observer pinpointed three factors peculiar to Finland which provided fertile ground for the Lapua movement: the close proximity of the national and ideological enemy, the nationalist fervour and anti-communist militancy of the clergy, and the plight of the small farmer, who was worse hit by the slump than other producers. Alapuro, who also considers the crisis in agriculture a major factor in the growth of Lapua, has however stressed the fundamental difference between the Finnish peasant, operating within and for the market economy and an essential and traditional element in the workings of parliamentary democracy, and the peasant of eastern Europe who was bound by tradition and economic backwardness. Unlike the east European peasant, the Finnish farmer was in the long run unlikely to turn to fascism, although there was an anti-capitalistic undercurrent prevalent in small farmer circles during the crisis years of 1929–32; and he was similarly unresponsive to the efforts of the Academic Karelia Society to forge links with the 'people'. The patriotic farmer, hard hit by the economic crisis which began in 1928 and angered by what he saw as a Communist plot to cripple the Finnish timber export industry, rallied to the Lapua movement at its inception: but popular support was already in decline by 1932, and the élitist and fascist I.K.L. was unable to secure the support of the small and middle farmers.

The economic crisis which affected the industrial nations of the world at the end of the 1920s set in somewhat earlier in Finland. The tremendous increase in output of timber by all the great timber-exporting countries between 1925 and 1927 caused world prices to fall as the market became glutted. In May 1928 the Finnish Sawmill Association agreed to restrict production by 10 per cent. Since timber exports constituted the lifeblood of the Finnish economy, the effect of the fall in price and reduced output was to reduce the farmer's income from stumpage and lumbering, cut domestic purchasing power as a whole, and reduce the gross annual value of industrial production. Unemployment reached an estimated peak of 92,000 at the beginning of 1932. Smallholders who could not afford the harder conditions for short-term loans were forced to sell up their farms, and many small businesses went bankrupt. Yet the Finnish economy was able to recover earlier than many others. When wholesale prices rose in the West as a result of the devaluation of the U.S. dollar, the increase was less marked in Finland, which had experienced its greatest upsurge in prices in 1931–2. Moreover, as the foreign purchasing power of the mark fell below its internal purchasing value, this helped make exports more competitive and together with strengthened tariffs, discouraged imports. Finland was indeed able to enjoy a favourable balance of trade from 1930 to 1936, and was able to redeem foreign debts with the accumulated trading surplus, thereby winning a reputation in the U.S.A. as the nation which paid off its debts. Finland also left the gold standard shortly after Britain, and was thus able to retain her competitiveness in British markets. The demand for building materials in Britain greatly aided the recovery of the timber industry, although this was overtaken in the 1930s as the major export industry by the paper and pulp industry. By 1935, Finnish industrial output had regained pre-depression levels, and productivity was to forge ahead at an even more rapid pace than in the first decade of independence.

The governments of the period followed a strictly orthodox policy of deflation; any attempt to reflate would anyway have been opposed by the majority of the members of the *Eduskunta*. The government made economies in public spending rather than by resorting to borrowing; it preferred to pay off foreign debts rather than use the accumulated trading surplus to buy imports and stimulate consumption and investment. One powerful reason for the ending of prohibition in 1932, after a national referendum had narrowly supported this move, was the hope of extra income from a state-controlled liquor monopoly. By 1935–6, 14 per cent of the state's tax revenue came from alcohol. Attempts were made to provide public relief works and to bolster agricultural production, but all three governments between 1930 and 1936 were distinguished by their fiscal orthodoxy.

In neighbouring Sweden, the Agrarian Party concluded a government pact with the Social Democrats, committed to an expansionist programme of combating the depression, in 1933. Although the Finnish Social Democratic Party conference in 1933 called for steps to be taken towards implementing a planned economy, no such deal was concluded in Finland, although the circumstances were not unpropitious. The Finnish Agrarians withdrew from the Sunila government at the end of 1932 in protest at its policy of credit squeeze: both the Agrarians and Social Democrats had earlier joined forces in compelling the government to alleviate the credit crisis facing small farmers. The Social Democrats were however reluctant to support a policy of reflation by an increase in the note circulation, which the Agrarians had been persuaded to adopt by the 'crisis movement' of debt-ridden small farmers. Behind the socialists' reluctance lay memories of rampant inflation in 1917–18, and a deep suspicion that the policy was designed to push up the price of dairy produce—which it was, although this might have been offset by a general resurgence of the economy. The net result of the governmental crisis caused by the collapse of the Sunila ministry was a return to the old pattern of minority government, although this centrist administration managed to survive for four years, largely through Social Democratic support. Although the Kivimäki government was all too evidently the creation of capitalist and banking interests, and pursued fiscal and economic policies in accordance with the desires of its bankers, it represented a lesser evil to the Social Democrats, who feared the alternative would be a minority National Coalition—I.K.L. government.

The labour movement had been gravely weakened during the years of crisis. The S.A.J. trade union movement had been banned, and the Social Democratic S.A.K. was numerically weak and, despite its pronounced 'Western' policies, was shunned by the employers' federation. Its role during the depression was strictly defensive, and it was utterly unable to prevent the termination or renunciation of collective agreements by the employers. Strike activity was so weak that the *Vientirauha* strike-breaker organisation was not called upon once between 1930 and 1933. President Svinhufvud let it be known that he would not countenance socialist participation in government, and the right-wing parties threatened to terminate the party's legal existence. In these circumstances, the party felt it had little option but to support the Kivimäki government. The tenseness of the political situation prevented the emergence of a government enjoying broad popular support; as one Social Democrat speaker during the debate on the government's agricultural policy remarked in 1934, an Agrarian-socialist government was far more realistic, but was ruled out by the Agrarians' continuing attachment to the right. The Social Democrats were so afraid of the alternative that they even supported measures which were distasteful to them in order to keep Kivimäki in office, such as the proposal to establish an economic council which would have allowed big business interests an opportunity to supervise the government's economic policies.

There was, however, growing opposition to continued support of the minority government within Social Democratic ranks. One section of the party wanted to forge closer links with the Agrarians, along similar lines to those pursued by the Swedish Social Democrats: left-wingers such as Karl Wiik and the members of the student socialist society sought to steer the party towards a more clearly-defined socialist policy, eschewing party alliances. The idea of a 'peasant-worker' alliance was also mooted in Agrarian circles, but there was still widespread mistrust of socialist intentions, in addition to the fundamental clash of producer and consumer interests which had led to bitter debates in former years. Socialist indifference towards the language question, which occupied a great deal of parliamentary time in 1935, also alienated the more nationalistic Agrarians. The Social Democratic Party leadership came in for much criticism for its continued support of the Kivimäki government at the party conference in 1936, and although it managed to win the day, it was sufficiently persuaded of the feeling of the party that it declared on the eve of the elections that the government would be toppled at the first suitable opportunity.

The Social Democratic Party had increased its mandate from sixty-six to seventy-eight seats in the 1933 elections, and in the 1936 elections obtained eighty-three seats. The Agrarians with fifty-three seats formed the second largest party, whereas Kivimäki's Progressive Party managed to hold on to a mere seven seats. The election results finally persuaded the socialist leader Väinö Tanner that the time was now ripe for a new government. Negotiations were entered into with the Agrarians, and the Social Democrats flexed their muscles in readiness to topple Kivimäki's government. In the end, it fell over an issue of its own making. Since President Svinhufvud set his face against socialist participation in government—although the party had officially declared its intention of seeking office a further spell of minority government was inevitable. In February 1937, the socialists managed to defeat Svinhufvud's renewed candidature for the presidency by switching their votes on the second ballot in the electoral college from Ståhlberg to the Agrarian Kallio. The new President had no objections to socialist participation in government, and in March 1937 a coalition of Progressives, Agrarians and Social Democrats was formed under the Progressive A. K. Cajander.

The 'red earth' Cajander government was not a popular front of the kind forged in Paris and Madrid and blessed by Moscow. Tanner had vigorously opposed all attempts to create a popular front with what remained of the Communists in Finland, and the party had even expelled the left-wing leadership of the student socialist organisation for sailing too close to the Moscow wind. Tanner was less concerned with the defence of democracy (although he had spoken out with great courage against the Lapua movement) than with practical politics. He was therefore prepared to strike a bargain with the Agrarians in order to effect social and economic reforms in government. A number of necessary reforms were passed, although some of these had been set in motion by the Kivimäki government; but the lack of a comprehensive programme of reforms, the conflict of interests between farmer and consumer, and the fact that the Social Democrats were very much 'on trial' in government placed the Cajander government in a very different category to that of its Swedish counterpart. Whereas Per Albin Hansson's government had taken the first steps towards the creation of a welfare state, the Cajander government showed little sign of economic, social or fiscal innovation.

The Cajander government did declare one of its aims to be the strengthening of the democratic order. In 1938 the *Eduskunta* approved an order banning the I.K.L. made by the Agrarian Minister of the Interior, Urho Kekkonen. However, this order was later overruled in the courts. The tide had begun to turn against the extreme Right even during the time of the Kivimäki government, which had passed legislation against incitement and the wearing of uniforms for political purposes. The I.K.L. was attacked by a number of leading bourgeois politicians as anti-democratic. In 1934, J. K. Paasikivi had returned to active politics, and within a year had steered the National Coalition Party away from its alliance with the I.K.L. The involvement of the I.K.L. youth organisation (*Sinimustat*) in the planning of a *coup d'état* in Estonia at the end of 1935 was generally condemned by all the other political parties, including the National Coalition, and the I.K.L. drifted into further isolation as a pale imitation of fascism.

In spite of the rejection of right-wing authoritarianism by the bourgeois parties, the political scene in Finland was firmly set on the right. Communist attempts to create a popular front in which bourgeois progressives might be included met with little success. A human rights league set up to rally support for the communist Toivo Antikainen, who was accused in 1934 on rather dubious grounds of murder during the war in Karelia in 1922, came to a natural end in 1936. Arrests and trials of Communists continued throughout the 1930s. Not even the Minister of Agriculture in the Kivimäki government was above police suspicion, as was revealed in a secret memorandum on Communist popular front activities. Socialists were still subject to harassment and suspicion, and their presence in the Cajander government says as much for the determination of Väinö Tanner as it does for the willingness of the non-socialist parties to consider such a coalition.

The inter-war years—a summary

At a time when the lights of democracy were going out in so many European countries, the formation of a Centre-Left government with a strong parliamentary majority in the new republic of Finland was hailed with relief by the upholders of free democratic principles. It seemed as if Finland, having narrowly escaped the threat of fascism, was on the road to recovery and reorientation. In the words of one contemporary observer:

The confidence of the people in its Socialist-Agrarian Government was shown at the elections of July 1939 when the Socialist and Centre parties gained at the expense of the I.K.L., who lost half their seats. The Finnish people were prosperous, contented and united in the summer of 1939; if there was trouble to come, it would not come from inside Finland.[5]

When viewed from the vantage point of forty years on, however, the contours of the 1930s appear somewhat smoother than they did to contemporaries. Perhaps the most striking feature of the Finnish political system during the inter-war period was its resilience, which was rooted in a deep soil of constitutionalist conservatism. The democratic systems planted in many eastern European countries in the years immediately after 1918 all too often lacked this nourishment, and consequently they soon withered and died. The men who guided Finland's destiny had matured during the fight to preserve Finnish constitutional liberties from autocratic oppression. It was very unlikely that they would willingly surrender these liberties as the price for crushing communism. It should also be remembered that the 1919 Constitution made provisions for a strong executive. The Finnish President was no mere figurehead, but 'a real head of state, in whose hands firm governmental power would be concentrated'.[6] The first President, Ståhlberg, provoked controversy but also gradually gained respect for the office by firm action, such as the dissolution of the *Eduskunta* in 1924 in the face of opposition from its non-socialist majority and the Kallio government. His successors were perhaps not of the same calibre, but they were nonetheless able to exercise considerable authority by virtue of their office. A strong presidency was probably a major safeguard of parliamentary democracy in Finland. In Latvia, Estonia and Lithuania, where governmental power was in the hands of factious legislatures, authoritarian régimes were created by heroes of the fight for independence; in Finland, the authoritarian White hero Svinhufvud was able to exercise authority within the framework of a conservative constitution.

It must also be said that the buoyance of the Finnish economy was in marked contrast to the backward agrarian economies of many other eastern European countries. This in itself was a powerful safeguard of the democratic *status quo*, since economic growth inevitably carries positive social and financial benefits in its wake and is far less likely to create reservoirs of discontent for extremist political groups to tap. It is true that there was a marked lack of industrial democracy in Finland, especially in contrast to Sweden where the 1938 Saltsjöbaden agreement was a notable landmark in industrial relations, but the trade unions continued to function and the Cajander government did introduce a few modest reforms (such as paid annual holidays) which marked a step forward towards proper recognition of the worker's rights in society. Not only the organised labour movement but the whole working class suffered from the stigma it had incurred in the civil war. What some writers have termed the 'first Finnish republic' (1918–44) was indisputably a White republic, in which socialists were tolerated but never fully integrated.[7]

The scars of 1918 also took a long time to heal on the Red side. The Finnish Communist Party and its adherents in Finland were sworn enemies of the White bourgeois republic, which the Social Democrats also regarded with suspicion. A number of emotional issues, such as the granting of amnesties to Red prisoners, served to remind socialists of what had happened in 1918, as did the 100,000-strong *Suojeluskunta*, which specifically barred socialists from membership. The post-1918 Finnish Social Democratic Party was a victim of circumstance. It inherited an insurrectionary (or, in the White view, a treacherous) tradition which it could not entirely disavow. The hostility of the non-socialist parties tended to preserve the old reluctance to participate in the running of a bourgeois state, although the political constellation of the 1920s did offer a real chance for socialist participation. It was not easy for the party to define its role, although the virtual elimination of Communism as a political rival in the 1930s did make this task somewhat easier. Party membership fell from 67,022 in 1919 to around 25,000 in 1925, and remained around this figure for much of the 1930s. The loss of urban members was particularly noticeable, and although many former leasehold farmers began to drift away from active party membership, the party was still dominated by the rural worker. In spite of a declining or at best stagnant membership, it managed to attract an increasingly higher share of the polls in national elections after 1930, winning over half a million votes in the 1939 elections. This electoral success is comparable to the gains made by the Scandinavian social democratic parties; but it would be incorrect to describe the Finnish party as 'Scandinavian'. Its very existence was threatened in the early 1930s, and it felt compelled to support a minority bourgeois government for four years for fear of a worse alternative. Even in the Cajander 'red earth' government the Social Democratic Party was something of a junior partner on trial. As one commentator has recently noted, Finnish social democracy in the 1930s tended to adapt to a right-wing society and in doing so allowed its ideology to become confused.[8] Instead of seizing the political initiative as a radical party of reform, like the Swedish and Danish Social Democratic Parties, it was content to play second fiddle for much of the time in the White orchestra.

The Finnish Social Democratic Party cannot accurately be described as 'Scandinavian', since apart from anything else, the political system and situation in Finland were very unlike those of her western neighbours. Communism posed no severe problem to the body politic in the Scandinavian countries, which had not experienced civil war and its aftermath, and did not share a long frontier with a potentially hostile country. Many of the political issues which were of deep concern to Finnish socialists either did not exist or were of secondary importance in Sweden and Denmark. There was one major political issue in Finland which caused ructions in Scandinavia but this was a matter of little concern to Finnish socialists: the language question, forcefully dismissed by Tanner as a 'sixth-rate issue'.

The focus of the language controversy was the University in Helsinki. Although new single-language institutions of higher education were founded on private initiative, their intake was small: the majority of students still found their way to Helsinki, where teaching was in Finnish and Swedish. This meant that a young man from the Finnish-speaking hinterland might find himself suddenly exposed to tuition in what was for him a foreign language, learnt at school. Not unnaturally, this created resentment, which was exacerbated by the problem of finding suitable employment, which was increasing along with the numbers of university graduates. Finnish-speaking students tended to favour teaching, the Church ministry and the civil service. In all these careers, promotion was often hard to achieve, and the civil service in particular had suffered a sharp decline in real earning power. Swedish-speaking Finns showed more interest in commerce and industry, where the Swedish-speaking establishment was still strongly entrenched. Hamalainen has estimated that in the early 1930s only four out of every six graduates found a job immediately, while many took ill-paid jobs which did not allow them to repay the loans they had obtained in order to study. Poverty, insecurity and loneliness in the alien big city all helped to draw the Finnish-speaking student to the Academic Karelia Society, which from 1924 took up the cause of finnicisation of the University. The older generation of Finnish nationalists was alarmed by the radical and at times intolerant demands of the A.K.S., and sought to preserve the *status quo* in the University. The 1923 university legislation proved unsatisfactory; by the end of the 1920s, the three non-socialist Finnish-language parties had adopted noticeably more uncompromising programmes on the language question. The Agrarian Party was perhaps the most outspoken, going so far in 1932 as to demand a one-language state, but it failed to push through finnicisation of the University in 1933–5, and in 1937 was associated with legislation which limited the number of Swedish-speaking professors to fifteen. Throughout the long and wearisome debates in the *Eduskunta*, Finnish nationalist students demonstrated, struck, held protest meetings and otherwise showed their feelings by painting out Swedish road signs, barracking or boycotting Swedish-speaking teachers and generally spoiling their case in the eyes of the older generation.

The language conflict can be seen as a clash between two different concepts of national integration, between the centre and the periphery, or as a conflict of generations; but its root cause was social. The struggle against Russian oppression had had the effect of masking the socio-economic tensions created by the challenge of an aspiring Finnish-speaking educated class to the established and overwhelmingly Swedish-speaking élite, but with the winning of independence these tensions became even more acute. What in the nineteenth century had been little more than a narrowly-confined conflict within the educated class now acquired much broader dimensions with the expansion of the public services and the emergence of modern political parties. More than anything else, the language conflict in the inter-war period was caused by the growth of an urban Finnish-speaking middle class and exacerbated by the unwillingness of politicians and intellectuals to recognise this fact.

In a very real sense, the issue was one not of language, but of status. The educated class (*sivistyneistö*) which had so completely dominated public life before independence now began to feel the keen winds of economic and social change; as a committee report in 1941 put it: 'Formerly our adored educated class truly dominated public life. Now capitalist circles impose their imprint upon it.'[9] The old social order of rank and status had begun to crumble before the impact of capitalism and industrialisation at the end of the nineteenth century, but it had preserved its political form until 1906. Even parliamentary reform did not destroy the conservative structure of government and administration, with its emphasis on loyalty and service towards the ruler. The first years of independence removed the kingpin of this structure. The new republic had to come to terms with harsh political and economic realities in an increasingly competitive world; but many of its citizens were unable to follow suit. Hence the appeal of an ardent nationalism which offered a vision of an organic, traditionalist community bound together by blood ties and honest peasant values. It is no coincidence that high-ranking civil servants, clergymen, students and intellectuals formed the backbone of extreme nationalist groups, since it was these elements who felt the loss of status most sharply. The civil service came under frequent attack from anti-urban and anti-bureaucratic elements of the Agrarian Party. Expansion of the bureaucracy at the lower levels, together with a decline in real income for civil servants, provoked conservatives to speak of the 'proletarianisation' of the public service.

As we have seen, a large number of students with academic qualifications found it difficult to obtain employment at the level they felt suitable. The University was no longer the open door to high-status employment. A commercial or technical education was far more likely to lead to a rewarding job, but the Finnish-speaking student showed more reluctance to follow such a course than his Swedish-speaking compatriot. The Church, traditionally a major employer of Finnish-speaking students, had suffered a great decline in its authority with the crumbling of traditional social and political values. Furthermore, the events of 1905 and 1917–18 had shattered the romantic nationalist illusion of the 'people', although the civil war did produce a new myth of the sturdy, honest peasant fighting for his country against the eastern foe. This myth gained a further lease of life in the Lapua movement: and yet the nationalist right-wing educated class failed to forge a lasting bond with the peasantry. The typical small farmer with a few acres of forest had become an element of the market economy, and his problems stemmed from this fact. Nationalist idealism had in the end precious little to offer him.

Yrjö Ruutu, a leading proponent of state socialism in the 1920s, identified Finland's basic problem when he called for the educated middle class to take the lead in advancing social reform. Finland lacked a strong middle class, or rather a social group which was willing to recognise itself as such. The historical imprint of the society of rank remained very strong.[10] Captains of industry and entrepreneurs had remained on the fringes of that society and were not easily integrated into the social and political framework of inter-war Finland. Government and administration was still very much controlled by the academic élite; a glance at the professional background of the ministers who served in inter-war governments confirms this. A businessman or industrialist in government was a rare phenomenon. At a time of unprecedented economic development, it is perhaps paradoxical that the affairs of the nation should be guided by politicians, many of whom had still not properly come to terms with the class society, and who hankered after *Gemeinschaft* in a *Gesellschaft* world.[11]

Nowhere were the ideals and aspirations of Finnish nationalism more closely reflected than in literature. Writers who were critical of the social order had difficulties in finding a publisher. There was a lack of translated foreign contemporary literature: many writers, such as Romain Rolland, John Steinbeck and Ivar Lo-Johansson were virtually unknown to the Finnish reading public, since their works were regarded as unsuitable for translation. Erkki Vala was jailed for publishing translated selections of *The Good Soldier Švejk* in his journal *Tulenkantajat*. Right-wing and church opposition prevented the staging in Helsinki of *God's Green Acres*. The introspective and even xenophobic tendencies of Finnish literature were succinctly expressed in a statement by the Finnish Writers' Guild in 1935: 'We must hearken to the whisperings of the spruce under which we dwell, and not to the many siren songs of foreign vogue, to whose tempo we so easily and clumsily dance. We shall attain our triumph by drawing from the noble depths of our own Kalevalan spirit.'[12]

The 'Kalevalan spirit' was certainly an invaluable and inexhaustible fount of inspiration for the propagators of Finnish nationalism, historians, poets and pamphleteers alike; it was perhaps less a source of great literature. With a few exceptions, such as the Nobel prize-winner F. E. Sillanpää, Finnish writers were virtually unknown outside their native land. In the field of music, Sibelius had acquired a European reputation even before independence, but his fame tended to overshadow a younger generation of Finnish composers. Only in architecture and at a popular cultural level, in sport, did Finland truly attain international recognition. Even if the man on the Clapham omnibus had not heard of Sibelius and Alvar Aalto, he knew of Paavo Nurmi.

What was less well known was that sport, like so many other aspects of Finnish life, was organised along class lines. The labour sports alliance (T.U.L.) rejected the idea of collaboration with the non-socialist S.V.U.L. in 1932 and thereby forfeited a state subsidy. On several occasions, tracksuited T.U.L. athletes were accused of contravening the ban on political uniforms; they were also frequently denied facilities available to the rival S.V.U.L.

The consumers' co-operative movement was also split into the 'neutral' S.O.K. and 'progressive' O.T.K., in which Väinö Tanner played a leading role. The achievements of the two movements were far more lasting than their political rivalries, and were widely admired abroad. Not only did the consumers' co-operatives provide a bridge between a backward rural economy and the modern consumer society, but they also performed a vital role in education. It is perhaps not too much to say that in offering a wide range of cheap, good-quality consumer goods in their shops and in helping to educate the ordinary Finn to cope with the mundane but necessary tasks of everyday modern life, such as book-keeping, domestic science and animal husbandry, the co-operative movement as a whole performed a vital function as an agent of national integration.

The subject of living standards is a contentious one, but all the evidence clearly suggests that the lot of the average Finnish man and woman was a good deal better in 1930 than it had been twenty years before. Average life expectancy had increased, and infant mortality had decreased. The average family in 1940 was spending less in proportion on food than it had done, and could afford to spend proportionately more on clothing, entertainment and leisure activities; it was also smaller than the average family of pre-independence days. During the inter-war years, the proportion of Finns between the ages of fifteen and sixty-four, the classic productive age-group—remained high, rising from 62·3 per cent in 1920 to 67·2 per cent in 1940. The great majority still lived on and obtained their living from the land, although the industrial labour force doubled between 1920 and 1940, and the urban population rose from just over half a million to nearly a million. Agriculture's share of the gross domestic product in 1930 was 47 per cent, compared with 13 per cent for Sweden. Although there was a swifter *per capita* growth of the Finnish gross domestic product than in the other northern countries during the inter-war years, the level of national wealth so produced was a good deal lower. In comparison with Sweden, Finland had a relatively undeveloped and predominantly agrarian economy; in comparison with most east European countries, however, it was further on the way towards industrialisation, with a sound farming industry and a higher standard of living.

The land reforms of the 1920s dramatically diminished the proportion of tenant farmers, although it helped to perpetuate the small farmer class which suffered severely during the depression. Notable advances in technique, fertilisation and cultivation brought about impressive increases in grain yields. Wheat, which had hardly been grown in any quantity before 1920, became a favoured crop in the 1930s. On the eve of war, Finland was virtually self-sufficient in bread grains, a welcome contrast to the situation in 1914. Milk yields also rose enormously, thanks to improved breeding and better provision of fodder and silage —the Virtanen method of making silage came into widespread use in the 1930s—and Finnish dairy products were marketed abroad. Horse-drawn machinery became increasingly common, though tractors were few and far between and large areas of eastern and northern Finland were without electric power.

The dominance of the wood-processing industries over all other branches of manufacture continued throughout the inter-war years. By 1939, the productive value of the paper and pulp industry exceeded that of the timber industry. Pulp and paper products were also respon-sible for nearly half Finland's earnings from foreign trade by the end of the 1930s; together with the exports of sawn timber, they comprised over three-quarters of the total value of Finnish exports. There was also expansion in the metal and mining industries, largely due to increased domestic demand. Finland's major trading partner in the 1930s was Great Britain, which even displaced Germany as the major exporter of goods to Finland.

In spite of rapid economic expansion, Finnish industry suffered from structural rigidity, which government support for agriculture in the form of loans and the creation of new farms did little to ease. As a recent survey of economic developments in northern Europe rightly concludes, 'it was not until the post-war period that Finland could really be called an industrialised country'.[13]

The growth of Finnish export industries, rising consumer demand and improved communications all brought Finland into closer contact with the outside world; yet in many respects Finland remained as isolated from world events and developments as she had been in the nineteenth century. Mention has been made of the paucity of translated contemporary literature available. For his appreciation of what was happening in the world, the Finnish reader had to rely mostly on agency reports and dubbed newsreels. There were few able news analysts and no tradition of on-the-spot or investigative journalism. Little was written or said about what was happening in Soviet Russian cultural life; Finland's eastern neighbour was almost as remote as Outer Mongolia. Pro-German and conservative sentiment certainly tended to omit the unpleasant features of the Nazi régime from the image of contemporary Germany. The diplomatic corps was inadequately financed and very inexperienced, and simply could not hope to present a balanced world picture to the government at home. Many leading diplomats of the 1920s owed their positions to their political activities during the war years; and not a few continued to pursue these activities while serving abroad. It is perhaps inevitable that a small, newly-independent nation anxious to establish its credentials will be over-concerned with its own existence; certainly this was so with Finland. A glance at press debate and literary polemics of the inter-war years quickly reveals the introspective and obsessive side of the Finnish national character, which perpetuated a number of rigid attitudes regarding Finland's position in the world, and as the supposed frontier-post of Western values.

As the 'low, dishonest decade' of the 1930s drew to a close, it might have seemed that a new chapter of domestic politics in Finland, was about to open, with the socialists participating in a strong government in which rising young politicians such as Urho Kekkonen and Karl-August Fagerholm were to make their mark. The old heroes of 1917–18, whose granite monuments now stand around the *Eduskunta* building, seemed to have outplayed their parts. Svinhufvud retired to his country estate after his defeat in the presidential elections of 1937; Ståhlberg remained in the background as a kind of liberal conscience of the nation. In the Soviet Union, Stalin's purges scythed down most of the old leaders of the Social Democratic Party who had converted to Communism, with the notable exception of O. V. Kuusinen.

Two leading figures of 1918 made a return to public life in the 1930s: J. K. Paasikivi as chairman of the National Coalition Party, and Mannerheim as chairman of the Defence Council, a post created specially for him. Few could have foreseen the crucial roles which the ex-imperial Russian army general and the former Old Finn Senator still had to play in the destiny of the nation.

6

FINLAND AND HER NEIGHBOURS
1920–1948

Tuo kaunis Kalevan poika	That fair son of Kaleva
läksi taitellen sotahan	went with music off to war
iloitellen ihmisihin	rejoicing off among men
ilon taiten tappeluhun,	playing joy into battle
sano kohta mentyähän	said as soon as he'd arrived
suurelle sotakeolle	upon the great battlefield
miesten tapputanterille:	on the slaughter-lands of men:
'Hiietki yhen urohon	'Even the demons will guard
sovissahan suojelevat	a hero with their war-gear
kaavuissahan kattelevat	will cover him with their cloaks
suurilla sotakeoilla	upon the great battlefields
miesten tappotanterilla.'	on the slaughter-lands of men.'
Jo tuolla tuli tuhua	Now destruction came
pääty päiviä pahoja:	evil days befell:
jo Kullervo kukistettihin	now Kullervo was conquered
kaattihin Kalevan poika	Kaleva's son was struck down
suurille sotakeoille	upon the great battlefields
miesten tappotanterille	on the slaughter-lands of men.

Sotaanlähtö 'The warrior's departure'
(*Finnish Folk Poetry Epic. An anthology in Finnish and English*,
edited and translated by Matti Kuusi, Keith Bosley and Michael
Branch, Helsinki, London and Montreal 1977, pp. 492–3)

Between the wars (1919–1939)

Finnish foreign policy in the inter-war years was essentially a search
for security against the possible hostile intentions of the Soviet Union.
In Finnish eyes, Russia was the traditional enemy, and the Soviet
Union was a constant threat to Finnish independence. Little or no

attempt was made to come to terms with geographical reality by seeking better and more durable relations with the Soviet Union. The story of Finnish foreign policy between 1918 and the conclusion of the mutual assistance treaty with the Soviet Union thirty years later is one of tragic failure to appreciate the apprehensions and desire for security of an isolated great power—and of an inability to understand that, in spite of its isolation, the Soviet Union *was* a great power. Given the deep antipathy towards all things Russian of the Finnish ruling élite, it is perhaps understandable that a more flexible or positive policy towards Moscow did not emerge. Nor did the actions and attitudes of the Communist régime exactly prepare the ground for cordial relations with bourgeois-capitalist states. At best Finland and the Soviet Union were reluctant neighbours; at worst, their disagreements were to lead to war.

As J. K. Paasikivi once acidly remarked, there was little real understanding of foreign affairs in Finland. Very few politicians showed any interest or deep knowledge. Finland's representatives abroad, particularly in the first years of independence, were political figures rather than professional diplomats. The establishment of a diplomatic corps was made difficult both by financial stringencies and by political wrangling. This in itself made the task of creating any sort of consistent foreign policy difficult. Jorma Kalela has argued that the desire to avoid isolation was the guiding theme of Finnish foreign policy between the wars, and that the means to this end lay in procuring outside aid. In the 1920s, this took the form of seeking to ensure the *status quo* in the Baltic, if possible with the help of the major powers, which Kalela sees as the proper context in which to view the so-called 'border states' policy. By the late thirties this had been pushed into the background as Finland sought to identify herself with the Scandinavian countries and thereby obtain the protection of the western powers. Nordic neutrality in itself was an insufficient guarantee of Finnish security, as Rudolf Holsti, Foreign Minister from February 1937 to December 1938, realised; the only hope for Finland lay in the support of Britain and France for the *status quo* in northern Europe.

In the event, neither the Baltic nor the Scandinavian policy brought lasting security for Finland. The reasons for this failure will be analysed in due course, but the major aspect of Finland's security problem, her relationship with the Soviet Union, was at the heart of the matter. Finnish security was also a Russian concern, and as long as the Finns refused to accept this harsh fact, the problem remained. It was the rock on which Finnish foreign policy finally foundered.

That the only possible threat to Finnish territorial integrity came from the east was axiomatic in military thinking throughout the inter-war years; indeed, no other possibility was ever seriously considered. This of course raised the problem of how a small country with limited manpower and financial resources could best defend itself. The main conclusion of the defence review committee, which presented its report in 1926, was that the armed forces should be sufficiently formidable to make any potential aggressor think twice before attacking, and strong enough to repel any attack, or at least to hold it off long enough for political or military aid to arrive. The committee suggested the creation of a field army of thirteen divisions, fully equipped and with ammunition for at least two months' campaigning. In the event of war, it was envisaged that as many as 300,000 men might be called to arms. However, the committee's recommendations were never put through the *Eduskunta*; instead, the government had to resort to emergency programmes, none of which came near to matching the original estimates of the 1926 committee report. The armed forces were under-equipped, and much of the equipment was surplus stock which was difficult to repair or replace. Since the politicians insisted on the army relying on domestic industry, which in many instances simply did not exist, this problem continued to plague the military chiefs.

In October 1938 Mannerheim, who had been appointed chairman of the Defence Council in 1931 with the secret undertaking that in the event of war he was to exercise supreme command, warned President Kallio of the inadequacies of the armed forces, and asked for extraordinary expenditure, which neither government nor *Eduskunta* was prepared to grant. Mannerheim in fact offered his resignation in June 1939 when the government refused to grant the full amount suggested by the Defence Council for the defence of the Åland islands, and was only persuaded to stay on when the government agreed to consult him first in future on all defence issues. His 'shopping list' costing 1,181,531,000 marks, which would have equipped the thirteen-division field army, was not taken up either, with the result that the Finnish army was, in his view, incapable of serious resistance to a determined attack when the crisis in relations with the Soviet Union broke in the late autumn. On the other hand, Finland was not afflicted by the 'defence nihilism' which in Norway led to the reduction of military service to eighty-four days in 1933 and a serious running-down of the armed forces' basic capacity to offer resistance to an invader. The term of military service in Finland never fell below 365 days, and this remained higher than in all the other northern countries. Although in the 1920s the Social Democratic Party opposed long-term military service and still clung to the idea of a militia as a cheaper and more democratic form of defence, its leaders at least had at last come round by the 1930s to acceptance of the necessity of meeting the costs of national defence. In government in 1938, the Social Democrats supported a re-equipment programme of considerable financial magnitude. Nevertheless, the left and many cost-conscious Agrarians tended to oppose high spending on defence throughout the first two decades of independence; although they came to see the need for a properly organised armed force, they were reluctant to meet the costs. The inadequacies of Finland's defences necessarily compelled a peaceful foreign policy, as the 1926 defence review recognised. What was not realised was that the Soviet Union might construe this weakness as a sign of Finland's inability to resist pressure from a belligerent Germany seeking a base from which to attack Russia.

Unlike the Scandinavian countries, whose wartime experience led to a fairly general national consensus on neutrality as the basis for foreign policy, Finland failed to find a generally acceptable policy with which to tackle the basic question of security. As Paasivirta has noted, every political tendency in Finland at the outset of independence suffered setbacks and disappointment in their attempts to set a course in foreign policy. The advocates of force as a means of resolving Finland's security problems found little support in government circles, but they were strongly represented in nationalist organisations such as the A.K.S. and they often attracted the attention of the Soviet press. The policy of co-operation with other states similarly threatened by Soviet Russia foundered on the impossibility of creating a durable defensive alliance, and the policy of neutrality was in a sense a non-starter, since unadorned neutrality was no answer to Finland's security problems. There were also those who advocated some sort of policy of *rapprochement*, or understanding of the Soviet Union but their voices carried little weight.[1] Finland's failure to find a satisfactory and lasting solution to her security problem was not unique; it was a fate shared by all the newly-independent eastern European countries. Finland alone was to escape the political consequences of occupation during the war which engulfed these former imperial appendages— which emphasises the country's dual geopolitical position as a Baltic neighbour of the U.S.S.R., and as a frontier zone of Scandinavia, with its long Atlantic coastline and the Western maritime powers relatively near at hand. This duality was a constant feature of Finnish and Russian relations during the inter-war years.

These relations had got off to a bad start in 1918–19, and the signing of the Tartu peace treaty was in many respects a temporary necessity rather than a satisfactory conclusion of outstanding issues between the former imperial power and the newly-independent state. The treaty certainly did not assuage Russian fears about the security of Petrograd. A hostile naval power could use the Finnish harbours in a campaign against the revolutionary capital, as the British had done in 1919. The Soviet Union had lost all the advanced bases of the old imperial Baltic fleet; it had also been excluded from the discussions on the future of the Åland islands and was not a signatory to the 1921 agreement, which effectively strengthened the demilitarisation of the islands which had first been agreed to in 1856 without permitting the Finns to take effective steps to defend the islands should they come under attack. Finland's insistence on having some say in the future of the East Karelia area (and support for dissident groups there, as in the autumn of 1921 when rebellion broke out in the area) and her activities in concert with the other border states annoyed the Bolshevik government and added to its conviction that Finland was a hostile country.

In the course of 1918–19, Finland also succeeded in alienating a number of other countries, such as Britain and Sweden. Even relations with Estonia were strained, as the Estonians, in the wake of the Finnish volunteer brigades sent in the winter of 1918–19, discerned unmistakable signs of a Finnish desire to establish commercial and economic dominance in Estonia. These volunteers, some 3,500 strong, were sent with Finnish government approval, as a part of the general fight against Bolshevism. Ethnic solidarity played some part in recruitment propaganda, but as Zetterberg has shown, there was on the whole less interest shown in Finland than in Estonia in the idea of a closer union between the two Finno-Ugrian peoples. Proposals for some sort of political union were indeed put forward in 1918–19 by leading Estonian politicians, but as Estonian independence became more likely in the spring of 1919, these plans fell into the background. They were considered by the Finnish government, but at no time was a closely defined 'Estonian policy' formulated. The general political situation was in any case too fluid for any such policy to emerge.

By the summer of 1919, it appears that the Castrén government was more willing to follow the lead of the Entente powers than to act independently. It deferred its decision on *de jure* recognition of Estonian independence and came round to the idea of some sort of joint front of the Baltic states as advocated by Britain—although in Foreign

Office eyes such a league was to be aimed as much against possible German penetration as against Soviet Russia. In September 1919 the Baltic states agreed to present a joint front to the Russian offer of peace negotiations, after Estonia had initially agreed to enter into discussions with a Soviet delegation. This front lasted as long as there was hopes of Yudenich's forces reaching Petrograd; the collapse of the offensive in October–November and the consequent threat to Narva forced the Estonians to go it alone and to seek a settlement with the Soviet government, which had signified its willingness to recognise their independence. In this regard, the policy of the three Baltic states differed from that of their northern neighbour, for although Finland had secured Entente recognition and could therefore afford to go along with whatever the Entente powers chose to regard as a policy towards Russia, its own political existence had received no guarantee from the Western powers. A peace settlement with Soviet Russia which guaranteed political independence was therefore of prime importance to the Baltic states.[2]

This difference goes a long way towards explaining why no lasting Baltic league emerged. Whereas Finland lay on the periphery—albeit an important one—of the Russian security zone, the Baltic states were right in the centre, between Russia and Germany. Furthermore, the southernmost state, Lithuania, was in conflict with Poland over Vilna, an issue which the Finns rightly felt might embroil them in a war outside their own sphere of interest. Also, whereas Finland had close traditional ties with Germany, there was little cause for Estonia and Latvia to seek the friendship of a nation which had traditionally played the role of oppressor rather than protector. Finally, there was always a question-mark over the eventual survival of the small Baltic states. Finland was in a different league, and was aware of this fact. Hence the caution with which many of the schemes for Baltic or Scando-Baltic collaboration concocted by Baltic statesmen were treated by Finnish governments and *Eduskunta* alike.

Any hopes for a viable Baltic bloc of states were dealt a severe blow when Polish troops occupied Vilna in October 1920. Not one of the five Baltic littoral states signed the political treaty, with its provisions for defensive military collaboration, which their representatives had drafted at the Bulduri conference of August 1920. A further attempt to create some sort of defensive military agreement was made at the Warsaw conference in March 1922, attended by delegations from Poland, Estonia, Latvia and Finland. The Warsaw accord was immediately attacked by the Right-wing press in Finland, since it would

equally involve Finland in conflict with Germany as well as with
Soviet Russia. The Social Democratic Party was also unwilling
to bind Finland to Polish designs. Although the government dropped
Article 7 of the accord, which obliged the signatories to confer in the
event of unprovoked aggression by a third power, the *Eduskunta*
refused to ratify it and passed a vote of no confidence in Holsti, the
Foreign Minister, who had tried to press the Warsaw accord as an
integral aspect of a border states policy. This brought about the
resignation of the government, and killed all hopes of the accord being
developed into a viable alliance. It did not spell the end of the Finnish
border states policy, since consultation and limited collaboration still
continued, but it did convince leading Finnish policy-makers that no
sort of military alliance with the Baltic states was possible.

If the border states policy did not bear fruit, attempts to forge closer
relations with Sweden were equally unsuccessful. Sweden was primarily concerned with strengthening her neutrality, and had shown
on a number of occasions her unwillingness to become involved in
Baltic affairs which concerned Russia. The Åland islands dispute, which
was finally resolved by the League of Nations in Finland's favour in
1921, and the language conflict in Finland prevented the establishment
of close relations at an official level. Swedish opinion was largely
unresponsive to suggestions of some sort of defensive alliance with
Finland, either in the form of a grand Baltic alliance or under the
auspices of the League. When the Swedish Foreign Minister
Hederstierna, in a speech given in October 1923, welcomed the idea of
a Swedo-Finnish defensive alliance, the public outcry in Sweden was
so great that he was compelled to resign. Nevertheless, the idea of a
defensive alliance was viewed more favourably by the military. A
commission headed by the Swedish chief of general staff concluded in
July 1923 that in the event of Soviet aggression against Finland,
Sweden would be obliged as a member of the League of Nations to
assist Finland. This was at odds with the thinking of the Swedish
foreign office, which was reluctant to bind Sweden to any sort of
military collective security agreement. In the League of Nations,
Sweden tended to follow the British line of disarmament rather than
the French policy of collective security, to which Finland adhered.
There was nonetheless a steady increase from 1923 onwards in contacts
betweenSwedish and Finnish army officers. Certain training facilities
were arranged for Finnish officers and cadets, and therewere informal
discussions and exchanges of information. In 1930 a group of young
Swedish army officers published a pamphlet entitled *Antingen—eller*

(Either—or), arguing forcefully for Swedish military support under League of Nations auspices in the event of Finland being attacked by the Red Army. It is thus clear that a section of the armed forces in Sweden did favour some sort of intervention on Finland's behalf in the event of Soviet aggression; but as events were to show, Sweden's political leadership was less willing to undertake this kind of commitment.

At an official level, little or no progress was made towards closer ties between Sweden and Finland during the 1920s. President Relander's state visit to Stockholm in 1925 was an indication that old wounds had healed, not of a new orientation in the foreign policy of either country. At the end of that year, the leader of the Finnish delegation to the League suggested the creation of a northern Locarno group, consisting of Sweden, Finland and the three Baltic states. This was little more than a revival of the old idea of a grand Baltic alliance, minus the military implications and the complication of Poland. It was also one more attempt to create a security system for Finland which left out the one major threat to her security, the Soviet Union. In 1922, the latter had accomplished a major diplomatic breakthrough with the signing of the Rapallo pact with Germany, and had also succeeded in concluding a frontier agreement with Finland in the aftermath of the Karelian uprising of 1921–2 whereby, in the event of troops crossing the frontier from the Finnish side, or of the Finnish government failing to prevent such an occurrence, the Soviet Union would be justified in regarding Finland as having entered into hostile activity against the Soviet state. From the Soviet point of view, this agreement marked the final fulfilment of the terms of the Tartu peace treaty and the end of the East Karelian question. But for the Finnish government, this was not so easy. The compulsory evacuation of thousands of Finnish-speaking Ingrians from the Leningrad area in connection with the collectivisation programme in 1931 aroused a storm of protest in Finland. After an initial silence, the Finnish government sent a note to Moscow protesting against the evacuations. The Soviet government, which was anxious to conclude a non-aggression treaty with Finland at the time, adopted a cautious attitude in the face of these protests, and the crisis soon ran into the sand. Nevertheless, one protest meeting had been graced by the presence of President Svinhufvud, members of the government and high-ranking army officers, and a leading advocate of uncompromising belligerence towards Soviet Russia had declared that in order to be truly powerful Finland lacked only Ingria and East Karelia. This was hardly likely to assuage Russian suspicions of the true intentions of her western neighbour.

Having obtained some degree of security at Rapallo, and with the 'border state' policy in ruins after the Warsaw accord, Soviet Russia sought to create a more favourable security system through negotiated arms reduction. The Red Army had been scaled down from over 5 million to an 800,000-strong force by 1922, but for financial and economic reasons the Soviet government wished to reduce the size of the army still further. This could only be done within the framework of a general reduction in armed commitment within the entire Baltic area, which would moreover help to bring the Baltic countries more closely within a security system dictated by Russia. The Soviet proposals revived co-operation between the Baltic countries. At a meeting of military chiefs in Tallinn in August 1922, counter-proposals were drafted, many of which were clearly unacceptable to the Russians. The disarmament conference foundered when it became evident that the Poles had no intention of seriously reducing their forces, although Soviet willingness to consider the proposals for non-aggression pacts and arbitration as a means of enforcing 'moral' disarmament did seem to offer a basis for more profitable negotiations between Finland and Russia. Finland rejected a Polish attempt to revive the Warsaw agreement in 1923 and again in 1925; Finnish reluctance to become tied to Poland was noted with satisfaction in Moscow. Soviet Russia sought to counter the Locarno pact by non-aggression treaties, such as that concluded with Turkey at the end of 1925, and offered to Latvia and Estonia in May 1926. The Finnish conditions for such a treaty were such that Moscow could not accept, and were an attempt once more to present a united Baltic front. However, Soviet offers to negotiate separate treaties relating to the Åland islands and the settlement of disputes were sufficient to deflect Finland from the united front, although the joint negotiations in Helsinki foundered in the Finns' unwillingness to shift from their original conditions for a non-aggression treaty.[3]

At the end of the 1920s, Finland's foreign policy was characterised by Hjalmar Procopé, Foreign Minister from 1927 to 1931, as one of 'splendid isolation'. This was more a reflection on the failure of the policy of co-operation with other states than a statement of what Finnish foreign policy ought to be. The border states policy came to a formal end with the discontinuation of regular consultations in 1926. In practice, the policy had been stillborn, killed by the petty rivalries of the Baltic countries and the determination of Russia and Germany to prevent any moves towards meaningful collaboration. Sweden had rebuffed Finnish approaches, and neither the Western powers nor Germany appeared willing to offer guarantees of Finnish security. The major Finnish initiative in the League, an attempt to create a system of providing financial help for victims of aggression, failed to win support.

Finnish attempts to obtain security on her eastern frontiers within the framework of the League of Nations Covenant merely aroused Soviet hostility, since the League in Moscow's eyes was tantamount to the capitalist great powers. The wave of anti-Communist and anti-Russian sentiment created by the Lapua movement, and the agitation over Ingria in 1931 were again hardly calculated to improve relations with Soviet Russia; nevertheless, the Soviet Union and Finland signed a non-aggression pact in January 1932. This was something of a personal success for one of the few advocates of better relations with Moscow, a former minister to Russia and Foreign Minister in 1931–2, A. S. Yrjö-Koskinen, although in the end it was brought about by developments on the broader European scene. France opened negotiations on a non-aggression treaty with Russia in the summer of 1931; Poland and the Baltic states followed suit, and Finland finally ratified her pact with Soviet Russia when it was made clear that Moscow would not tolerate any binding obligation to conclude similar treaties with the other Baltic countries. The agreement made no mention of the Åland islands, nor of arbitration of disputes, although it recognised the international obligations of each side. Aggression was defined in broad terms, although Finland's signing of the London Protocol of 1933, which defined aggression more precisely, was noted with satisfaction in Moscow.

The early 1930s marked the beginning of a new phase of Soviet diplomatic activity, designed to end the isolation of the 1920s. This is the context in which the 1932 non-aggression treaty with Finland should be seen, rather than as an indication of better relations between the two countries. The Soviet Union was still the only security threat in Finnish eyes, and there was as little understanding of Russian security needs in the 1930s as there had been in the previous decade. The Finns were hostile to the whole idea of an eastern security system constructed by Moscow which might involve them in conflicts outside their own sphere of interest and which would have undercut the basis of a Nordic constellation towards which Finland was now moving. Finnish hostility was interpreted in Moscow as an indication of Finnish collusion with the two powers that eventually wrecked the idea of an eastern Locarno, Poland and Germany; this impression was strengthened by the Finns' apparent unwillingness to welcome Soviet Russia as a member of the League in 1934.

The Finnish reaction to the Soviet proposals for an eastern security system was to move closer to the Scandinavian neutrals. This new orientation of foreign policy had other causes. For commercial reasons Finland had signed the Oslo agreement on tariffs in 1933, an indication of her desire to remain competitive *vis-à-vis* Western markets. In 1931, Finland had unsuccessfully sought to obtain assurances of deliveries of war matériel from Sweden in the event of war: the inadequacies of the Finnish army being a compelling reason to seek closer relations with a major manufacturer of arms and equipment. It might also be that Finland felt a closer affinity with the Scandinavian democracies than with the authoritarian régimes which had established themselves to the south of the Baltic, and which in the past had proved fickle negotiating partners. The Baltic policy thus gave way to a Nordic orientation. Many of the factors which had earlier kept Sweden and Finland apart, such as the Åland question and differences over the security policy of the League were now less significant. The resurgence of Germany caused the Swedes to re-assess their Baltic policy and to value more highly the desirability of aiding Finland in her attempts to stay out of conflict among the great powers. The talks between the Swedish and Finnish Foreign Ministers, and the attendance of the Finnish Foreign Minister for the first time at the Nordic Foreign Ministers' Stockholm conference in 1934 were the first steps towards this new course, which resulted in a declaration of Finnish solidarity with the Nordic neutrals being issued in December 1935. In 1936, Finland also adhered to the Oslo declaration of the northern neutrals which absolved them of obligations under Article 16 of the Covenant to aid fellow-members of the League who were the victims of aggression.

The League had failed to provide adequate security for Finland; but neutrality was not an end in itself, but a means to avoid conflict. Beyond the Nordic bloc, Finland hoped to secure the support of the West. Her professions of neutrality were distrusted by her Scandinavian partners, and by Soviet Russia, albeit for different reasons. Some commentators such as Ilkka Seppinen have argued that the Nordic orientation was little more than a continuation of the old line of seeking co-operation with potential allies. Others, like Max Jakobson and President Kekkonen himself do not question that the Finnish government genuinely desired to pursue a policy of neutrality, although they criticise it for failing to win the confidence of the Soviet Union. In a survey of Finnish foreign policy, Kekkonen remarked in 1961: 'No state can remain neutral if its will for neutrality and capacity to stay neutral are not trusted. Confidence is the alpha and omega of neutrality.'[4]

The Soviet Union's patent lack of confidence in Finland's ability or willingness to remain neutral was demonstrated in a number of ways. In the summer of 1935 the Soviet minister in Helsinki informed Prime Minister Kivimäki that in the event of conflict between Germany and the Soviet Union in Central Europe, his country might be compelled to protect itself by occupying parts of Finland. In their utterances, the Soviet press and high-ranking figures such as Molotov and Marshal Tukhachevsky linked Finland with German plans of aggression. In November 1936, in a speech to the Soviet congress which received international coverage, Andrey Zhdanov gave a clear warning that if the border states drifted into the Nazi sphere of influence, the Soviet Union would not stand idly by. According to one observer, 'they [the border states] could find themselves experiencing the strength of the Soviet Union, and the Soviet window might even be opened wider.'[5] Kivimäki was extremely worried about the parlous state of Soviet-Finnish relations in the last months of his premiership. Moscow was well aware of the pro-German sympathies of President Svinhufvud, and was suspicious of the Finnish drift into Nordic neutrality, at a time when developments in Europe such as the German-Polish rapprochement and the Anglo-German naval agreement seemed to bode ill for the Soviet Union. The formation of a new government by Kyösti Kallio in which Rudolf Holsti was recalled as Foreign Minister marked a new phase of better relations with Moscow. Holsti was the first Finnish Foreign Minister to visit Moscow, in February 1937, and his declaration that Finland would resist any attempt by a third power to use Finnish territory for hostile purposes against the Soviet Union was welcomed by his hosts. However, personal verbal declarations were not enough for the Russians, and the Finns for their part were unwilling to enter into a formal agreement. The improvement in relations occasioned by Holsti's visit did not last. The visit of a U-boat squadron to Finnish waters in August 1937 and Holsti's trip to Berlin two months later raised yet again in the Soviet press the spectre of White Finland sliding into the Nazi camp.

The growing Sudetenland crisis in the spring of 1938 prompted a new Soviet attempt to secure its frontier with Finland. The man entrusted with this task was Boris Yartsev, a relatively minor official in the Soviet embassy in Helsinki. After warning Holsti that the Soviet Union would not stand idly by should German troops land in Finland as part of an all-out offensive against his country, Yartsev then offered a military and economic assistance pact. The highly unorthodox manner in which this approach was made—without the knowledge of the Soviet foreign ministry, and initially via the Finnish Prime Minister's secretary—and the evident haste displayed by Yartsev is some indication of the importance attached to the conclusion of an agreement by Stalin, then in the midst of the purges. Not unreasonably, the Finnish government failed at the time to appreciate the importance of Yartsev's proposals, which were seen as yet another attempt by the Soviet Union to drag Finland into its security system. At the same time as the Yartsev negotiations were taking place, Finland and Sweden had begun serious discussions on the question of the defence of the Åland islands. On the issue the Soviet Union was to play a major role, since it was highly unlikely that the Finns could persuade the Swedes to agree to a joint defence programme in the face of Russian opposition. Finnish reluctance to admit that the Åland question was of major importance to her eastern neighbour was to result in failure to reach any lasting agreement, in the same way as the inability to appreciate Soviet security needs brought about the collapse of the talks with Yartsev in 1938.

The Finnish reply to the Soviet initiative, presented by the acting Foreign Minister Väinö Tanner in August, merely reiterated Finland's intention of preserving her territorial integrity against all potential aggressors and sought Soviet approval for Finnish plans to defend Åland. Yartsev replied by presenting a new offer; his government was now willing to accept Finnish assurances that they would repulse any German attacks and were prepared to accept military aid from the Soviet Union to this end. The U.S.S.R. was willing to accept the fortification of the Åland islands, provided that it could participate and send observers to oversee the work; in return for this concession, the Soviet Union should be allowed to build a fortified air and sea defence base on Suursaari, an island in the eastern waters of the Gulf of Finland. Finally, the Soviet government offered to guarantee Finnish territorial integrity, to provide military aid on favourable terms if the need should arise, and to accept a trade treaty which would offer extremely favourable terms to Finland.[6] These new proposals represented a significant shift in Soviet strategic thinking, with the emphasis now on the role to be played by the Baltic fleet. As Suomi has pointed out, the proposals would have created a double security system for the

Soviet Union, with armed assistance to the Finnish army as a fallback should German troops actually land in the country.

The Finnish government replied by standing firm on its determination to defend Finland's territorial integrity against any would-be aggressor. Yartsev then suggested that secret negotiations could be continued in Moscow at the same time as official negotiations for a trade agreement. For the Russians, political agreement was all-important: this the Finns were unwilling to accept, preferring to believe that better trade relations would lead to an improvement in diplomatic relations. In the light of this fundamental difference, the Moscow talks were doomed to failure.

During the year of negotiations which terminated in March 1939, the Soviet Union made it clear that it regarded Finland as a special case. Finland's Nordic connections and its strategic position placed it in a different category from the Baltic states; but this was not to be the case in the autumn of 1939. In 1938, before the Munich agreement, the Soviet Union offered a military assistance pact, and then military assistance if necessary, whereas in 1939, the main Soviet demand was for territorial concessions in the form of bases. In the face of these various demands, the Finnish government remained committed to its intentions, first mentioned to the Soviet leaders by Holsti during his Moscow visit. There was throughout an inability to understand the Soviet Union's scepticism about the Finns' ability or willingness to defend their territory. Unlike the Russians, the Finns could not believe that Germany entertained any serious thoughts of aggression via Finland. In consequence, the Yartsev talks proved fruitless. Whether they offered a real chance for Finland to resolve her security problems is an open question; but having failed to come to terms with the Soviet Union in 1938, Finland found herself in a much more perilous situation in the autumn of 1939. In 1938 Moscow was prepared to reach a mutually acceptable agreement with Finland at a time of great internal crisis and diplomatic isolation for the Soviet Union. In 1939, Finland was to become just another pawn in the game of great-power politics.

The Winter War (1939–1940)

In the early months of 1939 a number of significant political moves were made. The occupation of Bohemia and Moravia by German troops in March 1939, and the Lithuanian acceptance of the sudden and brutal German ultimatum for the transfer of the Memelland to the German Reich which followed only a few days later were sufficient indications that Hitler's appetite had only been temporarily appeased at Munich. The Anglo-French guarantee to Poland, and the replacement of Litvinov by Vyacheslav Molotov as Soviet Foreign Minister marked the end of the policies of Western appeasement and collective security and a return to traditional great-power politics. In the spring of 1939, tripartite negotiations between Britain, France and the Soviet Union were initiated. Although the British reluctantly accepted the Soviet demand for guarantees for the border states, they were highly suspicious of the introduction of the concept of indirect aggression in the Soviet draft proposals. As Lord Halifax said on 6 July, 'The use of the term "indirect aggression" would confirm the worst suspicions of the Baltic states, whose objection to the proposed Treaty rests largely on the fear of Russian interference in their internal affairs.'[7]

In consequence, no clear-cut agreement was 'made, and the military delegation sent in August was specifically instructed not to discuss the defence of the Baltic states, but to refer home for instructions. From the Soviet point of view, however, the defence of the Baltic was the first priority. The Soviet military delegation proposed that a strong Anglo-French squadron be sent to the Baltic, where Britain and France would seek permission for the temporary occupation of naval bases from the Åland islands to Liepaja. The Anglo-French delegation argued that Britain and France would make a more useful contribution by meeting and destroying the enemy outside the Baltic, and then sending a naval force through the Sound.

While the military talks were proceeding, the Soviet Union was seeking a swifter and more brutal way out of its security dilemma. On 23 August 1939 a non-aggression pact with Germany was signed in Moscow. The secret protocol placed Latvia, Estonia and Finland within the Soviet sphere of interest. Within a month, German troops had overrun Poland and the Soviet Union had taken the first steps to secure its frontiers by demanding a military pact with Estonia, which would allow Red Army units to man strategically important bases there. By 10 October, all three Baltic states had been compelled to sign similar treaties, which left them still independent but at the mercy of their eastern neighbour. Five days earlier, Molotov had invited the Finnish Foreign Minister to Moscow to discuss 'concrete political questions'. Finland's time of reckoning had come.

Although the Soviet Union had ceased in 1939 to regard Finland as a special case and had lumped it with the Baltic states in the security package sought unsuccessfully from the Western powers and swiftly conceded by Nazi Germany, it is nevertheless clear that Finland did retain a rather different status from Estonia or Latvia. For its part, the Finnish government made it clear that a pact of the kind imposed upon the Baltic states would be resisted. The army was mobilised by 10 October, and instead of the Foreign Minister Eljas Erkko, J. K. Paasikivi was seconded from his duties as minister in Stockholm to represent Finland in Moscow. He was cordially received, and the talks on 12–14 October were held in an informal and friendly atmosphere. The Soviet demands put forward by Molotov were for territorial concessions and base facilities within the framework either of a mutual assistance pact or a more limited agreement on joint defence of the Gulf of Finland. These demands were specified, and were referred back to Helsinki by Paasikivi. Similar though more modest territorial demands had been made in the winter of 1938–9, and Erkko had decisively rejected them. In the far more dangerous atmosphere of autumn 1939, he still refused to make any concessions. Paasikivi had been instructed that neither any frontier changes nor the establishment of military bases on Finnish territory would be tolerated. The minor concessions which the Finnish government was prepared to make were regarded by the Russians as insufficient, although they were willing to make counter-concessions to keep the talks open.

In spite of the pessimistic forecasts of the military experts, who pointed out the inadequate state of Finnish defences to resist a full-scale Soviet attack, the politicians persisted in their belief that right was on their side and that the Soviet Union would not engage in full-scale war to achieve its ends. The third round of talks in Moscow at the beginning of November proved as fruitless as the previous two rounds; the Finns would not shift on the issues of vital concern to Soviet security, the establishment of bases in the Gulf of Finland and the readjustment of the frontier on the Karelian isthmus. By 13 November, the talks had broken down. There then followed a fortnight of silence, during which the Finnish politicians grew increasingly confident that nothing was going to happen. Upton has suggested that Stalin had not included the breakdown of the negotiations in his calculations, and was at a loss what to do next until persuaded to resort to war by the hard-line faction led by Zhdanov, the party leader in the Leningrad region. Zhdanov had made pugnacious utterances in previous years, and he may also have been impressed by Finnish émigré Communist illusions of an oppressed Finnish working class ready to to rise up and welcome the liberating Red Army. At the end of November, the Soviet press started a campaign of vilification against the Cajander government, which was accused of being a mere puppet of the imperialists; the Finnish people were urged to get rid of their government if they wished to avoid disaster.

An incident on the frontier on 26 November provided the Soviet Union with the excuse to begin hostilities. Four days later, Red Army units began crossing the frontier. A puppet government under the leadership of the exiled Finnish Communist O. V. Kuusinen was set up in the border town of Terijoki, and a mutual assistance treaty was concluded with this government on 2 December, whereby the Soviet Union obtained all it had sought in the autumn negotiations, in return for the unification of Soviet Karelia with the future People's Republic of Finland. Although Cajander had been persuaded to resign in order that a new government might attempt to reopen negotiations, the formation of the Kuusinen government and the conclusion of the mutual assistance treaty seemed to indicate that for the Soviet Union at least, the way back to the negotiating table was closed.

Although the obduracy and unrealistic attitudes of the Finnish politicians played a part in bringing about the breakdown of talks in the autumn of 1939, the tragedy of the Winter War should more properly be seen in the light of the previous two decades of mutual distrust and failure to resolve a vital security problem. In the event, it is clear that in its determination to resist what were considered to be unjustifiable Soviet demands, even at the risk of war, the Cajander government echoed the feelings of the nation. The price of resistance was a heavy one. In the three and a half months of fighting, 25,000 men were killed and 45,000 were wounded. Although corresponding Soviet losses were probably much higher, such casualties were a heavy blow for a country of less than 4 million people.

That the Finns were able to put up a fight which aroused worldwide admiration and support owed much to the inadequacies and errors of their opponents. The forces deployed by the Red Army early in the war were poorly trained and ill-equipped for combat in bitterly cold conditions, and the Finnish forces were able to inflict severe defeats in battles fought in the Karelian isthmus and at Suomussalmi in northeast Finland in December and January. These victories concealed the harsh truth that in a prolonged campaign between two vastly uneven sides, the stronger was bound in the long run to wear down the weaker. Once the Red Army command had realised its mistakes, and had settled down to a strategy of driving back the Finnish troops in the Karelian isthmus with its superior and concentrated firepower, defeat for Finland was only a matter of time. The only hope was that envisaged in the defence review of 1926: that Finnish resistance would hold up the enemy long enough for outside help to be obtained.

This hope was considerably blunted by the fact that the one major power in a position to offer effective assistance had concluded a non-aggression pact with the Soviet Union, and had made it clear in early October that Finland could expect no support in negotiations with the Soviet Union. Individual high-ranking Germans urged the Finns to give way to Russian demands, and even tried to persuade the Scandinavian governments to put pressure on Finland to this end. It seems that the Germans had not bargained for the outbreak of hostilities, but official policy remained one of cold aloofness towards Finland and benevolent neutrality towards the Soviet Union. For its part the Soviet government did not seek German recognition of the Kuusinen government, which would seem to strengthen the view that the formation of this government was a cunning diplomatic move rather than a serious commitment to the idea of 'liberating' Finland. A Russo-Finnish war was not in German interests, even though the failure of the Red Army to break Finnish resistance was noted for future reference by the German high command. It threatened to upset the stability of the north, an area of vital importance to the German war industry, with its heavy dependence on Swedish iron ore, and it offered the Allies an opportunity to fish in troubled waters. This had indeed been quickly realised in London. Although the British had advised caution to the Finns, they were by no means averse to the prospect of a conflict which might direct valuable Russian supplies away from Germany to the Finnish front, and might cause friction between Moscow and Berlin and arouse American indignation. Unlike Poland, Finland did not involve Britain in war. The British could therefore afford to be generous in their sympathy to the gallant underdog fighting the Russian aggressor. They could also use the conflict as a means of exerting pressure on Germany's vital link with the Swedish ore-fields.

Sweden occupied a key position during the Winter War. Despite Finland's adherence to a 'Nordic' foreign policy in 1935, there remained a great deal of mistrust of Finnish intentions in leading political circles in Stockholm. Finnish attempts to secure a firm commitment on arms supplies in the event of war were unsuccessful; although agreement on the defence of the Åland islands was reached in January 1939, the Swedes reserved the right to determine whether or not to participate in the joint defence plan in the event of war, and insisted on obtaining Soviet consent for the plan. In October 1939, the Swedish government offered little more than diplomatic support for the Finns. Although there was some support in military circles, and even in the ruling Social Democratic Party, for a policy of military intervention should Finland be attacked by the Soviet Union, this was decisively defeated at a meeting of the Swedish cabinet on 22 October. The Finns were told five days later by Per Albin Hansson, the Swedish Prime Minister, that 'Sweden would not, by taking part in the defence of the Åland islands or in any other way, take the risk of becoming involved in conflict with the Soviet Union.'[8]

Hansson's policy of keeping Sweden out of the conflict won the day. On 2 December, his government decided to inform Finland that Sweden would not participate in the defence of the Åland islands. Richard Sandler, the Foreign Minister and principal advocate of aid to Finland, immediately resigned and was replaced in the new coalition government by Christian Günther, whose views on aid to Finland were similar to those of Hansson. The main aim of the Swedish government was to bring about an end to the conflict as soon as possible. Although it allowed the recruitment of volunteers to fight on the Finnish side and the sale of considerable quantities of arms and supplies to Finland, it also had to take note of external pressures. Towards the very end of the war, for instance, Günther warned the Finnish government that the supply of military equipment might well dry up should the situation become more serious. The possibility of Russian troops overrunning Finland was a worry to the Swedish government, but the fear of becoming involved in open conflict as a result of Allied plans for intervention exercised a much greater influence on its deliberations, since it soon became clear that the real purpose of such intervention was not to aid Finland but to secure the Swedish iron ore fields and thereby cut off supplies to Germany.

The idea of embarking upon some sort of action in northern Europe to deprive Germany of Swedish iron ore had been taken up as early as September by Winston Churchill, on becoming First Lord of the Admiralty, and by the middle of December the possibility of resolving the iron ore problem by means of a military expedition, ostensibly sent in response to the League of Nations' appeal for assistance to Finland, was being discussed in Allied circles. On 27 December, the Allies sent identical notes to Oslo and Stockholm, in which they spoke of sending indirect and unofficial aid to Finland, and alluded vaguely to the desirability of Scandinavian aid for Finland and the Allies' willingness to defend the integrity and independence of Norway and Sweden. No mention was made of troops. Nevertheless,

Holma, the Finnish minister in Paris, having been summoned to high-level discussions with French officials after the meeting of the Supreme Allied War Council on 19 December, telegraphed to his government in Helsinki that if Sweden and Norway were to take Finland's side in the war, the Allies would send troops. This interpretation was swiftly denied by the British Foreign Office, but it was transmitted to Oslo and Stockholm via the Finnish ministers in the two northern capitals before the Allied note of 27 December was even despatched. Sweden and Norway thus got wind of the Allies' intentions before the final commitment to armed intervention was made. The responsibility for this seems to have lain with Holma and Pakaslahti, head of the political section of the Finnish Foreign Ministry, both of whom were anxious for a more active Finnish policy to secure armed foreign intervention on Finland's behalf. The Finnish government made no move to obtain Allied armed assistance, although the possibility of Allied intervention was discussed from the beginning of the war as a line of action.

The Finns seem not to have become fully aware of the extent of the plans for intervention until February 1940. At a meeting of the Supreme Allied War Council on 5 February, the final details of the plan of intervention were settled. The plan depended in the first instance on the Finnish government issuing a formal request for aid to the Allies, who would then ask Norway and Sweden to permit the transit of an expeditionary force of 'volunteers'. Two brigades were to land at Narvik and secure the vital railway line to the Gällivare orefields, and then go on to Finland, where they would operate under Finnish command on the Lapland front. To meet the threat of a German attack, five brigades were to occupy positions around the ports of Trondheim, Namsos and possibly Bergen, and up to four divisions would occupy central Sweden. It was envisaged that the landings would take place on 20 March, and that some 100,000 men and 11,000 vehicles would have to be transported across the North Sea, starting on 12 March. These plans had been drawn up despite the fact that the Swedish and Norwegian governments had made it clear to the Allies that any violation of their neutrality would be resisted.

The main task of the Ryti government, which was formed on 1 December, was to bring an end to the conflict as soon as possible. This task was made difficult by Soviet unwillingness in the first weeks of the war to contemplate anything other than a military solution, and as the war dragged on, by the involvement of the Western Allies. The 'strong man' of the government and its virtual creator was the

Foreign Minister Väinö Tanner. In Paasikivi's view, Tanner always needed facts before he could act; for this reason, his appreciation of the situation during the October negotiations had lacked judgement. The outbreak of war provided him with a factual starting point on which he was willing to begin negotiations and, if necessary, make concessions. Tanner was dismayed by the expulsion of the Soviet Union from the League of Nations, which he feared would only serve to bring Berlin and Moscow closer together, and he was reluctant to entertain any plans which would have dragged the Scandinavian countries into the war.

The two most outspoken supporters of Allied intervention in the Finnish government were the Agrarians Niukkanen and Hannula, who tended to see the conflict in terms of the defence of democracy against dictatorship. Tanner was suspicious of the Allies' real intentions from the beginning, and preferred to pin his hopes on Swedish mediation. Ryti, who had been reluctant to form a government and had only agreed to do so on Tanner's insistence, tended to side with his Foreign Minister although he was willing to put pressure on Sweden by the threat of appealing for Allied aid. The commander-in-chief Marshal Mannerheim had seriously doubted his army's ability to withstand the Soviet attack in the early days of the war, but the successful repulse of the Red Army offensive in the second week of December encouraged him to declare that with substantial foreign aid peace was no longer the only alternative. The defeats suffered by the Red Army at the end of December, the hostile reaction of world opinion to the Soviet attack on Finland, and the probable awareness of Allied interest in northern Europe as a theatre of operations also seem to have disposed the Soviet Union to consider a peaceful solution to the conflict.

On 29 January, the Soviet government announced via Stockholm that it had no objection in principle to concluding an agreement with the Helsinki government. The Kuusinen government was quietly abandoned and the way was opened for further territorial bargaining. On 5 February, the first official contact was established in Stockholm between the Soviet minister, Aleksandra Kollontay, and the Finnish Foreign Minister Väinö Tanner. Two days later Tanner learned of the decision of the Supreme War Council, and in consultation with Prime Minister Ryti and Mannerheim's confidant, General Walden, decided not to reply to the Soviet demands for the time being. Instead, three options now seemed to be in the offing: a negotiated peace on favourable terms, and continuation of the war either with active Swedish material support or with the support of the Allies. On the question of making peace concessions the government was evenly divided, with Ryti, Tanner and Paasikivi in favour and Niukkanen, Hannula and Söderhjelm, their three colleagues in the governmental foreign affairs committee, opposed to any further concessions. In the end, Tanner was sent once more to Stockholm to seek a Swedish commitment to aid Finland—though he was also authorised to inform Mme Kollontay of the concessions which the Finnish government was now prepared to make.

The optimism of the Finnish leaders was soon to be dashed. The Soviet government announced that it would not be satisfied with less than the leasing of Hanko as a base and the cession of the Karelian isthmus, thereby making the Finnish concessions irrelevant. The Swedish government also declared that it was not prepared to extend the level of assistance to Finland, nor was it prepared to grant the right of transit to Allied troops. The breakthrough of the Red Army in the isthmus during the first two weeks of February only underlined the urgency of the situation. The Finnish government received alarming reports of the exhausted state of its troops, falling back on the isthmus before the overwhelming firepower of the Soviet artillery. On the other hand, it was given the impression that Allied aid would be forthcoming if only Finland were to ask for it. The harshness of the Soviet peace terms, which a substantial element in the government found totally unacceptable, compelled Tanner to prevaricate, even though he placed little faith in the Allies' offer of aid. On 28 February, the British minister in Helsinki admitted to Tanner that the number of Allied troops to be sent to Finland could only be half of what General Ling had led him to believe four days earlier, and they would not arrive until the second half of April.[9] The Finnish Foreign Minister had just been told yet again by Per Albin Hansson that his government would oppose any attempt by the Allies to intervene via Sweden, and could offer no further aid to Finland. He had also been given forty-eight hours by the Soviet government in which to decide whether or not to open peace negotiations. News of a massive Red Army breakthrough on the isthmus on 29 February tipped the scales. Late that night the Finnish government agreed to enter into discussions with Moscow.

News of this decision triggered a speedy and unilateral action in Paris. Daladier, the Prime Minister, promised to send 50,000 men and 100 bombers to Finland by the end of March. This was a 'thoroughly dishonest' promise, as Upton has observed, but it persuaded the Finnish government to back-track. On 1 March, it cancelled its reply to the Soviet government and asked for further clarification of terms. The Swedish government was to be told that Finland was seriously considering asking for Allied aid. The French offer of intervention was soon revealed to be a desperate leap in the dark. All that the British minister in Helsinki could offer Tanner on 3 March was 6,000 men at the beginning of April, provided the Finns make a formal request for aid by 5 March. He was unable to say what the Allies would do if Norway and Sweden should refuse transit for the expeditionary force. This was enough for Tanner. Finland had now reached the end of the line, and had no alternative but to swallow the bitter necessity of making peace. There followed two nervous days of waiting for news from Moscow, during which further conflicting offers reached Finland from Paris and London. On 5 March the Finnish government agreed to open peace negotiations, although it left open the possibility of appealing for Allied assistance before 12 March should the talks fail (the deadline had been extended by the Allies on hearing of the Finns' decision to sue for peace).

Negotiations began in Moscow on 8 March. The Soviet demands included territory not mentioned in the original proposals made at the end of February. These terms caused Mannerheim, hitherto convinced of the military necessity of making peace, to suggest making an appeal for Allied aid as a means of forcing the Russians to climb down. At the same time, however, he forwarded an alarming report on the exhausted state of the army, which concluded that at best the front would hold for only another week. This determined the fate of the negotiations, in which the Russians refused to consider any concessions. On 11 March, the Finnish government and foreign affairs committee of the *Eduskunta* authorised the delegation to conclude peace. As the British and French governments strove desperately to induce the Finns to issue the appeal which would allow them to take the initiative against Germany in northern Europe—and the Germans set up a timetable for an invasion of Norway—peace was signed on 13 March in Moscow. By the terms of the peace treaty, which was approved by the *Eduskunta* two days later, Finland ceded to the Soviet Union Suursaari and the islands to the east in the Gulf of Finland, the Finnish portion of the Rybachy peninsula on the Arctic, the Salla enclave in northern Finland and the whole of Karelia up to the frontier of 1721, which included the towns of Viipuri, Käkisalmi and Sortavala. The Hanko peninsula was to be leased for thirty years as a naval base. In addition there was a mutual non-aggression clause and provisions for the improvement of trade between the two countries. Finland's only consolation was the return of Petsamo, with its access to the Arctic.

During the edgy winter of the Phoney War, Finland's fight, likened by Harold Macmillan to a Thermopylae every day, aroused the admiration of the world. Whether or not it could have been avoided is another matter. As a result of the war, the Soviet Union obtained rather more than it had sought in the negotiations during the autumn of 1939. It is true that Finland retained her independence and probably won the healthy respect of the army and political leaders of the Soviet Union, but it is by no means proven that Moscow had any plans to deprive Finland of that independence in October–November 1939. What is certain is that the obduracy of Finnish political leaders such as Erkko made the chances of agreement in 1939 extremely unlikely. This wilful blindness to reality was not cured by the events of the Winter War, which served to strengthen the feeling of moral righteousness which was deeply embedded in the government and the *Eduskunta*. In the bitter aftermath of the war, there was a widespread feeling that Finland had been let down, particularly by Sweden. At the same time, the heroic deeds of the mid-winter battles at Summa and Suomussalmi were remembered. The belief that with a little more aid from outside for Finland's just cause, right might have won the day—or at least that the unjust claims of the Soviet Union might have been thwarted—was potentially very dangerous, as Upton has pointed out. Finland survived in 1940 because of her tough fight and the fact that she was not of primary strategic significance; the basic lesson of the Winter War was that will and morale cannot compensate for material weakness in the face of the big battalions. In the rapidly changing northern European war scene of 1940, this lesson was soon forgotten in Finland.

Settling accounts: 1940–1948

Less than a month after the conclusion of the Winter War, Hitler launched his attack on Denmark and Norway. The Allied troops sent to Norway to hinder the German advance were finally withdrawn in June. By this time, the German war machine was rolling to victory over the plains of Flanders and northern France. In the Baltic, the Soviet Union further strengthened its frontier by incorporating the three Baltic States as new Soviet republics in August 1940. Within a few short months, the war situation had fundamentally altered. Faced already with the difficulties of adjusting to peace, Finland still had to cope with the continuing war which threatened her own security.

The fifteen months of 'interim peace' between the Moscow peace treaty and the renewal of hostilities in the summer of 1941 has been the subject of much bitter controversy among historians. The crux of the debate has been the extent to which Finland had a choice of action in 1940–1. It is perhaps correct to say that the theory that Finland was caught like a floating log in the flood of war is no longer seriously defended by any historian. Jutikkala, a leading protagonist in the controversy sparked off by the publication of Upton's *Finland in crisis* in 1964, now maintains that Finland was more like a kayak, which could only shoot the rapids if it were steered vigorously and with skill. It is not clear whether Jutikkala believes that the craft of state *was* cleverly guided or not, but Upton's argument would suggest that it was not, and that the policy pursued by the inner circle which had begun to emerge as the effective war leadership in the Winter War was not entirely consonant with public opinion.[10]

It is certain that there was a great deal of bitterness in the aftermath of the Winter War. Although the government, and Mannerheim in his proclamation to the nation at the end of the war, sought to divert energies into the task of reconstruction, they did nothing to create an atmosphere that was more conducive to lasting friendly relations with the Soviet Union. Anti-Soviet feelings were further exacerbated by the attempts of the Soviet government to bring pressure to bear on Finland in the summer of 1940.[11] It is also certain that many Finns believed that the peace was merely an interlude, with the final reckoning still to come. For many, Germany was the ultimate salvation, notwithstanding the shock and disappointment of the Nazi-Soviet pact. An attempt to create some sort of Nordic defensive alliance in March had foundered on Soviet opposition. In a situation of extreme isolation, when it was widely feared in Finland and abroad that Finland was about to share the fate of the Baltic states, it was perhaps natural that the Finns should seek the support of Germany. On 4 July, the Finnish Foreign Minister told the German minister in Helsinki that pro-German feeling in Finland was snowballing and that public opinion was much influenced by the idea that with German aid, Finland could recover territory lost to the Soviet Union. Hitler's declaration on 19 July, in which he specifically disclaimed any German interest in Finland, seemed calculated to dash the Finns' hopes; yet within a fortnight, he had changed his mind and had given the order for plans to invade the Soviet Union in the spring of 1941. In these plans Finland was to play a clearly defined role.

The first step towards this new policy was taken in August, when a retired air force colonel and arms dealer with many contacts in Finland, Josef Veltjens, was chosen to undertake a secret mission to Finland. Here he met Mannerheim, Prime Minister Ryti, Foreign Minister Witting and Defence Minister Walden, and as a result of his mission, a secret transit agreement, allowing German troops to pass through Finland to northern Norway, was concluded. In return Germany would supply Finland with arms and equipment. This agreement was never submitted to the Finnish government or the *Eduskunta*. It is true that Finland also concluded a transit agreement with the Soviet government, allowing the passage of unarmed troops in sealed trains to the Hanko base; but the agreement with Germany allowed for the presence of armed German troops and camps on Finnish territory, and in effect drew Finland into the German orbit. As one of the Finnish officers involved in drawing up the agreement noted in his diary on 21 August: 'This has been a momentous week for Finland. Our course has been steered parallel to that of Germany.'[12]

Ryti later denied having authorised Mannerheim to make such an agreement, although in the autumn of 1940 he told the Permanent Under-Secretary of the British Ministry of Economic Warfare that he had concluded the agreement himself in secret and admitted that the Germans were building up their forces in northern Norway to block any Anglo-Russian countermove in the area. Mannerheim for his part gave the British to understand that the Germans had presented some kind of ultimatum to Finland. Although the British briefly cancelled the 'navicert' agreement on shipping to Petsamo, they tended to discount the transit agreement as an offensive military pact, and were content to lift the ban when British inspectors approved by Finland reported that Germany was not receiving imported commodities. Petsamo thus remained open, and was important for the importing not only of consumer goods and foodstuffs, but also of arms and equipment for the Finnish army. The nickel deposits in the Petsamo area also offered Finland a useful opportunity to resist Soviet pressure for a mining concession and to gain German support.[13]

The political turning-point in Russo-German relations occurred in November, when Hitler made it clear to Molotov during talks in Berlin that nothing less than complete acceptance of his terms by Moscow would satisfy him. In the words of State Secretary Weizsäcker, the Führer had placed Finland under his umbrella. On 18 December, General Order No. 21 aimed at the destruction of the Soviet Union under the code-name Barbarossa was issued in Berlin. Barbarossa's success necessitated not only the involvement of Finland in the German war plans, but also a degree of control of Finnish policy. Finland must do nothing to antagonise the Soviet Union before the time set for attack, nor could she be allowed to escape into neutrality. For this reason the Germans did not wish to see the formation of a political union between Finland and Sweden, an idea advanced by certain members of the Swedish government and taken up in Finland during the autumn of 1940; this plan had finally foundered on Soviet opposition, and was not taken up again by Ryti, who was elected President on 18 December 1940. Whether or not the union plan was a viable alternative is open to question—especially in the light of fierce Finnish resentment at the role played by Sweden during the Winter War—but its failure certainly left the Finns at the mercy of the two great powers in the Baltic area. Both Goering and Hitler gave the Finns to understand that they were lukewarm to the idea of a union, which would turn Finland into a Swedish province, the fate of which would be a matter of indifference to Germany.

In mid-December, General Talvela visited Berlin for political and military conversations. General Halder's diary entry *'Ich bitte um Auskunft über Zeitbedarf unauffälliger Angriffsbereitschaft nach Süd-Ost'* (I want to know how much time is needed for inconspicuous preparations for an attack to the south-east [i.e. the Karelian isthmus]) has been taken by some commentators to mean that he actually asked Talvela the question, although others such as Upton maintain that this was a later note jotted down by Halder, who was hardly likely to have risked revealing German plans so early in the day. Halder was later to deny that any exchange of information had taken place during the visit of the Finnish chief of staff, and the evidence would at least suggest that the Finns were deliberately kept in the dark about German military planning right up to the spring of 1941.[14] On the other hand, it must have been increasingly obvious to the Finnish high command that Germany was planning moves against the Soviet Union, in which Finland would play a role. Visits by high-ranking German officers such as the chief of staff of the army in Norway, who had been intimately involved in the drawing up of plans for Operation Silver Fox —which assumed the full-scale co-operation of the Finnish army in an offensive against the Soviet Union—were bound to cause speculation, and the Finns no doubt drew their own conclusions from the hypothetical questions which their visitors fired at them. The details of the Barbarossa plan were never revealed to the Finns; as Krosby remarks, 'the Germans simply assumed that Finland would be a participant when the time came.'[15]

On 20 May a German Foreign Ministry official, Karl Schnurre, revealed to Ryti that German-Soviet relations had lately deteriorated, and he suggested that a Finnish military delegation be sent to Germany to discuss co-ordination of military measures should the Soviet Union launch an attack. Schnurre also revealed that during his visit to Berlin in November 1940 Molotov had demanded a free hand to deal with Finland, and added that this had been refused by Hitler. This was not the whole truth, nor was the assertion that Hitler did not want war with the Soviet Union, but it was enough to persuade the inner circle that military talks should be initiated. High-level military discussions were held in Germany and Finland between 25 May and 5 June. German unwillingness to reveal the full details of the Barbarossa plan, and Finnish sensitivity about being committed to German plans for an aggressive war, has led some Finnish commentators to maintain that the Finnish reply to German recommendations was a negative one. This was certainly not the impression made upon the German military leaders, although they were aware of the Finns' desire not to be seen as aggressors. It is clear that at the beginning of June Finland was committed to the German plans, and that the approval of the military arrangements by the foreign affairs committee of the Finnish State Council on 14 June was something of a political formality. The date for the offensive was not officially revealed to the Finns until 19 June; three days later, the Germans launched their attack against the Soviet Union. The Finns were saved the embarrassment of openly appearing as aggressors by a series of Soviet air attacks on Finnish towns on 25 June, which provided the formal *casus belli* for the Finnish government, whose armed forces were due to complete mobilisation by 28 June.

The course of Finnish foreign policy during the interim peace has been a subject of fierce controversy. The Soviet Union appears to have adopted a far more conciliatory attitude in the spring of 1941, indicating for instance that it no longer held any objections to the creation of a close alliance between Finland and Sweden; but such gestures came too late. Roy Medvedev has accused Stalin of calmly watching the predictable triumph of revanchist tendencies in Finland, which led Finland into the German camp. It is certain that by the spring of 1941, the Finns were reasonably assured of the Führer's protection; but they were still in the dark regarding his real intentions, and the unease which many felt but could not express—since the true state of affairs was never revealed—was to give the lie to the myth of national unity forged during the Winter War, and provided the foundation for an opposition which was to grow in the course of the Continuation War.[16] It may well be that by May Finland had no real alternative but to go along with Germany; German troops not only surrounded her northern frontier but were inside the country by virtue of the transit agreement; and furthermore Finland had become economically dependent on Germany. The evidence suggests, however, that Finland was by no means an unwilling partner, that the inner circle of leaders banked on a German victory and were willing to follow the path dictated by Hitler, and that they did not seriously consider any alternative policy.

The Finnish army on the eve of the so-called 'Continuation War' was much larger, much better equipped and better prepared for war than it had been in November 1939. The period of compulsory military service had been doubled to two years in December 1940, and the number of military districts increased from nine to sixteen, each providing one infantry division. Thanks mainly to the Germans, the army had acquired much-needed new equipment, for which the hitherto reluctant politicians were now only too willing to pay. When fully mobilised, the Finnish army was 400,000 strong, and numerically superior to the opposing Red Army units, since the Karelian front had been stripped of troops needed to stem the main German advance.

The main thrust of the Finnish offensive launched in July 1941 was north of Lake Ladoga and in the Karelian isthmus, and by the end of August, the pre-1939 frontier had been regained. South of the Gulf of Finland, the German *Heeresgruppe Nord* had begun to draw the net around Leningrad. Hitler pressed the Finns to participate in the siege of Leningrad, even threatening to cancel delivery of 15,000 tons of grain if Mannerheim refused to commit his troops, but Mannerheim refused to be drawn, claiming that the war effort was already straining the fibres of the Finnish people and that his forces were neither strong enough nor sufficiently well equipped for a lengthy siege. In the end, Hitler did not press his demand, having in the meantime decided to concentrate his main military thrust against Moscow and to starve Leningrad into submission. Polvinen has argued that the German high command backed down over Leningrad because it did not wish to antagonise the Finns, whose troops were playing a useful role on a secondary but long northern front, and because a Finnish advance to the river Svir', where it had been agreed that they should 'shake hands' with German forces, was of more importance. This advance began on 4 September, as General Jodl was trying for the last time to persuade Mannerheim to advance against Leningrad. Within a matter of days the Svir' had been reached. On 1 October 1941 the capital of the Karelian-Finnish S.S.R., Petrozavodsk, was occupied. By the end of the year the Finnish army was in occupation of an area bounded by the Svir' and Lake Onega and with a front running north some 80–160 kilometres inside Soviet territory. The Karelian front thus established remained virtually unchanged until the major Soviet offensive of June 1944.

The nature and extent of Finnish-German collaboration has provoked much controversy, which shows no signs of dying down. It is clear that the Barbarossa plan envisaged a subordinate military role for Finland, and the Germans certainly assumed that Finland would play that role when the time came. It is also clear that the Finnish political and military leaders were not unwilling to enter into a 'war of compensation' against the Soviet Union as co-belligerents of Nazi Germany. What is not certain is the extent to which the Finns were prepared to strain their limited resources in order to accomplish the overall German objective of defeating the Soviet Union. There can be little doubt that such an objective was highly desirable to the Finnish leadership, or that it was hoped that Finland would acquire a sizeable share of the northern territory of a defeated Soviet Union. On 11 September 1941 President Ryti defined the ideal territorial limits for Finland in a conversation with the German minister. Finland should have short and easily defended frontiers on the Svir' and the Neva—since it was the Germans' intention to raze Leningrad to the ground—and should possess the whole of East Karelia and the Kola peninsula, with Germany occupying the adjoining territory between lake Onega and the Dvina river. These views were never publicly formulated as Finnish war aims, but they can be taken as representative of the thinking of the Finnish leadership.[17]

One of the reasons why Finnish war aims were never clearly defined was that Finland continued to maintain that she was fighting a defensive war against Soviet aggression, as a co-belligerent but not as an ally of Germany. Thus, when American suspicions were roused by Mannerheim's order of the day issued on 11 July but prepared a week earlier, in which he reiterated his pledge of 1918 not to replace his sword in its scabbard until East Karelia was freed, Foreign Minister Witting informed the American minister that this was done without the knowledge of the government as an inspiration to the army and dissociated the government from any idea of conquering East Karelia, although he did not rule out smaller territorial accretions. The occupation of East Karelia compelled the Finns to adopt a different line, in which the necessity of a more secure frontier featured prominently. This was the tenor of Mannerheim's reply to Churchill's personal appeal to cease hostilities at the end of November. It was also the argument used to stem the growing disquiet within the Social Democratic and Swedish People's parties. Unfortunately, the attempts by the Finnish war leadership to explain the purpose of the war in purely military and strategical terms merely confused the issue still further. Ryti's speech to the nation on 25 June 1941 left unanswered the question of how far a defensive war against the threat in the east would be pursued, but at the time it probably summed up the willingness of the majority of the Finnish people to fight a limited war to regain the old frontiers.

The crossing of these frontiers in the autumn of 1941 was a turning-point. To many it seemed as if the government was embarking on a policy of territorial expansion: others saw this as clear proof that Finland was in some way inextricably bound up in the German military plans and would not be able to disengage herself easily from the world war. The nationalists of the Academic Karelia Society, which exercised a preponderant influence among the officer corps, the clergy and the university-educated élite, saw the advance into East Karelia as a golden opportunity to fulfil Finland's historic mission as the national home of all the Finno-Ugrian peoples. Propaganda among the troops and on the home front was imbued with these nationalistic ideals, which took little account of the grim realities of the war situation. Finland had strained her resources to the utmost in the autumn of 1941. Her German partner had been unable to deliver the decisive blow in Russia. The port of Murmansk remained in the hands of the Red Army, and the German units operating in Lapland had encountered serious difficulties during their slow advance towards the Murmansk line. This vital railway link was never taken. Mannerheim's proposed joint attack against the junction at Belomorsk failed to get off the ground. The German and Finnish rendezvous on the Svir' was doomed never to take place. In July, diplomatic relations between Britain and Finland were broken off as the result of German pressure on the Finnish government. Britain came under increasing pressure from Stalin to declare war on Finland, and finally did so on 6 December. The U.S.A. maintained diplomatic relations, although pressure was brought to bear in the autumn, when Cordell Hull, the U.S. Secretary of State, warned the Finns on three occasions that his government was on the brink of breaking off relations. The Americans had failed to apply such pressure in August as Stalin had requested, in an attempt to draw the Finns out of the war with promises of concessions on the Soviet side. No further offer of peace with concessions was to be made by Stalin.

By the end of 1941 the Finnish war leaders were beginning to realise that the speedy German victory on which they had calculated would not materialise. Although Finnish troops occupied East Karelia, this had only been achieved by pushing the nation's material and manpower resources to the limit. The lack of labour to run essential industries and till the fields compelled the release from the front of 180,000 reservists by June 1942. A further extension of thefront was virtually impossible, as Mannerheim well knew. Finland's fate rested in the hands of the great powers who were engaged in a mighty global struggle. Ryti's outburst to the American minister in September 1942 that 'Finland was determined ... to follow its present policy at any cost ... and neither we [the Americans] nor anyone could alter it because Finland knew Russians and we did not as our existence was not at stake and existence of Finnish people [was]' illustrates how convinced Ryti and other Finns were that they were fighting for their very existence as a nation. Equally it reveals an inability to understand that as the global conflict grew, Finland was in no position to determine her own fate.[19]

In his talks with Anthony Eden, the British Foreign Secretary, in Moscow in December 1941, Stalin demanded territorial concessions by Finland but promised to respect Finnish independence. Paasikivi was also mentioned as a suitable new head of government with whom the Russians could negotiate. In 1942, the Soviet government began to apply pressure on Sweden to act as a channel for talks with Finland. In the autumn of that year Yartsev resurfaced, offering terms via a Swedish journalist this time. The Soviet Union declared its willingness to take the 1939 frontiers as a basis for discussion. The terms offered by Yartsev did not correspond with those outlined by Stalin to Eden, and the method of approach chosen was probably intended to avoid the embarrassment of a leak as had occurred with the Soviet peace initiative in 1941. The initial Finnish response was not unfavourable, but Ryti managed to persuade his colleagues that Germany should be involved in an attempt to negotiate a general peace. The Germans were unwilling to take up this line, and persuaded the Finns to let the matter drop.

The surrender of the remnants of the German Sixth Army at Stalingrad on 1 February 1943 had a powerful impact in Finland. At a meeting called by Mannerheim on 3 February, the inner circle of ministers unanimously agreed that Finland should try to get out of the war, in which Germany appeared to be heading for defeat. The re-election of Ryti as President in mid-February for a further two years— after an attempt to promote the candidature of Mannerheim as a more acceptable peacemaker had come to grief—was accompanied by the formation of a new government under the National Coalition chairman, Edwin Linkomies, in which the notoriously pro-German Witting was replaced as Foreign Minister by the anglophil Henrik Ramsay. These changes prompted the United States to offer its good offices as a mediator between Helsinki and Moscow. The minimum armistice terms proposed by Molotov were however considered by the Americans to be unacceptable as a basis for negotiations in Helsinki, and they refused to transmit them to the Finnish government.[19] In the meantime, the Germans had got wind of the American offer. On 26 March, the German Foreign Minister Ribbentrop demanded the immediate cessation of talks with the Americans and the signing of an agreement by the Finnish government not to make a separate peace. After much agitated discussion, the Finnish government informed the United States on 10 April that since negotiations with the Soviet Union without any assurances of permanent guarantees for Finland's future were unacceptable, Finland had no alternative but to fight on. This was interpreted in Washington as a result of German pressure, and the United States government decided to break off diplomatic relations. At the last minute, the rupture in Soviet-Polish relations over the Katyn affair caused the State Department to cancel its instructions, and the tenuous diplomatic link between Washington and Helsinki remained.

The deterioration in relations between the Western Allies and the Soviet Union during the summer of 1943 effectively nullified any hopes of renewed American mediation. Discussions in Lisbon between George Kennan and the Finnish chargé d'affaires about the possibility of an Anglo-American landing in Lapland were dismissed by the Americans as politically unwise and logistically impracticable, although Ramsay privately informed Cordell Hull that Finland would not consider such an operation as directed against her and would begin negotiations with Germany to bring about the withdrawal of German units from Lapland. The Finnish government clearly hoped that American or Swedish forces would replace the Germans, an idea which neither Washington nor Stockholm was prepared to entertain.

By the late autumn of 1943, the war situation in Europe had swung decisively in favour of the Allies. Anglo-American forces were advancing towards Rome, while the Red Army was driving relentlessly through the Ukraine after the decisive battle of Kursk. Diplomatic relations between the Western Allies and Moscow were symbolically restored at the meeting of foreign ministers in October, when the formula of unconditional surrender by Germany and her allies was worked out. Finnish anxieties about this formula, which Soviet and British press releases implied would apply to Finland, were relieved on 20 November when the Soviet minister in Stockholm, Mme Kollontay, informed the secretary-general of the Swedish Foreign Ministry, Erik Boheman, that her government had no intention of violating Finnish independence or sovereignty unless compelled to do so by the future policy of the Finnish government. She also announced that Finnish negotiators would be welcome in Moscow to discuss peace terms. Boheman transmitted this offer to Helsinki, and the Finnish government replied by offering the 1939 frontier as the basis for negotiations. This was unacceptable to Moscow, as soon became evident. At the Teheran conference, Stalin repudiated any Soviet designs on Finland, but laid down the following peace terms: the restoration of the 1940 frontiers as stipulated in the treaty of Moscow; a naval base to be leased at Hanko, or the annexation of Petsamo; 50 per cent compensation for damage caused by military activities; the breaking off of relations with Germany and the expulsion of German troops from Finnish territory; and the demobilisation of the Finnish army. In her reply to the Finnish note on 20 December, Mme Kollontay informed Boheman that her government stood by the 1940 frontiers as the basic precondition for negotiations.

The Swedish government, which had finally freed itself of the embarrassing transit agreement with Germany in August 1943, now began to exert pressure on the Finns to enter into negotiations. The Red Army offensive towards the river Narva in 1944 left the Finnish front in the isthmus dangerously exposed. In February there were major bombing raids on Helsinki and other towns in southern Finland. Mannerheim for his part urged the government not to delay any longer. In the end, it was decided to send Paasikivi to Stockholm to sound out the Soviet position. In secret meetings with Mme Kollontay at a hotel in Saltsjöbaden, he ascertained that before any negotiations began, Finland would have to break off relations with Germany and intern German troops, and would have to withdraw behind the 1940 frontier. Paasikivi recommended acceptance of these terms, but they were vigorously opposed by the Agrarians and the right wing in the government and *Eduskunta*. The Finnish government was persuaded by Swedish pressure in March to drop its rejection of the Soviet conditions and to offer to negotiate without any definite commitment to the terms put to Paasikivi. This was deemed unsatisfactory by the Soviet government, which demanded a more positive answer within a week—otherwise it would regard the Finns as having rejected their terms. The Finnish *Eduskunta* and government refused to negotiate on the terms laid down; however, on 19 March Moscow let it be known that it had no objection to receiving a Finnish delegation in order that the Soviet terms might be further explained. Paasikivi and Carl Enckell were sent by the Finnish government, and soon discovered that the terms envisaged in Moscow were a good deal tougher than those relayed to Helsinki via Stockholm. In particular, the sum of $600 million was mentioned as the amount to be paid by Finland as compensation for war damage. The terms brought back were rejected as too high a price to pay for peace, although the Finnish government let it be known that it was still anxious to conclude peace with the Soviet Union.

As Carlgren has pointed out, the basic requirements for success in Swedish efforts to bring about peace were not as propitious in 1944 as they had been in 1940. The Finnish army was still standing its ground in Karelia; there were some 150,000 German troops in the country, and Germany was able to exercise considerable pressure to keep Finland in the war. The British position seems to have been that third-party mediation would not bring about peace, and that Finland and the Soviet Union should be left to settle their own differences. Churchill voiced Britain's opposition to the Soviet demand for reparations, which he felt Finland would be unable to pay—and which would also mean that Finnish pulp and timber supplies vitally needed in Britain after the war would be seriously diminished—but it was clear in 1944 that Britain was in no position to impose demands upon the Soviet Union with regard to Finland. In a memorandum of 9 August 1944, Eden assumed that Finland would enter the Soviet sphere of influence, and that Britain had neither the ability nor any powerful reason to oppose such influence, although it was hoped that Finland would retain her independence and parliamentary system.

The United States had kept open diplomatic channels to Helsinki and had sought to mediate, but without success. This link was much valued by the 'peace opposition' in Finland, and the threat to break off relations did have a certain influence on the Finnish government.

Nevertheless, German counter-pressure was in the end of much greater importance. It was sufficient in the spring of 1943 to persuade the Finnish government to break off discussions with the Americans— although it must be said that the American initiative had already foundered on the unacceptable terms offered by Molotov—and to give anxious assurances that the *Waffenbruderschaft* would continue. Ribbentrop's demands for a political treaty binding Finland to Germany for the duration of the war were eventually satisfied by a speech given by Linkomies on 10 May 1943, in which he declared that Finland would fight to the bitter end rather than throw herself at the mercy of her eastern neighbour. But relations between Finland and Germany were not improved by demonstrations of sympathy with occupied Norway and Denmark in the Finnish press, or by the frequent public assertions of Finland's right to end hostilities when a suitable moment arose.[20] The news of Paasikivi's secret conversations in Stockholm provoked an angry reaction from Ribbentrop, who informed Ramsay that any attempt to make a separate peace would be viewed by Germany as 'clear treason'. According to Tanner, this destroyed all hopes that Germany would 'understand' such an action, a view apparently transmitted to Mannerheim by General Jodl of the German armed forces command (O.K.W.).[21] In April 1944, apparently angered by a protest by Finnish academics against the evacuation of the art collections of the University of Tartu in Estonia, Hitler banned all arms exports to Finland with the exception of deliveries absolutely essential to maintain the frontline defences. This ban was not lifted until 12 June 1944, three days after the Red Army launched a major offensive on the Karelian isthmus, after one of the most intensive artillery bombardments of the whole war. By the end of June the Finnish army had been driven back beyond Viipuri, but with the aid of German dive-bombers, shore batteries and anti-tank weapons, the front held. On 15 June, the order was given to withdraw troops from East Karelia to form a reserve defence beyond the Vuoksi river.

Faced with military disaster, the Finnish government was caught between the stark alternatives of surrender, presented by the Soviet government on 23 June, or of binding Finland to Germany in a political treaty which would ensure further supplies of matériel and troops. This latter alternative was pressed on the Finns by Ribbentrop, who flew to Helsinki for this purpose on 22 June. Previous attempts to persuade Mannerheim to take over the presidency had failed. Tanner tried to persuade his colleagues to negotiate a surrender with Moscow, and appears to have won over President

Ryti. Linkomies in his memoirs claims that his opposition to a negotiated surrender saved the day for Finland. In the event, no message was
sent to the Soviet Union. On 25 June, Hitler cabled to Ribbentrop
that unless Finland issued a public statement on its political relationship
with Germany aid would cease forthwith. Mannerheim pressed the
government to make an agreement in order to obtain vital supplies
and aid. After much hair-splitting over the legal niceties of an agreement, with Socialist and Swedish Party opposition making it unlikely
that the *Eduskunta* would accept it, Ryti, in his personal capacity as
President, finally signed an agreement not to make a separate peace.
Ribbentrop for his part consented to drop the idea of a formal agreement in favour of a personal letter of assurance to Hitler.

The Ribbentrop-Ryti agreement led to a breach of diplomatic
relations between Finland and the United States and prompted the
Swedish press to speculate about more binding arrangements and
political coups, but the truth of the matter is that it gave Finland a
breathing space and much-needed German military assistance. For
Ryti it was an act of political suicide, but it was equally an admission
of Germany's inability to force Finland into a truly binding treaty.
Ribbentrop had considered the idea of a coup by pro-German elements in Finland, but was informed by Blücher, the German minister
in Helsinki, that both a leader and the thousand reliable men envisaged
as the agents of such a coup by Ribbentrop were lacking. Germany
was in no position to seize power in Finland as she had done in
Hungary. In the end, Ribbentrop had to be satisfied with the personal
assurance of the Finnish President. As Polvinen remarks: 'Accustomed
to an authoritarian way of thinking, Ribbentrop clearly did not at
the time fully appreciate the back-doors of the Finnish democratic
system.'[22]

It was through one such back-door that Ryti resigned to make way
for Mannerheim, who assumed the presidency on 4 August. The front
had stabilised in early July. Stalin had decided on 12 July to suspend
offensive operations on the isthmus, and to press on to Berlin. On
25 July, Mme Kollontay informed the Finns through Boheman that
they could count on a peace agreement which would preserve their
independence and political system. Pressure had been brought to bear
on Mannerheim by Finnish politicians and the Swedish Prime Minister
to assume the leadership of his country and lead Finland out of the
war. On 17 August, the new President informed Field-Marshal
Keitel that he did not regard himself or his new government as bound
by the agreement made by Ryti. Mannerheim was not in any hurry

to open discussions with Moscow, however, to the evident annoyance of the Swedes, who declared themselves willing to offer economic aid to Finland after the war and refuge to the inhabitants of Lapland in the event of conflict between Finnish and German troops. Contact with the Soviet Union was established through Swedish mediation on 25 August: the Soviet government demanded the breaking of relations with Germany as a prerequisite for peace negotiations. German troops were to be evacuated within two weeks of Finland's acceptance of this precondition, or by 15 September at the latest. By 108 votes to 45, the *Eduskunta* voted to accept the Soviet Union's preliminary terms on 2 September, and Mannerheim sealed the breach with Germany in a letter addressed to Hitler that same day. The evacuation of German units from southern Finland proceeded peacefully, but a German attempt to seize the island of Suursaari on 15 September led to fighting, while German troops had to be driven out of Lapland in some of the bitterest fighting of the war.

The terms of the armistice agreement, which were accepted by the *Eduskunta* on 19 September, were described by Mannerheim as militarily disastrous, and were seen by the Swedish government as reducing Finland in practice to the status of a Soviet vassal state. In addition to the restoration of the 1940 frontier, the surrender of the Petsamo area, the disarming of German troops and demobilisation within two and a half months, Finland agreed to pay reparations of 300 million dollars' worth of raw materials and machinery within six years and to lease a naval base at Porkkala, a short distance to the west of Helsinki. However, Hanko was returned. There were also a number of sinister aspects to the treaty. Airfields in southern Finland were to be placed at the disposal of Soviet planes engaged in operations against German units and ships in the northern Baltic. All 'pro-Hitler' and fascist organisations were to be immediately dissolved, as well as organisations peddling anti-United Nations and in particular anti-Soviet propaganda. Finland also agreed to co-operate with the Allied powers in arresting and trying persons guilty of war crimes. To supervise the implementation of the armistice, an Allied Control Commission was to be set up.

The armistice terms were harsh, but Finland was escaping the fate of occupation which befell every other eastern European country between Minsk and Berlin. Her political institutions remained intact, and she was fortunate in having leaders of the calibre of Mannerheim and Paasikivi, aged conservatives who enjoyed the respect of Moscow and who were able to set about the unpleasant task of reconstruction in an atmosphere of political bankruptcy. Paasikivi, who took over the premiership on 17 November 1944, told the nation on Independence Day the same year that Finland had to face up to reality and strive for peaceful and good neighbourly relations with the Soviet Union. This message he was to repeat constantly over the years of uncertainty between the armistice and the final conclusion of peace.

By the summer of 1944, the race to Berlin had assumed far more importance for the Soviet leadership than the elimination by military means of a diminishing security threat on their north-western border. The Finns had been pushed back almost to the 1940 borders, although they had fought hard and were by no means defeated. In early July, the order was given to halt the Red Army's advance on the isthmus and to transfer troops to the Narva front. The announcement made in Stockholm on 14 July that the Soviet Union was still prepared to negotiate a peace with Finland indicated that any plans for a military occupation had been rejected. It is in fact hard to find evidence of Soviet plans for an occupation of Finland. According to Djilas, Zhdanov in 1948 thought that the Soviet Union had made a mistake in not occupying Finland, but he did not say if such a move had ever been contemplated. Molotov's contemptuous rejoinder, 'Finland— that is a peanut', perhaps indicates the extent of the threat which the Soviet leaders saw in Finland in the post-1945 era. As P. Winterton observed in July 1945, 'The Russians have learnt that the Finns are an indigestible people, but they also know that they do not have to swallow Finland in order to get what they require.'[23]

The situation in 1944–7 was in some ways reminiscent of 1809–12 when Alexander I, in the midst of a major European war, settled Russian security problems on the north-western borders. The 1809 settlement had resolved the problem by uniting Finland to the Russian Empire, and had sought to win over Finnish loyalties by the creation of an autonomous political status for the Grand Duchy. Recognition of Russia's great power interests had been a key feature of nineteenth-century Finnish nationalism, as expounded by Snellman and Yrjö-Koskinen, and the septuagenarian Paasikivi was the conscious latter-day embodiment of that tradition. During the last years of imperial Russian rule, he had been an adherent of the policy of appeasement and 'bridge-building' advocated by Yrjö-Koskinen and Danielson-Kalmari. During the war years he had argued the necessity of coming to terms with the Soviet Union, to the extent that he was regarded in many circles as dangerously 'soft' towards Moscow. Paasikivi himself had a low opinion of his fellow-countrymen's grasp of political realities, as his numerous private and public utterances clearly show. His own position in the post-war years was clear: the establishment of good relations with the Soviet Union was the vital prerequisite for Finland's continued political independence, and to achieve this end, internal as well as external changes had to be made.

The parallel between 1809 and 1944 is a valid one, which Paasikivi himself recognised, but there were also significant differences. The Soviet Union was not imperial Russia, nor had Finland till recently been a possession of the Swedish crown. If for the Soviet Union the Finnish problem was essentially military-strategic, as it had been in 1809, the dimensions were vastly different in the age of the super-powers. There was also an ideological aspect which had hardly existed 150 years before—although Finnish patriots had voiced alarm at the prospect of different cultural and political values being forced upon them. Finland had passed from Sweden to Russia in 1809 after a political settlement had been arrived at between the Estates and the Emperor. In 1944 independent Finland had concluded an armistice, but not a settlement. The whole question of what limits might be placed upon Finland as an independent, sovereign republic was therefore still unresolved as the Soviet Union sought to strengthen its position in Europe.

The Soviet-dominated Allied Control Commission, the task of which was to supervise the implementation of the terms of the armistice, arrived in October 1944, and did not leave until the autumn of 1947. The presence of a large complement of Soviet officers and officials in a hotel in the centre of Helsinki caused great unease in an already tense atmosphere. Incidents such as the shooting of a Russian officer in a suburb of Helsinki in November 1944 typified the edgy atmosphere of the time. There were a number of clashes between the Finnish government and the Commission (headed by Andrey Zhdanov) over the interpretation of the terms of the armistice. The Finns were compelled to return to an army strength of 37,000 men, and to disband the paramilitary *Suojeluskunta*. They were forced to give in to the Soviet demand for reparations to be paid at 1938 prices, after Zhdanov had threatened to take over all the industrial concerns of eastern Finland unless agreement were reached. The most difficult aspect of the terms of the armistice was the implementation of the war-guilt clause, which afforded the Soviet Union a clear opportunity to interfere in internal Finnish politics. Nevertheless, the fact that the Finns were able to conduct their own war-guilt trials—albeit under pressure—is an indication of the difference between Finland and other occupied eastern European states. This difference was clearly recognised at the time by foreign observers. The American representative in Helsinki pointed out in 1945 that Finland was not under occupation, and still retained control of the media and communications, which was not the case in other countries under an Allied Control Commission. When it was revealed in the summer of 1945 that an order had been issued by the army command in November 1944 for secret arms dumps to be set up around the country, a high-ranking 'Anglo-Saxon' diplomat apparently expressed his surprise to Paasikivi at the remarkably mild manner in which the Soviet Union continued to treat Finland.[24]

Many Finns—though not all—were also cautiously optimistic about future relations with their eastern neighbour. The veteran social democrat Väinö Voionmaa, for example, wrote to his son in August 1945 that the Paasikivi government was in firm control, and expressed the hope that the final peace settlement would be as good as could be expected. The easing of tensions may have encouraged the Finnish government to seek amendments to the armistice agreement. In discussions in Moscow during the summer of 1946, Stalin gave the Finns to understand that the reparations burden might be eased, but that no territorial concessions would be made. In spite of this, Foreign Minister Enckell made obvious allusions to the desirability of the return of Finnish Karelia in his speech to the Paris conference on 15 August 1946. Molotov's reaction was sharp. He accused the Finns of trying to enlist Western support, and rejected out of hand any changes in the terms of the armistice. The final peace treaty was in fact modelled along the lines previously determined by the Allies for the settlement of relations with former satellite states of Nazi Germany. The Finnish delegation played no part in this.

According to Jakobson, the treaty was 'off the peg', and seriously dashed Finnish hopes of the West's ability or interest in supporting democratic Finland against her totalitarian neighbour. In addition to the territorial clauses and the stipulations concerning the payment of reparations, Finland was obliged to limit her defence forces to 41,900 men, with a maximum floating tonnage of 10,000 tons and an air force of no more than sixty aircraft. In addition, there were restrictions on the types of weapons and equipment to be used by the armed forces. Article 6 decreed that Finland should take all necessary measures to guarantee full civil and human rights to Finnish citizens; all organisations hostile to the Soviet Union or other members of the United Nations had been banned by the armistice agreement, and Finland was obliged in future to prohibit any such organisations which sought to deny the democratic rights of the people (Article 8). Article 9, which decreed that persons guilty of war crimes be arrested and tried, seemed to offer scope for Finnish citizens to be handed over for trial in foreign courts, contrary to the Finnish constitution. The Paris treaty, which finally came into force on 16 September 1947, also decreed that Finland should not participate in any alliance directed against the Soviet Union. This stipulation was to be greatly strengthened by the conclusion of the treaty of friendship, co-operation and mutual assistance between the Soviet Union and Finland in April 1948.

The treaties of 1947 and 1948 were concluded at a time when political tension in the world was growing. For the Soviet Union, both treaties were clearly intended to eliminate the possibility of Finland becoming a threat to Soviet security in the future. The 1948 treaty also provided a useful means of controlling Finnish foreign policy. The implications of the 1947–8 settlement for Soviet-Finnish relations will be examined later, but in the uncertain world of the Cold War this settlement was widely interpreted as placing Finland firmly under the control of the Soviet Union, without much hope of ever being able to exercise a truly independent foreign policy. The presence of Red Army units at the Porkkala base seemed to deny any claim to neutrality, as Paasikivi later admitted. The huge reparations bill was still to be paid off. The adherence of Norway and Denmark to NATO in 1949, and Swedish hesitations, seemed to dash Finnish hopes of some sort of Nordic defence bloc which might stand between the two great power blocs. The post-war settlement was furthermore imposed upon Finland. The Finnish people had to accept it, as they had had to accept the Peace of Moscow in March 1940, but in a spirit of negative submission rather than as a positive basis on which to develop relations with their eastern neighbour. Paasikivi was fond of saying that in the history of Finland, the pen has had to repair that which the sword had torn asunder. Time has, perhaps proved him right; but in 1948, with the thunderclouds of war massed over central Europe and the Far East, the sword still seemed to be hanging over Finland.

7

RECASTING THE MOULD

1940–1960

'Ziffel:

[. . .] Die Leut in diesem Land werden also nicht nur von den Gutsbesitzern und
Fabrikanten beherrscht, sondern auch von sich selber, was Demokratie genannt
wird. Das erste Gebot der Selbstbeherrschung heisst: das Maul halten. In der
Demokratie kommt dazu die Redefreiheit, und der Ausgleich wird dadurch
geschaffen, dass es verboten ist, sie zu missbrauchen, indem man redet. Haben
Sie das verstanden?
Kalle:
Nein.'

Bertolt Brecht, *Flüchtlingsgespräche*
(Suhrkramp edition, Frankfurt-am-Main 1961, p. 127)

Counting the cost of war

The cost of war for Finland was heavy indeed. Some 86,000 men had
been killed, and another 57,000 permanently injured or crippled.
There were nearly half a million refugees from the ceded or leased
territories, in addition to over 100,000 inhabitants of Lapland whose
homes and property were destroyed by the retreating German forces
in the winter of 1944–5. By the peace terms Finland lost important
factories and refineries, the port of Viipuri, the Saimaa canal, 17 per
cent of the national railways, 22 per cent of the timber needed by the
wood-processing industries, 286,000 hectares of cultivated land, over
3 million hectares of forest—in total, some 13 per cent of the national
wealth. There was also the burden of reparations—300 million dollars'
worth of specified goods and commodities to be handed over to the
Soviet Union within five years at 1938 prices. Reparations amounted
to some 10 per cent of the gross national income in 1945, according to

148

Hyvämäki—a proportion four times greater that of the German gross national income devoted to reparations under the Young plan of 1925–30.

For a small nation with limited resources, the strain of maintaining up to half a million troops in the field for more than four years had been immense. There was a chronic labour shortage, despite the introduction of compulsory labour service in October 1939 and its extension in 1942 to cover all industries and trades essential to the national economy and welfare, and despite the release of older reservists from active duty at the front in the spring and summer of 1942. Agriculture in particular suffered from a lack of manpower. Bad weather and the lack of fertiliser meant that the volume of grain harvested during the war years was well below pre-war levels. Animal husbandry also suffered from the lack of fodder and the non-availability of foreign concentrates: many beef cattle were also lost during the evacuation of Karelia in 1939–40. Milk yields were only around 65 per cent of pre-war levels. Export industries were particularly hard-hit during the war although, as in the First World War, the metal industry prospered: by 1944, it was employing nearly 30 per cent of the national industrial labour force, and its output increased substantially above pre-war levels. The reforms of 1940 in the structure for managing the war economy and for production of armaments and munitions, in addition to the supplies of arms and equipment from Germany and the greater willingness of the *Eduskunta* to vote supplies (the defence budget for 1941 was 45 per cent of total expenditure), meant that Finland was far better prepared for war than she had been in 1939. Nevertheless, the Continuation War began at a bad time. Food stocks were low, due to bad harvests and the loss of 11 per cent of the total cultivated land area and 33 per cent of the nation's livestock, and they could not be replenished by imports.

Finland's dependence on Germany for vital foodstuffs was indeed an important factor in the course of the war. Increased consumption, and the lack of imports to replenish rapidly diminishing stocks, caused severe shortages of vital raw materials such as rubber. Fuel was in especially short supply. Foreign trade slumped dramatically, and was confined almost entirely to Germany and occupied Europe. Deprived of vital imports, the Finns had to resort to substitutes: wood-burning devices were attached to motor vehicles, and wood was used with some ingenuity in the manufacture of clothes and shoes. Roasted rye grain, dandelion roots and chicory were poor substitutes for coffee, the lack of which was undoubtedly the most remembered hardship. Sugar and coffee were the only items rationed during the Winter War, but in 1940–1 rationing spread to other foods. At the height of the period of rationing—which did not end till 1953— a non-manual worker would obtain 2 decilitres of milk a day, 150 grammes of butter a month, 433 grammes of meat a month and four packets of cigarettes a month. Such rationing allowed him a minimum daily intake of 1,000–1,500 calories, well below the level of 2,000 calories generally considered to be the minimum necessary to keep body and soul together (manual workers were allowed up to 2,800 calories per day). As a result, 'private enterprise' (the rearing of pigs, rabbits, etc.) flourished, as did the black market—which, as the writer Olavi Paavolainen noted in January 1942, was 'the only way to get decent food'.[1]

The privations, frustrations and harassments of the war years imposed strains upon the sense of national unity which had been forged by the experience of the Winter War. Then, Finns from all walks of life had shared the vicissitudes of war and the bitterness of defeat, as Mannerheim generously and wisely acknowledged in his Order of the Day of 14 March 1940. But the Continuation War of 1941–4 was not a struggle for national survival until the final months. The confused and tense atmosphere in which Finland re-entered the war in 1941 was vividly portrayed in an Opinion Survey report of 24 June:

A section of the public think that we do not know what to do and are drifting along with the tide more or less accidentally, others on the basis of differing foreign news broadcasts which have become distorted by word of mouth believe that we are fully at war, others assume that everything has been settled beforehand and that Finland is following a predetermined timetable, while others believe that we will remain resolutely neutral in defence of our democratic position throughout the entire conflict.[2]

However, once the country was at war there appears to have been a general acceptance of the need to fight to regain the pre-1939 frontiers, and there was also a good deal of confidence in a German victory in the east. When a speedy victory did not materialise, doubts began to grow. These were not dispelled by the often vague and contradictory utterances of the war leadership concerning Finland's objectives in the war, and they were increased by a growing war-weariness— although, as the Opinion Survey reports indicate, grumbles about shortages and inadequate rations began to give way to serious doubts about the whole future of Finland after the decisive German defeat at Stalingrad.

The façade of national unity had begun to crack at the end of the Winter War. The signing of the peace treaty was bitterly opposed by a number of politicians, especially Karelians, and two Agrarian ministers resigned from the government in protest. Memoirs written after the war by leading political figures clearly reveal deep personal rivalries which often date from the aftermath of defeat in 1940. During the interim peace, the Finnish-Soviet Friendship Society, a pro-Soviet organisation set up by dissident Left-wing socialists and Communists which in its heyday had over 35,000 fully paid-up members, caused some alarm for the government. Not until the end of 1940 did the government feel sufficiently assured of German protection against possible Soviet reaction to be able to ban the activities of this association. A second group of Social Democrats, who had for some time been critical of the party leadership and its attitude towards the war, was suppressed in the early months of the Continuation War when six of its leaders were given prison sentences on highly contentious treason charges.

In spite of these cracks in the surface of political unity, national morale survived the bitterness of defeat remarkably well. The way in which the resettlement of some 420,000 Karelian refugees was accomplished with the minimum of friction testifies to the willingness of the Finns to unite in an effort to conquer the problems of reconstruction, as Mannerheim urged them to do in his Order of the Day of 14 March 1940. Unfortunately Mannerheim also dwelt heavily on the sense of outrage felt by his countrymen at the harsh peace terms. Paasikivi, in maintaining that the war had been a costly mistake caused by an inability to appreciate the harsh realities of life with a mighty neighbour, was exceptional. It was widely assumed that the war had not been fought in vain and that the evidence of the past offered ample proof that injustices did not endure. The strong outburst of moral outrage which greeted the signing of the peace treaty was an essential aspect of national unity and morale, but it also blinded the eyes of many to the meagre limits within which Finland could conduct a lengthy war against an overwhelmingly superior enemy force. This blindness and the reluctance of the Finnish political leadership to accept the peace as permanent helped lead Finland into the paths of collusion with Germany.

Gratitude for German support and a boundless confidence in a German victory were marked features of Finnish press coverage of the early months of the war in the east. The socialist press, which had stressed the need to observe neutrality to the end, was more reserved and it was here that the first open signs of disagreement with the conduct of the war appeared. Otherwise, support for Germany was so strong that the censorship had on occasion to curb the enthusiasm of the press. As late as the autumn of 1942 a public opinion poll showed a clear majority in favour of a final German victory, even among supporters of the Social Democratic Party; a year later, however, the balance had swung decisively in favour of the Allies. There was a strong traditional pro-German sympathy among the educated class, and in the early stages of the war a number of public figures expressed their sympathy for Hitler's concept of the 'new Europe'. On the other hand, hardline Nazi sympathisers were few, and politicians and press alike tended to keep their distance from the fascist I.K.L. On the whole the Finnish press and politicians were at pains to show the difference between Finland's political traditions and war aims and those of Nazi Germany, though many hailed Germany as a partner in the 'crusade' against communism. The war against 'godless bolshevism' was taken up with enthusiasm by the Lutheran clergy. The persecution of the Jews and the harassment of the clergy in occupied Norway and Denmark were largely ignored by the Finnish church, which was excessively preoccupied with the destiny of the Finnish people and the conversion of the 'heathen' Karelians to the ways of the Lord. The evils of Nazism were simply not comprehended by the strongly pietistic Finnish clergy.

Although official pronouncements on war aims were cautious in regard to the idea of 'Great Finland', right-wing nationalists showed no such inhibitions. The conquest of East Karelia, the land between the river Svir' and the White Sea coast, was seen as the fulfilment of Finland's 'historic mission' to unite the Finnic peoples. The geographer V. Auer and the historian E. Jutikkala also suggested in *Finnlands Lebensraum* (1941) that the annexation of this territory was an economic necessity for Finland. Although the Swedish People's Party and the Social Democratic Party were less enthusiastic about the extension eastward of Finland's frontiers, some right-wing Swedish Finns and socialists championed the idea of annexation. Enthusiasm for Great Finland began to wane from 1942 onwards, as it became increasingly evident that the course of the war was swinging towards the Allied side. The press had virtually abandoned the theme by September 1943, when the censorship imposed a ban on discussion of annexation. The largest national daily, the moderate *Helsingin Sanomat*, which had earlier been a keen supporter of the future victory of Germany, joined the ranks of those newspapers which voiced such criticism of the government and the war as the censor would allow. The 'opposition' press sought to stress Finland's right to make a separate peace, and voiced cautious hopes of an Anglo-American victory in the west which might save Finland from Soviet domination. Heavily censored though it was, the Finnish press had abandoned its initial pro-German sentiments clearly enough by 1944 to provoke complaints from the Germans that they felt they were dealing with an enemy country.

The first signs of opposition to the war came from the troops. There is evidence to suggest that many Finns viewed the prospect of renewed warfare with little enthusiasm. Having observed the 'cynical indifference' of working-class troop units on parade in June 1941, Paavolainen noted in his diary how unexpected and inexplicable the approaching war was to the Finnish people at large and how they would tend to regard it as '*herrojen*' *sota*, a war imposed on them by the ruling class. More than 300 soldiers are known to have refused to cross the old frontier during the advance in the autumn of 1941. Although physical and psychological weariness was thought to be the main reason for their refusal, a large number of those investigated did feel that their duty did not extend beyond the defence of the 1939 frontiers and many also felt that they had been deceived by false promises of a speedy end to the war. Undoubtedly such feelings played a part in prompting others to desert or go absent without leave between 1941 and 1944.[3] As Salminen's study shows, there was a great deal of suspicion in the ranks that the war was being prolonged merely to serve Germany's expansionist interests or to satisfy the extreme demands of Great Finland chauvinists.

The crucial test of army discipline and morale came in June 1944, when the massive Red Army onslaught on the isthmus created something like a state of utter panic. Over 19,000 men of the Fourth Army Corps were deemed to be lost or to have deserted; 800 men of the Sixth Division were charged with desertion, and four were executed for cowardice in the face of the enemy. This collapse shook the previously-held assumptions of the army command that the Finnish soldier was immune to enemy propaganda and the defeatism of the home front, and would fight to the last. However, once the German armies were in retreat and it became clear that the integrity of the fatherland was now truly at stake, morale in the ranks stiffened. The cheerful assertion by the working-class soldier at the end of Linna's novel *The Unknown Soldier* that the Soviet Union had won the war but brave little Finland had come a good second perhaps typifies the sense of relief felt by men of his class and background. The real defeat suffered in 1944 was not that of the Finnish people, who preserved their national independence at a price, but that of Great Finnish nationalism which had provided a cherished ideal for most of the educated ruling class for the previous two decades. Not only was the dream of a Greater Finland shattered, but also an image of national unity which had falsely assumed that the nation as a whole supported this ideal.

On the home front, national unity became ever more fragile as the war dragged on, and the ultimate defeat of Germany became only a matter of time. A victorious wartime leadership can be forgiven many things, but in defeat there is no forgiveness. The political changes, the war guilt trial, the bitter recriminations which followed Finland's departure from the war and the irrevocably altered circumstances in which Finland now finds herself all tend to colour judgements of the wartime leadership. Nevertheless, a few general observations should be made.

First, it is clear that those who entertained doubts about the wisdom of Finland's political course during the Continuation War were under severe pressure to conform or keep silent, not merely from the government. The *Eduskunta*, which returned from the isolated town of Kauhajoki (to which it had been evacuated in December 1939) to Helsinki in February 1940, appears to have been kept singularly ill-informed by the government of major developments, but few members raised their voices in complaint. On the whole, they accepted without demur the statements and policies of successive governments and ministers, and frequently rounded on those with the temerity to voice criticism. Very few of them were interested in or had any understanding of foreign affairs, although the claim that the Speaker and his deputies were themselves satisfied with the information given to them by the government 'particularly as it occurred over dinner, when coffee, a wartime luxury, was served' seems unnecessarily cynical.[4] Those who were to form the opposition to the war complained that the government had failed to keep the *Eduskunta* informed of its policies and actions, and had presented it with a *fait accompli* on 25 June 1941. The government and its defenders countered by emphasising the necessity for secrecy in wartime; vital information, it was claimed, could easily be leaked abroad if discussed too freely. This was stated rather bluntly by Väinö Tanner in a speech in September 1943, when he quoted approvingly a former Norwegian prime minister's advice to his countrymen during a delicate stage in negotiations with Sweden over the dissolution of the Union to keep their mouths shut. Unfortunately, such statements simply served to alienate the opposition, especially in Tanner's own party where his somewhat overbearing manner was greatly resented.

Secondly, there does appear to have been an unwillingness in political circles to face up to unpalatable truth. This is especially evident from 1943 onwards. A sombre military analysis of the likelihood of German defeat, which concluded that a new peace treaty with Moscow was in the circumstances the best policy, was received 'coldly, even hostilely' by the *Eduskunta* in February 1943, so much so that Colonel Paasonen had to present an altogether more optimistic review two days later.[5] Even the 'peace opposition', which began to organise itself after the decisive German defeat at Stalingrad, was motivated more by a sense of unease that Finland was drifting into the arms of Nazi Germany, and a desire to align with the Western democracies, than by a recognition of the necessity of coming to terms once and for all with the Soviet Union—the line which Paasikivi represented and which Urho Kekkonen was to take up in 1943.[6]

Thirdly, the calibre and quality of the men who occupied high office during the war may be questioned. Paasikivi, whose own comments on the members of the government were critical to say the least, was widely feared as a defeatist and 'soft' towards the Soviet Union and he was not given office in spite of his proven abilities and experience. Urho Kekkonen, whose talents had been revealed in the Cajander government and who was not initially regarded as a defeatist—he had voted against the signing of the Peace of Moscow in 1940—was similarly passed over, probably as a sop to the I.K.L. which he had attempted to ban in 1938. A number of ministers and officials with pronounced pro-German sympathies were removed or sent to less influential places in the reshuffle of the administration following Ryti's re-election as President in 1943. It was a matter of evident pride to Linkomies that his government contained a higher number of members with high academic qualifications than that of his predecessor, but to judge from his own remarks and those of others, some of these people were not very well suited to high office. Few served in government right through the war years: even the indispensable Väinö Tanner was compelled to resign from the Ryti government in August 1940 in an effort to ease relations with Moscow. The vital Ministry of Public Welfare, set up in September 1939, had six different ministers between 1939 and 1944. No other new ministries were created, and the structure of government remained virtually the same as in peacetime.

The real direction of the war effort rested with the army high command and the 'inner circle', the government's foreign affairs committee, in which a major role was played by three men; Mannerheim (with his confidant General Walden, the Minister of Defence), Ryti and Tanner. None of the three was above manipulating others to suit his own purposes. Walden was commonly regarded as the stalking horse for the commander-in-chief, and the prime mover of his candidature for the presidency in 1943. Mannerheim was supported by those who felt Ryti to be too compromised to be able to conclude peace, by those who had a strong personal dislike for Ryti, and pre-war opponents of his economic policies as director of the Bank of Finland. For his part, Mannerheim let it be known that he would stand only if he was certain beforehand of being elected. The unwillingness of the socialists to support him, and the premature leaking to the press of the Agrarian's commitment to him caused the commander-in-chief to withdraw, and Ryti was re-elected with 269 out of the possible 300 votes. Tanner played a major role in these manoeuvres, as in the formation of the 1939 Ryti government; even when his political star had fallen, he still exercised considerable influence. He attended discussions on the formation of a new government in September 1944, and later recorded: 'The discussion was dragging on and didn't seem to be getting anywhere, since everyone who spoke merely raised objections to others' candidates. Fed up with this, I wrote out a government list, which I first showed to Mannerheim in an adjoining room.' Mannerheim approved the list, and Tanner was thus able to claim the 'parentage' of the short-lived Castrén government.[7]

In the war-guilt trial of 1945-6, charges were brought against eight men.[8] Kivimäki, the former Finnish minister in Berlin, was accused mainly of abetting the conclusion of the transit agreement of 1940, but the other seven were charged for their part in directing—or misdirecting—the policy of their country while they had been members of the government's foreign affairs committee. The gravamen of the charges was that the accused had led their country into war in 1941, had neglected opportunities to make peace, had bound Finland to the side of Germany, and had misled the *Eduskunta*. In his defence speech—which was heavily censored—Ryti claimed that Finland had been drawn into the war by external circumstances, and that he and his colleagues had merely been doing their duty in working for the defence of their country. Since the trial was essentially of a political nature, these arguments were rather academic. The evidence which has emerged since the war would suggest that Finland was not an unwilling partner of Germany in 1941 and clearly hoped to gain from a German victory in the east; that information was withheld, and opportunities to make peace were bungled, as much by clumsiness as anything else. This is not to say that Ryti and his co-defendants were a clique of conspirators intent on drawing their country to destruction. Their failings were human, and they suffered the consequences. The Finnish war leadership, caught up in a major global conflict in which they believed they were in some way free agents, were simply unable to extricate themselves or their country. Rather than accept the unpalatable truth, they preferred to take refuge in public pronouncements based on moral rectitude. In rejecting the terms offered by Moscow in March 1944, for example, Linkomies declared to the *Eduskunta*: 'Rather than consent to such terms, the Finnish people will continue the unequal struggle, placing its confidence in that which has given us strength in these years: the rightness of our cause and our unsullied record.'[9] Many speakers echoed his words from the floor. In his memoirs Linkomies claimed that by choosing to fight on rather than accept the Soviet terms, Finland managed to emerge from the war with her independence intact, having fought an honourable fight. This assumption is questionable. Morale posturing in dire straits is a feeble cover for non-existent policies. But if the government can be criticised for a lack of realism, the opposition was not much better. The peace address signed by thirty-three public figures in August 1943 exhorting Ryti to initiate new measures to bring Finland out of the war—which was 'leaked' to the Swedish press by one of the signatories—may have made the general public aware of the existence of an opposition in Finland, but it was also a sign to the enemy of internal division. The peace opposition was demonstrative rather than a serious practical alternative. In the spring of 1944, after the collapse of the peace negotiations, it appears that plans were made for a refugee government in the event of an occupation of Finland. Paasikivi, who was approached as a possible head of such a government, rebuffed the idea on the grounds that it might provoke a violent German reaction and possibly a civil war in Finland. Mme Kollontay also let it be known that Stalin felt the peace opposition would be better employed in working to place Mannerheim at the head of a 'peace' government.

Moral rectitude, a sense of national pride and identity and a devotion to duty on the one hand, and an insistence on the necessity of preserving basic democratic freedoms on the other both played a part in saving Finland from the maelstrom of events in 1944. But in the end, both sets of values were rooted in the political traditions of a past age.

Paasikivi represented a third tradition, stretching back to the Finnish 'national' line of Snellman and Yrjö-Koskinen, one which saw the necessity of living at peace with a mighty neighbour. In the first two decades of independence, this tradition had been submerged. Now, with the collapse of the dreams of a Great Finland and with the very structure of Finnish democracy under threat, it was to reassert itself under the guidance of a man who first held government office in 1908.

In certain circles in Finland there seems to be a prevalent belief that we are back in the normal routine and that there is no longer any need to take any notice of anything except what we became accustomed to in the 'twenties and 'thirties when we were squabbling among ourselves. A grasp of political realism has not been one of the stronger points of the Finnish people, as our unfortunate policy of recent years has demonstrated. We believe what we wish to be the state of affairs and we act as if that for which we hope were true.[10]

This homily, delivered to the nation on Independence Day 1945, contains the essence of Paasikivi's political 'line', with its emphasis on recognition of political reality. It is perhaps the most fitting epitaph to an era which came to an abrupt end in 1944.

Change and restoration

The first fundamental change of political direction in Finland occurred some two months after the signing of the armistice with the appointment of the Paasikivi government. The Castrén government, which had been masterminded by Tanner, showed itself singularly ill-prepared to negotiate over the reparations question with the Allied Control Commission, and broke up with the resignation of its two peace opposition socialist members. Paasikivi was in fact imposed upon a reluctant President Mannerheim by the Allied Control Commission, and his cabinet included several known advocates of a radical break with the past, such as Urho Kekkonen and Mauno Pekkala, as well as a Communist, Yrjö Leino. On the other hand, eight had served in Castrén's government, five had served in wartime governments, and key posts such as foreign affairs and defence were held by professionals, both enjoying Mannerheim's confidence.

The principal task of the new government was to ensure the carrying out of the armistice terms. The Castrén government had already released more than 1,000 political prisoners and banned a number of organisations regarded as fascistic or anti-Soviet. The basic agreement over reparations was reached on 17 December, after Zhdanov, the head of the Allied Control Commission, had threatened to take over industrial concerns in eastern Finland if terms were not reached. Despite a number of minor problems, the stipulations laid down in the armistice were met, to the extent that the Allied Control Commission could express its satisfaction in the summer of 1945 and propose the normalisation of diplomatic relations. However, as Paasikivi pointed out on the eve of the general election in March 1945, Finland would have to pursue a new course of foreign policy in order to create lasting good-neighbourly relations with the Soviet Union. This in turn meant the rejection of past attitudes and prejudices, and the withdrawal from public life of compromised figures. To meet this requirement, Paasikivi was not averse to using whatever pressure and threats seemed necessary. In order to ensure the establishment of good foreign relations, Paasikivi was willing to override or ignore domestic considerations. He never ceased to emphasise that the Finnish people could no longer afford to think that they were able to do what they liked provided that the formal obligations of the armistice agreement were observed. In this he was diametrically opposed by many who refused to change, those whom Voionmaa characterised in December 1944 as thinking that since the Soviet Union had promised not to interfere in Finnish internal affairs, 'it had no right to stick its nose in, and should keep its hands off us', allowing the Finns to act and speak as they thought fit in their own affairs.[11]

The leading advocate of change in the Agrarian party was Urho Kekkonen. In a radio speech on 25 September 1944 he had warned his listeners that unless attitudes and prejudices changed, there could be no future for the Finnish nation, fated as it was to exist side by side with a mighty neighbour. Two days earlier, he had demanded a radical change of government and of party policy at the Agrarian central committee meeting. Within the party he was in a minority. In December, his views were decisively rejected and he failed to obtain a seat on the central committee. Although the party chairman Viljam Kalliokoski was compelled to stand down in June 1945, Kekkonen's candidate for the post failed to secure sufficient votes, and Kekkonen's resolution condemning wartime policies and the wartime party leadership was defeated. The party was reluctant to drop certain named leaders from its electoral lists in March 1945, and these men were only persuaded to withdraw when Paasikivi threatened to resign from office if they did not. For the Agrarian party, of which many of the leaders came from Karelia and which had been strong in the surrendered eastern territories, the loss of Karelia was an emotive issue which often clouded political judgement, as in August 1945 when a hapless delegation of Karelian politicians was given a lecture by Paasikivi on the folly of seeking the return of Karelia at the forth-coming peace conference.

The Social Democratic Party had become bitterly divided during the war, and was now faced with a new rival, the legalised Communist Party, which was making overtures towards left-wing and opposition socialists. At its first legal conference on Finnish soil in October 1944, the Communist Party committed itself to the creation of a broad popular front movement, and in negotiations with the left-wing socialists who had been expelled from the Social Democratic Party during the war—the peace opposition still in the party refused to attend—agreed to set up the Finnish People's Democratic League as the umbrella organisation for all popular democratic elements. Des-pite the wishes of the left-wing socialists, the new party's programme was democratic rather than socialist, in accordance with the desire of the Communists to create a broad 'anti-fascist bloc'. At the Social Democratic Party's nineteenth congress at the end of November 1944, the peace opposition lost control of the party executive. This dashed the Communists' hopes of capturing the Social Democratic Party, since the right-wing 'comrades-in-arms socialists' tended to agree with Väinö Tanner's view of Communism as poison to the Finnish people and unreliable as a defender of Finnish independence.[12] Dissi-dent socialists and local party branches thus broke away and joined the Democratic League, especially after the Social Democratic Party executive had narrowly rejected the offer of an electoral alliance in January 1945. This offer was supported by the Deputy Prime Minister Mauno Pekkala, who joined the Democratic League after its rejection.

The Finnish People's Democratic League went to the polls with a programme calling for a foreign policy consonant with the principles of the United Nations, democratisation of Finnish institutions and the elimination of fascistic organisations, full employment and the return of wage levels to 1938 standards. The Communist Party was thus committed to a popular front strategy, rather than its own revolutionary programme, and it was well pleased with the results. On a poll of almost 75 per cent, the People's Democrats secured forty-nine seats, and with the subsequent defection of two Social Democrats, it became the largest single party in the *Eduskunta*. The Social Democratic Party's mandate shrank from eighty-five seats obtained in 1939 to forty-nine (forty-seven). The third major party, the Agrarians, secured forty-nine seats, a loss of seven. Nearly half the returned members were 'new faces', mostly People's Democrats, though half the National Coalition mandate of twenty-eight, a third of the Agrarians and a quarter of the socialists were new to the *Eduskunta*.

The spectacular electoral success of the People's Democrats encouraged the Communist leadership to initiate discussions with the two other major parties on a joint programme. The so-called 'Big Three Agreement' was concluded in April 1945. The original proposals discussed by the Communists and Social Democrats were weakened in the final round of discussions between the Agrarians and Communists —for example, plans for nationalisation of the big banks, insurance companies and major industrial concerns were dropped. It appears that the Social Democrats were less anxious for Agrarian participation than were the Communists, who were prepared to accept a programme which was neither socialist nor communist in content as the price for a broad-based agreement. As Upton has pointed out, the renunciation of socialism for the immediate future left open the question as to whether the Communist Party could carry out its programme of democratisation in a government and a parliament which it did not control without resort to extra-parliamentary methods. An interesting analysis of the situation by the Agrarian veteran Juho Niukkanen assumed that the Communists lacked the basic organisation necessary to take over state power: hence they would seek to establish an hegemony by the creation of a broad front of workers, small farmers and intellectuals. Niukkanen feared that they would strive to increase their support in rural areas, and would precipitate new elections once they were confident enough of obtaining an absolute majority with the Social Democratic Party—which would then be swallowed up, allowing the Communists a free and constitutional hand to push through socialist policies in the *Eduskunta*. In Niukkanen's view, the Agrarians went into government with the other two partners of the 'Big Three agreement' in order to keep an eye on developments and gain time to strike back.

There can be little doubt that this was so, or that the Communists allowed themselves to become hostages to fortune by eschewing their revolutionary programme and seeking to work for socialism with a popular front tactic. Upton has pointed out the deficiencies in the Communist Party leadership, and has suggested that there was no Communist seizure of power in Finland because this was never the intention of the party leadership. Unlike other eastern European countries, Finland retained her political institutions intact, and there was no break in continuity in the political arena. What happened after 1944 was essentially a repair job on the body politic, not whole-sale reconstruction, and it would seem that as long as the Finns carried out these repairs satisfactorily, the Soviet Union was content. Social disruption would be bound to affect the delivery of the goods specified in the reparations agreement, a point well taken by the Russians. When Zhdanov expressed his concern, as a 'natural conservative', about rumours of the imminent break-up of the Big Three coalition government in 1947, he was probably expressing the desire of his master to preserve the political *status quo* in Finland. He knew well enough that such a hint would be taken seriously by the Finns.

Although the degree of direct Soviet pressure on Finland was surprisingly slight, the presence of the Allied Control Commission was a constant reminder that Finland was a defeated country under severe constraints. This in itself created further tension in a country labouring under grave social and economic difficulties. There were a number of incidents, such as the stoning of the Allied Control Commission headquarters, and the more serious episode of the secret arms dumps apparently set up at the end of the war on instructions issued by senior army officers, which resulted in the interrogation of over 5,000 persons and the arrest and trial of a number of army officers. On the whole, however, Paasikivi managed to steer a careful course and re-mained master of the situation. In this respect he was undoubtedly strengthened by the evident goodwill of Stalin, the incompetence of those who wished to interfere with this course and his ability to con-trol and manipulate the levers of power in a state with powerful constitutional safeguards. The acid test of his ability to steer Finland through dangerous waters was the question of the war-guilt trial.

Article 13 of the armistice obliged Finland to arrest and try those alleged to have committed war crimes. It soon became clear that the Soviet Union expected the Finns to try not only those charged with criminal acts contrary to international law, but also those politicians deemed to have led their country into war. In January 1945, a group of left-wing socialists in the *Eduskunta* sought to have the government investigate the possibility of charging those responsible for involving Finland in war on the side of Germany. Legal experts in Finland were of the opinion that the constitution did not permit the bringing of such charges, a view shared by the majority of the *Eduskunta*. The question was raised again in June–July, when the Communist Hertta Kuusinen openly named Ryti, Tanner, Rangell, Linkomies and Kivimäki as the principal figures responsible for Finland's involvement in the war. The publication on 8 August 1945 of the London agreement concerning the prosecution of war criminals, and the pressure exerted by the Allied Control Commission to bring Finland's war leaders to trial resulted in the passing of an enabling act by the *Eduskunta* in September. Paasikivi had earlier sought to satisfy the Russians by compelling politicians such as Tanner to withdraw from public life and by seeking to carry out Article 13 within the framework of existing Finnish laws. When it became clear that this was no longer possible, he argued the necessity of accepting extraordinary circumstances, but he also pointed to the wisdom of retaining control of the conduct of the trials. The eight men who were arraigned in November 1945 were tried by a Finnish and not an international tribunal, although the tribunal's decision was influenced by external pressure. On the final day of the trial, Paasikivi secured an adjournment after he had been given to understand by the Allied Control Commission that the sentences proposed were inadequate. Two days later, in a radio broadcast, the Speaker of the *Eduskunta* gave a warning that if the sentences did not satisfy the Commission, Finland would be deemed not to have fulfilled the thirteenth article. The final sentences imposed ranged from ten years for Ryti to two years for Kukkonen and Reinikka. None of the condemned men served his full sentence, and no-one was executed, as happened in other countries where similar trials were staged. Mannerheim was never brought to trial, although he feared that he would be. For much of the winter of 1945–6 he remained in Portugal for health reasons, a growing embarrassment to the government. He was finally persuaded to resign after receiving assurances from Zhdanov's second-in-command that he would not be brought to trial, and on 9 March 1946 the *Eduskunta* exercised the powers it had decreed the previous day by electing Paasikivi as his successor.

The fulfilment of Article 13 was an act of political necessity which the government and the Finnish people had to accept. That they did so, with the minimum of fuss—although with obvious reluctance—is a tribute to the efforts of Urho Kekkonen—who, as Minister of Justice, was largely responsible for steering the enabling legislation through the *Eduskunta*—and to the authority of the aged Paasikivi. When Paasikivi reminded an audience of journalists in February 1946 of Bismarck's dictum that the nation would have to pay for the panes of glass smashed by the press, he was not only reminding them of their responsibilities, but of Finland's still precarious situation. For much the same reason Kekkonen suppressed the publication of much of Ryti's defence speech at his trial. Public discussion of such delicate issues could endanger Finland's position; or, as Paasikivi put it on another occasion to the representatives of the fourth estate: 'I don't like phrases. In recent years we have uttered so many phrases, and we can now see what the result has been.'[13]

The most vociferous demands for the prosecution of those accused of crimes against peace came from the Communists, who at one stage threatened a general strike in support of their demand. By December 1945, the hitherto clandestine party had acquired a membership of 20,000, and through the Finnish People's Democratic League controlled over a quarter of the seats in the *Eduskunta*, occupied six posts in the government, and in the local government elections of that month obtained 274,000 votes (as against 265,000 for their Social Democratic electoral partners) and the control of 225 local councils. Through the efforts of the Communist Minister of the Interior, Yrhö Leino, the security police (*Valpo*) was also firmly in Communist hands, and was responsible for the interrogations of those involved in the arms concealment case. However, in spite of a number of resignations and dismissals, the regular police, army and judiciary remained virtually unchanged, and where the left wing did manage to acquire a toehold— as with the appointment of the left-wing writer Hella Wuolijoki as director-general of *Suomen Yleisradio*—it was not destined to remain there for long. In the spring of 1946 the Communist Party launched a mass movement, calling for thoroughgoing social reform and the democratisation of the army and civil service, which culminated in mass demonstrations in Helsinki in June. This movement failed to realise any significant changes, and probably strengthened the right wing of the Social Democratic Party, which won the day in the extraordinary party conference and compelled the withdrawal of the moderates from the party executive. The socialists were also able to order the postponement of the elections to the central trade union organisation (S.A.K.), alleging electoral irregularities, and when the elections were held in 1947 the socialists, having staged a strong and effective electoral campaign on an anti-Communist platform, were in the majority.

By the end of 1946, it was clear that the Communists were losing ground in the country and were becoming isolated in government. There was also friction within the party, which came to a head in 1948. The Social Democratic Party, elated with its victory in the trade union (S.A.K.) elections and the local elections of December 1947, and increasingly disenchanted with the Big Three agreement, sought to capitalise on the uncertainty caused by Stalin's suggestion of a mutual assistance pact in February 1948. Rumours of an impending Communist coup were not helped by the misreporting of a speech given by Hertta Kuusinen, in which she was taken to infer that the Czechoslovak example was the one to follow in Finland. Paasikivi was sufficiently alarmed to take security precautions, but no attemped coup ever materialised, and it is almost certain that the rumours were without foundation. With the ratification of the mutual assistance treaty by the *Eduskunta* at the end of April 1948, the alarm quickly subsided. One month later, the Communist Minister of the Interior, already in deep trouble with his own party, was forced to resign as a result of a censure motion relating to the return of war criminals, some of them Finnish nationals, to the Soviet Union in 1945. A mass strike failed to persuade Paasikivi to reinstate Leino, and the Communists had to be content with a ministry without portfolio for Hertta Kuusinen and the appointment of a non-Communist People's Democrat as Leino's successor. By this time the 'Big Three Agreement' was virtually dead. The socialists had formally withdrawn in May, and in the election campaign of June they fought on an openly anti-Communist platform. The People's Democrats only managed to secure thirty-eight seats, and when they were offered only four posts in government as against six each for the socialists and Agrarians, with the Ministry of the Interior explicitly ruled out, they decided to remain in opposition. They were to remain there for almost two decades.

The Communist-dominated People's Democratic League held office in government for three and a half years. In Italy and France, the Communists were eased out of government in 1947; in Finland they managed to hang on until mid-1948. The growing Cold War undoubtedly had much to do with the elimination of Communists from government in the Western democracies, although the tactics employed by the Communists themselves had also much to do with their failure to establish a lasting power base. In the case of Finland, the country had been on probation in Soviet eyes since 1944. Hence there was always a strong, albeit latent tension between the Communist Party—which was closely identified with the Soviet Union—and all other parties. The fulfilment of the articles of the 1944 armistice agreement, the final conclusion of peace in Paris and the withdrawal of the Allied Control Commission at the end of 1947 coincided with the growing crisis in East–West relations. No sooner did Finland appear to have acquitted herself of the most onerous political burdens imposed by the Soviet Union than she was faced with a new and potentially dangerous situation in February 1948. Stalin's request for a mutual assistance treaty similar to those concluded between the

Soviet Union and other eastern European countries was widely interpreted as an attempt to draw Finland into the Soviet satellite system. According to one of the eventual negotiators sent to Moscow, Paasikivi himself feared that the Soviet Union was seeking to take over military control in Finland and establish a Communist government. This pessimism was echoed in other quarters. Only the People's Democrats responded favourably to Stalin's proposals. The Social Democrats and the Swedish People's Party favoured negotiations, but argued that a military pact was not in the country's interests. The other parties were not even willing to enter into negotiations. The world press drew parallels between what had happened in Prague and the possible fate of Finland. Writing to his brother on 7 March, J. O. Söderhjelm gave his opinion that at best Finland might preserve her *de facto* autonomy, but that the unwillingness of the *Eduskunta* majority to enter into serious negotiations merely strengthened Soviet suspicions and offered the Communists an excellent opportunity to show that they were the only dependable group in Finland. 'I cannot see how Russian ambition and desire for absolute security can be satisfied with anything less than a Communist-Russian régime here too.'[14]

In the event, Stalin was willing to shelve his initial proposals and to accept those advanced by the Finns. Although the 1948 treaty bound Finland to the Soviet Union's eastern European security system, it did not have the same far-reaching implications as the treaties concluded by other eastern European countries. Moreover, there was no Communist takeover in Finland; as Paasikivi pointed out, Finland retained her democratic institutions and complete internal sovereignty. In a Europe rapidly dividing into two antagonistic military blocs, Finland occupied a strange position, linked by a mutual assistance treaty to her eastern neighbour, yet outside the power blocs and still retaining full control of her internal affairs. However, the extent to which Finland could exercise full and unhindered control of her internal affairs was open to question. Paasikivi on numerous occasions before 1948 warned his countrymen that the Soviet Union could not be indifferent to what went on inside Finland, and yet after the conclusion of the treaty he himself appears to have thrown his weight behind the parties seeking to oust the Communists from government and positions of power. The most likely explanation for this sudden swing to the right seems to be that Paasikivi considered the Soviet Union to be satisfied with the 1948 treaty; that he was well aware of the growing split between the superpowers, and that he counted on the West not letting Finland down in a crisis. There is some evidence to suggest that the United States offered economic aid to Finland as an inducement not to sign the treaty, and even offered support under Article 35 of the United Nations Charter should her territorial integrity be threatened. The United States also operated economic sanctions against Finland at the beginning of 1948, such as the suspension of export licences on goods deemed to have strategic importance. Once it became clear that the 1948 treaty had not 'bolshevised' Finland, American goods and credits began to flow again, and Finland was admitted to certain Western monetary institutions such as the International Monetary Fund and the World Bank. Even in 1948, *Literaturnaya Gazeta* accused Paasikivi of following the 'American road', and by 1950 he was being attacked as an imperialist warmonger along with Tanner and Fagerholm, whose Social Democratic minority government Paasikivi had actively supported following the 1948 elections.

The swing to the right—which, it must be remarked, occurred in other Western democracies at this time—was also a reaction to the tactics employed by the Finnish Communist Party. During the period 1944–8, Paasikivi had subordinated internal political considerations to the exigencies of Finland's delicate relationship with the Soviet Union. After April 1948 he was prepared to go along with the rising tide of internal political opposition to the Communists and to institute what might best be termed a period of restoration.

The failure of the Finnish Communists to establish themselves in a dominant position can be largely attributed to the strength of their opponents. Their partners in government pursued a policy of containment, and it is clear that the Communists were willing and indeed eager to shelve their programme for a socialist Soviet Finland in order to participate in government. The popular front tactic could only succeed if the Communists played a leading role and established an unrivalled hegemony. But in Finland the party's attempt to rally support round the democratic banner of the People's Democratic League failed to win over the Social Democratic Party, and even caused friction between Communist and socialist elements within the League. The tactics of mass meetings and demonstrations adopted in 1946 played into the hands of the right-wing socialists, as did the strikes inspired by the Communists, since these could be portrayed as deliberate sabotage of the obligations laid on Finland to deliver machinery to the Soviet Union in accordance with the reparations agreement. The heavy-handed tactics of the Communist-dominated security police

(*Valpo*) aroused protest and provided ammunition for the right-wing parties, which had largely been cowed into silence following the events of 1944–5.

The Social Democratic Party recovered quickly from the massive defections of 1944–5, and could claim a membership of 108,000 by 1950. Many of the older party members had either joined the ranks of the People's Democrats or retired from active politics; the party leadership was now in the hands of men whose political experience had been that of wartime national solidarity and for whom the class struggles and isolation of former decades had little meaning. The Communist Party leadership was still very much in the hands of Soviet-trained émigrés, who had little real understanding of the attitudes and experiences of the Finnish people, and whose uncompromising rigidity was ill-suited to the shifting political patterns of Finnish democracy. Much of the initial success of the Finnish Communist Party can be attributed to the broad-based appeal of the People's Democratic League, which seemed to offer a definite break with the past and the hope of a better future to many voters; but success at the polls and participation in government, although strengthening the party's resolve to pursue a parliamentary tactic, also made it a prisoner to bourgeois democracy. The party had allowed its programme to be watered down for the purposes of the elections and entry into government; the more opportunist Social Democrats were thus able to appear as a more 'radical' working-class party and to assault their partners in government with very effective propaganda —such as the slogan 'Enough of false promises, price rises and forced democracy!'—in the S.A.K. elections of 1947 and general elections of 1948. The Communists were also guilty of clumsy and inept tactics, which did not pass unnoticed in Moscow. The Soviet Union's intentions towards Finland will probably never be known, though in all likelihood the Finnish Communist Party was never more than a secondary element in Soviet policy. Upton's comment that as long as Stalin had Paasikivi he did not need the Finnish Communist Party, seems to have been not far from the truth.

The period 1944–8 saw a number of radical changes in Finland, largely a direct result of the war and its consequences, although the legislative achievements of the 'Big Three' governments headed by Paasikivi and Mauno Pekkala should not be belittled. One of the most momentous changes occurred in the field of labour and industrial relations. The trades union federation S.A.K. had achieved bargaining parity with the employers in January 1940, but in 1944 the employers' federation finally accepted the principle of collective agreements, which soon became general throughout industry and for which comprehensive legislation was enacted in June 1946. Union membership rose from around 80,000 at the end of the war to 340,000 in 1947.

This sudden increase in strength and the fact that Communists and left-wing socialists occupied leading positions in certain major unions helped to promote a resurgence of strike activity. During the war the government had decreed that wages were on average to be augmented by two-thirds of any rise in the cost of living. Under pressure from the unions the government agreed in January 1945 to the principle of wage increases commensurate with the rise in the cost of living. Acute inflation, which caused the government to devalue the mark three times in 1945, and the threat of strike action together brought about a second major wage increase in the spring of 1945 and a new order for the regulation of wages in June, which merely led to wage settlements over and above the maximum levels and a renewed wave of strikes in the spring of 1946. By dint of further regulation and amendment, price controls and the promise of tax reliefs, and the agreement of the S.A.K. to restrain its members, the government managed to regain control of the situation. However, it failed to work out a comprehensive or binding policy, with the result that in the autumn of 1947 a major wave of mostly unauthorised strikes reached its peak. Nearly half a million working days were lost, although socialist claims that the strikes were tantamount to sabotage of the reparations programme were dismissed by the commission administering the programme. The S.A.K. finally took up the cudgels on 20 September 1947, threatening a general strike if its demands were not met. The government in turn threatened to resign, but finally it gave way. The wages policy agreed not only allowed for general and immediate rises, but bound all future increases to the cost of living index, so that a five-points increase would trigger off a 5.5 per cent wage increase. In addition, a family allowance scheme was adopted.

The wages and prices spiral was made worse by the rapid depreciation in value of the mark, which by the mid-1950s was only one-fiftieth of its 1938 value, thanks to frequent devaluation and the fact that the state had sought to meet its commitments after the war by increasing the note issue. Foreign credits to meet the costs of reconstruction and economic revival were at first limited. For political reasons, Finland did not participate in the Marshall Aid programme, and although American credits did begin to flow in at an increased rate, they were carefully tied to industries and projects which would in no way benefit the Soviet Union. On the other hand, demand for Finnish exports, particularly paper and timber products and their increasing competitiveness on world markets as a result of the devaluations of the mark, brought about a rapid revival of trade, with export earnings helping to secure badly needed machinery and raw materials for industry. The Finnish post-war economy was dominated by the massive reparations bill; but as the bulk of this bill was paid off in the form of ships and machinery, the Finnish metal and engineering industries were transformed into major elements in the national economy by 1952, when the last delivery to the Soviet Union was made.[15]

In spite of advances in the industrial sector, Finland in 1950 was still a good way behind her western neighbour. Only one-fifth of the actively employed population in Sweden worked on the land: in Finland, agriculture was still the largest single employer of labour, providing a livelihood for 47 per cent of the actively employed population. Agriculture in post-war Finland has been as much a political and social as an economic issue; and it is reasonable to assume that further structural transformation of the economy has been hampered by the policies on agriculture pursued by successive governments. The 1945 Land Act offers a good illustration. Designed to resettle the large numbers of refugees from Karelia, most of whom were farmers and their dependents, the Act created some 142,000 new holdings out of 2.8 million hectares of land—mostly by compulsory purchase—but the creation of new and economically non-viable farms simply created problems for the future as the price for an equitable policy of resettlement. The average size of a farm in 1959 was 8.9 hectares, even smaller than it had been after the 1940 peace treaty.

The farmers' interests were well served by the Agrarian party and the agricultural producers' union (M.T.K.), which was not averse to using the threat of withholding farm produce as a means of influencing government prices policies in the post-war years. Grappling with inflation and seeking to satisfy the demands of powerful interest groups such as the S.A.K. and M.T.K. have been the lot of all post-war Finnish governments. The economic problems of the 1950s were particularly intractable and led to frequent clashes between the Agrarian and Social Democratic parties, the two major contenders for governmental office. The minority socialist government led by K.-A. Fagerholm, which succeeded the 'Big Three' coalition in July 1948, received public support from the S.A.K., but was also compelled to bow to other interest groups. An attempt to unseat the government in June 1949 over its unemployment policy provoked a public declaration of support from the S.A.K., which defended the wages paid to those on relief projects. As a result, the government survived with the support of the right-wing parties. However, it had to agree to a substantial increase in the price of grain paid to farmers, and devalued the mark twice in 1949 in an attempt to restore the competitiveness of Finnish paper and timber exports, badly hit by the recession. The subsequent rise in consumer prices, and the attempts of industry to adjust wages led to further industrial conflict. An attempt by a large pulp and paper mill in the town of Kemi to reduce piecework rates led to a strike, which soon acquired political overtones. Two strikers were shot by police rushed in by the government; a state of emergency was declared in the town, and Communist strike leaders were arrested. However, the Communists overplayed their hand, and in September the S.A.K. purged its ranks of those unions which had staged unofficial strikes, and the government ordered the trial of some 150 strike leaders in Kemi. The Communist Party had lost ground in the 1948 elections, and had failed to secure control of the S.A.K.; in addition, the Fagerholm government dismissed left-wingers and Communists from posts acquired in previous years and replaced the *Valpo* security police with a new force not under Communist control.

The minority government formed by Kekkonen after the re-election of Paasikivi as President in 1950 was beset with financial and economic problems. In January that year, the Fagerholm administration had decreed a return to free collective bargaining in January 1950. In opposition, the Social Democratic Party now backed the wage demands of the S.A.K., which threatened a general strike in the spring. Fagerholm acted as mediator, and the so-called 'F-agreement' of May 1950 awarded a general wage increase of 15 per cent with a 5 per cent threshold trigger linked to the cost-of-living index. This proved impossible to implement and more than 4.6 million working days were lost in subsequent strikes, three times greater than the previous record of 1927. A second threatened general strike was narrowly averted in the autumn; the government's attempt to impose a wages freeze provoked further demands from the S.A.K. with the result that Kekkonen broadened the base of his government with the inclusion of eight Social Democrats. In the autumn of 1951, a wide-ranging stabilisation programme was finally agreed. The cost-of-living index was revised with the base rate of 100 as from October 1951; direct

taxes and family allowances were removed from it. Although wages
were still index-linked, these measures afforded some kind of control,
as did the efforts of the government to keep down prices and cut
taxes.

This agreement took place against the background of world economic resurgence as a result of the Korean War. By 1952–3, however,
the fall in world prices for Finland's major export commodities
led to unemployment and further conflict over economic strategy.
In addition to the contending claims of the unions, employers and
agricultural producers, the formulation of an overall economic
strategy was gravely hindered by political rivalries. A wing of the
Social Democratic Party led by the party secretary Väinö Leskinen
opposed entry into a coalition headed by Kekkonen in 1953 and again
in 1954. Kekkonen himself had had to fight a long struggle within
his own party to gain reluctant acceptance of a new approach to
relations with the Soviet Union, and in government he frequently
clashed with members of his own party, as in 1952 when he threatened
to resign over Agrarian opposition to the imposition of price controls
on butter. It is a mark of his unassailable authority that no government
between 1950 and 1956, with the brief exception of the non-party
Tuomioja government, could be formed without him: as Hakovirta
has pointed out, only Kekkonen seemed to have the ability to create
a workable coalition between the Agrarians and Social Democratic
Party, and this made him virtually the first choice of the President
when a new cabinet had to be formed.

He was also able to use foreign policy as a means of pressure. In
November 1953, Paasikivi warned the *Eduskunta* that it would be
unwise to topple Kekkonen's minority government, which appeared
to be engaged in negotiations for a favourable trade deal with the
Soviet Union. However, the government was defeated and replaced
by a non-party caretaker administration under the director of the
Bank of Finland, Sakari Tuomioja, who was virtually jobbed into
office by the Social Democrats, as an alternative to Kekkonen: the
Agrarian's refusal to join this government left the Social Democrats
with no option but to remain outside government as well. Kekkonen
took the opportunity to publish the details of his talks with the Soviet
ambassador on trade agreements, which was seen in the press as an
attempt to undermine the Tuomioja government. Kekkonen returned
to office after the 1954 elections as Foreign Minister in a coalition
headed by Ralf Törngren of the Swedish People's Party. The government was unable to work out a satisfactory solution to the demands of

the S.A.K. for a reduction in the cost-of-living index or wage increases, demands reinforced by the threat of a general strike, and it was replaced by Kekkonen's fifth government.

The constant conflict of interests over economic policy came to a head in 1956, after right-wingers in the *Eduskunta* had managed to block the annual extension of the government's powers to control wages and prices in December 1955. As a consequence, there was a sharp increase in the cost-of-living index, occasioned by steep rises in the cost of dairy produce. The unions then demanded an hourly wage increase of 12 marks, which the employers were unwilling to meet. On the day when the newly-elected President Kekkonen took office, the fifth post-war threat of a general strike became reality. In protest, the M.T.K. called for the withholding of dairy produce, the sixth such threat since the war. The strike lasted for nearly three weeks, involving some 420,000 workers. Although the demand for a 12-marks-an-hour wage increase was conceded, subsequent price rises virtually wiped out the gains. The trade union movement was seriously weakened by the growing split in the Social Democratic Party, and was forced to agree to the government's two-thirds compensation in wage rises related to the cost-of-living index in 1957. A devaluation of 39 per cent in the autumn of 1957 helped to restore the competitiveness of Finnish exports, while the farmers were able, through the efforts of the M.T.K. to obtain better prices for their produce. In the three-cornered contest between workers, farmers and industrial interests, the decisive losers in the years 1957–9 were the workers, whose real earnings declined to the level of the early 1950s.

The split in the Social Democratic Party was not simply the result of conflict between left and right, and it is indeed difficult to trace the ideological divisions between the warring elements. The party had decisively broken with the Communists in 1947 and had maintained a strong suspicion of the Soviet Union ever since; neither side in the struggle which erupted in the mid 1950s showed any sign of wishing to deviate from this line. It is true that personal rivalries and internal conflicts for positions of influence in organisations such as the workers' athletic union (T.U.L.) influenced the form of the struggle, but they alone did not determine its outcome. The split in the party was essentially between the rural and urban party associations, the former wanting to continue support for a policy of high agricultural subsidies (which the low-paid workers in the cities also supported), the latter pressing for a policy of rapid industrialisation, the elimination of inefficient farms by rationalisation and the phasing-out of agricultural subsidies. Such a programme for industrialisation was proposed at the 1957 extraordinary party conference and adopted after the opposition walked out following the narrow victory of Väinö Tanner in the election for the party chairmanship. Tanner was the candidate of the party secretary Väinö Leskinen, who was also able to fill the party executive with his supporters. Tanner was more clearly identified with the Leskinen group, although he endeavoured to bring about a compromise solution to preserve party unity. The reluctance of the Leskinen group to reach agreement with the opposition killed almost all hopes of compromise, and Fagerholm, whose government included four members of the opposition, finally resigned office in May 1957. The Social Democratic Party majority attacked the emergency economic programme of the ensuing minority government of V. J. Sukselainen and sought to create a new government with the right-wing parties. The minority opposition of the Social Democratic Party finally entered Sukselainen's government in its third reshuffle in September 1957. The five members of the opposition refused to leave the government on the insistence of the Social Democratic leadership, and were thereupon expelled from the party. In the 1958 elections, the opposition campaigned under its own banner, although it was not till 1959 that it set up a separate party—the Workers' and Small Farmers' Social Democratic Union. The S.A.K. also broke up, despite Swedish attempts at mediation. The opposition retained control of the S.A.K. while the minority eventually formed, in 1960, a rival central trade union organisation (S.A.J.).

The split also had implications for Finland's relations with the Soviet Union. Although Leskinen had begun in 1954 to advocate a more active role for the party in fostering good relations with the Soviet Union, this was in all probability a tactical move designed to outflank Kekkonen and the Agrarian party, who were viewed far more favourably in Moscow than the Social Democratic Party. In the event, Leskinen was prepared to enter the anti-Soviet lists once more in 1956 in order to win over Väinö Tanner, whose return to politics after his release from prison in 1949 was viewed with deep suspicion in Moscow. Leskinen's anti-Agrarian electoral campaign of 1954 had failed to produce results, and his efforts to keep Kekkonen out of government not only failed but also deepened the conflict within the Social Democratic Party, one wing of which was still prepared to work in coalition with the Agrarians to maintain the price subsidies and index-linked wages policy forged by the Kekkonen government in 1951. The victory of the Leskinen wing and the election of Tanner as party chairman in 1957 were viewed in Moscow with alarm, which was further increased by the formation of Fagerholm's third government in August 1958. Although the left-wing parties secured an absolute majority in the 1958 elections—the People's Democrats increasing their mandate from forty-three to fifty—the Social Democrats rejected the attempts of President Kekkonen and the People's Democrats to form a new 'Big Three' government. Instead, Kekkonen was forced to accept a coalition of Social Democrats, Coalition Party conservatives and Agrarians, who were persuaded to enter government in order to preserve the farm incomes policy, in spite of warnings from senior party officials. Moscow had already showed signs of alarm when Tanner tried to form a government in 1957, and against a background of growing global tension showed its displeasure by not replacing the Soviet ambassador and virtually suspending important trade negotiations. When the United States began to show an interest and offered economic aid and a substantial loan via the World Bank, the Agrarians decided to pull out of the coalition, which resigned at the end of the year.

The so-called 'night frost' crisis highlighted the conflict of interests and attitudes which characterised Finnish politics in the immediate post-war decades. Although the Fagerholm government gave no indication of wishing to change the direction of Finnish foreign policy, it was clearly suspect in the eyes of the Soviet leadership. As Khrushchev remarked to Kekkonen when the two met in January 1959: 'As far as I know, Mr. Fagerholm has a broad back. But behind his back we can see Tanner and his supporter Mr. Leskinen and other persons well known for their antipathy towards the Soviet Union.'[16] The Soviet leader also drew attention to the number of anti-Soviet press articles which had appeared in Finland, a point made by Kekkonen himself in broadcasts at the end of the crisis. Such manifestations, although quite within the law, nevertheless created an atmosphere of mistrust and made the task of the nation's leaders in fulfilling the obligations of the 1948 treaty that much more difficult. In other words, public opinion, as voiced by the press and politicians, must be seen to be behind the policy of friendly relations with the Soviet Union.

The reaction of the Social Democrats to the 'night frost' crisis was understandably rather different. They attacked the Agrarians for not standing firm in the face of what they regarded as unwarranted Soviet interference in Finnish internal affairs. Kekkonen was criticised for exercising discriminatory powers in an anti-democratic manner—since the government had enjoyed majority support in the *Eduskunta*—and the tone of these attacks became more strident as the 1962 presidential election drew near. The re-election of Tanner as party chairman in 1960 was an open act of defiance, characterised by the Scandinavian correspondent of the *New York Times* as a sign of the worsening political crisis in Finland. The 1960 party conference continued the attack against Kekkonen, and the Agrarians for their part refused to enter government with the Social Democrats unless there was a radical change of policy. It was not until 1963, which saw the retirement of Tanner from active politics and Leskinen from the party executive, that the Social Democratic Party began to reconsider its position, and to realise that unqualified support for the Paasikivi–Kekkonen line in foreign policy was the first condition for re-entry into government. This was the lesson the Agrarians had learnt under Kekkonen's tutelage, and in consequence the Soviet press adopted a much friendlier attitude towards the party.

There is no doubt that Kekkonen's advocacy of an active policy of friendly relations with the Soviet Union met with vigorous resistance even within the ranks of his own party. As early as 1950, a secret club of conservatives, Social Democrats and right-wing Agrarians had been formed with the intention of preventing Kekkonen becoming president in 1956, and as he himself later remarked, the 1956 presidential campaign was essentially fought over the issue of foreign policy. The great drawback of the Paasikivi line was that it was forged in the bitterness of defeat, and was not accompanied by any radical changes in attitude among those who occupied positions of influence. The Communist Party's strategy of a popular democratic front failed to make inroads among the middle-class intelligentsia, and the party's devoted loyalty to Stalin tended to keep it isolated, with its steady hard-core working-class support, alienated and excluded from the mainstream of Finnish political life. The Social Democratic Party had become reconciled to bourgeois Finland during the war, and its internal conflicts were an indication of the changing structure and appeal of the party; but its leaders set their faces against co-operation with the Communists and grew increasingly antagonistic towards the internal and external policies of the Agrarians. The efforts of the party leadership in the late 1950s to form a coalition with industrial and capitalist political groupings in order to force through a rapid industrialisation programme met with opposition not only from the Communists and Agrarians, but also from the trade unions and the opposition within the Social Democratic Party itself. In the end, such a coalition was ruled out by foreign policy considerations.

Cultural and intellectual life in Finland throughout the 1950s remained conservative and resistant to foreign influences. The student body and student activities were still dominated by right-wing nationalist values, while the authoritarian structure of the university administration served to reinforce academic traditionalism. As one observer noted in 1960, culture in Finland was becoming the prerogative of the expanding middle class, but was still confined by an authoritarian, patriarchal framework. In consequence, it lacked the scope of free expression. Free discussion was indeed seen as in some way threatening national values, even independence.[17] This was very much the case with regard to discussion of Finland's immediate past. When the American Professor Leonard Lundin in 1957 dared to advance an interpretation of Finland's role in the Second World War which was at odds with the orthodox view, he was savaged by the Finnish historians, who had earlier regarded Paasivirta's pioneering work on the events of 1917–18 with something less than enthusiasm. The interpretation of Finland's recent past did pose something of a problem for her historians. One writer has suggested that the orthodox view of Finland drifting like a log into the maelstrom of war had to be rejected by the bourgeois intelligentsia if the latter were ever to break out of the political impasse in which they found themselves after the war. This also implied rejection of the historians, 'the traditional national prophets of the Finnish people'.[18] The vacuum thereby created was to be filled by the social scientist.

Even if this is somewhat to oversimplify, the late 1950s were to see a series of investigations of Finnish society which helped to foster a deeper understanding of the recent past. A number of deep-seated cleavages in Finnish society were revealed, although one which had caused friction in the inter-war years—the language question—had all but disappeared. Eskola's study of the attitudes of country- and city-dwellers towards each other revealed a number of illogical and superficial prejudices, although he also discovered a strong sense of continuity linking the two, which was only likely to be broken if the countryside was unable to keep abreast of developments elsewhere and the city-dwellers began to lose touch with their rural roots. Allardt has also argued that the rural-urban conflict is very largely regulated within the institutional framework of the political system. Class is still a potent feature of Finnish life, although the emergence of an urban middle class in the post-war years has tended to cut across the traditional division between workers and peasants on the one hand and bourgeois '*herrat*' on the other. In his study of backwoods

Communism in Kuopio province, Nousiainen concluded that social isolation and economic backwardness were probably less important than traditions in determining loyalties to the Communist Party. Allardt has questioned this by asking why Social Democracy has stronger support in the old 'Red' areas of Häme and south-west Finland, and has suggested that Communism is more likely to thrive in rural areas with weak social constraints—areas with a high level of migration, for example—whereas in industrial communities with weak social constraints—growing conurbations, for example—Social Democracy is more likely to recruit working-class support. Other studies tend to show that insecurity is a more marked feature of the Communist voter—hence the strong support given to the party by building workers, lumberjacks and small farmers in backward areas. Both Communists and Social Democrats regard their party as the best upholder of working-class interests; a sense of personal identification, rather than ideological preference, seems to be the foundation of support in both cases. There has also been a marked regional cleavage in Finland: the north and east have been traditionally more 'radical' than the more prosperous south and west. Agrarian members of the *Eduskunta* from the north and east have tended to adopt a distinctly anti-bourgeois and anti-urban line, in contrast to their colleagues from the south, who are more often identified with big farming and even business interests. The growth in Communist support in the north since the war can undoubtedly be ascribed to the immediate post-war flow of money to aid reconstruction and the boom in demand for timber—with which the Communists as partners in government could legitimately be credited—and the subsequent neglect of the peripheral and economically backward north by the governments of the 1950s.

An even more fundamental dilemma which faces Finland is posed by her position in the world. In brief, Finland is a multi-party democracy with a capitalist economy, and for political reasons she must always take heed of her eastern neighbour in determining policy. This is particularly so with regard to trade. During the 1950s, Finland's trade with western Europe increased steadily, while the amount of exports to the Soviet Union—which had accounted for something like 20 per cent of the total immediately after the final settlement of the reparations bills—had fallen to 15 per cent by 1959. Trade with West Germany in particular showed a sharp increase, and it is interesting that the crises in Soviet–Finnish relations occurred in the years when Finnish trade with West Germany increased and that with the Soviet Union fell.

The Soviet Union has been able to exercise sanctions to prevent Finland from becoming too closely involved in the economic integration of western Europe, as in 1958, when the suspension of imports and curtailment of deliveries of ships and machinery caused a sharp rise in unemployment in Finland. Although this can be interpreted as a sign of Soviet displeasure with the Fagerholm government, it was perhaps a warning to the Finns not to become too closely involved in the plans for integration which had been given force in the Treaty of Rome. Finland had already taken a significant step towards easing trade with the Western nations in 1957, when the 'Helsinki Club' protocol signed between Finland and the O.E.E.C. countries afforded an opportunity for easier payment arrangements. The creation of E.F.T.A. posed a particular problem for Finland: if she remained outside, the competitiveness of her major export commodities in Western markets would be seriously weakened. On the other hand, full membership of E.F.T.A. was politically out of the question, and in negotiating associate membership Finland would have to take account of the 1947 'most favoured nation' status accorded to the Soviet Union. Such an arrangement was concluded in 1961, after assurances had been made to the Soviet Union, which shared the tariff reductions introduced for E.F.T.A. countries trading with Finland.

The signing of the treaty of associate membership with the E.F.T.A. countries ensured that Finland's main exports to the West—timber, pulp and paper products—would remain competitive, and added a further dimension to the freeing of restrictions on imports, which had begun in the early 1950s. At the same time, however, the freeing of trade caused a balance of payments problem which has plagued Finland ever since. The Finn/E.F.T.A. treaty was also an important political victory, and a prime illustration of the balancing act which Finland has to perform in order to preserve her traditional export markets in the West and the continuance of good relations with the Soviet Union. During the 1950s, Finland also became more intimately involved with international organisations, which in turn added new dimensions to her role in the world.

Paasikivi's Finland was very much under the shadow of the Yalta agreement on the role of the defeated nations. The Soviet occupation of the Porkkala base even denied Finland the right to formal neutrality, as Paasikivi himself observed. In 1955, in return for a renewal of the 1948 treaty for a further twenty years, the Soviet Union returned the Porkkala base. Finland also became a member of the Nordic Council and the United Nations. Kekkonen thus entered office in 1956 in a situation vastly different from that which had faced his predecessor ten years earlier. This, as much as the personal qualities which Kekkonen brought to the presidency, was to prove decisive in the years ahead.

8

THE KEKKONEN ERA

'How often have we heard the plaintive cry 'Finland needs hard times, danger from without, before it can attain unanimity.' This sort of lament actually seems to conceal a hidden hope that evil days will come so that the old, longed-for conformity in society is achieved.

'But we do not need this sort of conformity and unanimity. National solidarity must be achieved and can be achieved by stretching out an open hand and by the co-operation which this brings about.'

Urho Kekkonen, 4 February 1967
(Urho Kekkonen, *Puheita ja kirjoituksia II*, Helsinki 1967, p. 445)

Finland's foreign policy since 1944

The end of the 1950s witnessed a heightening of global tension. In Europe this culminated in the Berlin crisis of 1961. Increasingly strident Soviet attacks on the role played in NATO by West Germany, and the seeming determination of the Soviet leaders to force through some sort of settlement of the Berlin question, were sooner or later bound to have consequences for Finland, as the chief of the general staff Lieutenant General Viljanen intimated to his government on 12 August 1961.

On 30 October the Soviet government proposed consultations in accordance with Article 2 of the 1948 treaty on measures for the defence of the borders of Finland and the Soviet Union against the threat of armed aggression by West Germany and her NATO allies. Although President Kekkonen, who happened to be relaxing on the beach in Hawaii at the end of a tour of North America when the Soviet note was delivered, sought to convince Finnish and world opinion that the note reflected the crisis in relations between the Western powers and the Soviet Union and insisted that it was not directed against Finland, there is no doubt that it caused considerable alarm in Finnish government circles. In the meantime, however, the note remained unanswered, and the Foreign Minister Ahti Karjalainen was sent for exploratory talks to Moscow. He was reassured by his opposite number Andrey Gromyko that the Soviet government had confidence in Finnish foreign policy, but fears were expressed as to the continuity of that policy—a clear reference to the anti-Kekkonen electoral alliance formed to contest the January 1962 presidential election. On 14 November, Kekkonen used his presidential powers to dissolve the *Eduskunta* prematurely, thereby bringing forward the date for the scheduled 1962 elections to February. This move was designed to remove some of the Soviet fears of a break in continuity in Finnish foreign policy, but it also served to weaken the alliance of Social Democrats and conservatives, since it was unlikely that this alliance would survive the January presidential electoral campaign.

Kekkonen's action failed to placate Moscow. On 16 November the Finnish government was reminded that it had not yet replied to the original Soviet note, and it was asked to send a delegation to Moscow to begin consultations. Kekkonen thereupon decided to see Khrushchev personally, as he had done during the 1958 crisis. The two men met in Novosibirsk on 23 November. Khrushchev was persuaded to postpone consultations, which Kekkonen claimed would merely serve to increase alarm and tension in Scandinavia. In return the Soviet leader expressed the wish that Finland should keep an eye on developments in northern Europe and the Baltic area and if necessary let the Soviet government know what steps it thought should be taken. The break-up of the anti-Kekkonen electoral alliance occurred on the same day, and Kekkonen was able to secure a comfortable victory on the first ballot of the electoral college after the January election.

The 'note crisis' of 1961 can be regarded not only as a personal political triumph for Kekkonen, whose position as head of state has remained unchallenged up to the time of writing, but also as a test-case and a turning-point in relations between the Soviet Union and Finland since the Second World War. These relations rest firmly upon the 1948 treaty of friendship, co-operation and mutual assistance, the provisions and implications of which have been the subject of much comment and analysis by Finnish and foreign observers.[1] The conclusion of a mutual assistance pact between the two countries had been raised by the Soviet Union during the abortive 1938 discussions, and was mentioned again by Zhdanov in discussions with Mannerheim and Paasikivi in 1945. The timing of Stalin's letter to Paasikivi on 23 February 1948, as the Communist take-over in Czechoslovakia was gaining momentum, was unfortunate, since it caused widespread fears that the real purpose of a mutual assistance pact was to enable the Soviet Union to establish military control over Finland as it had done over the Baltic states in 1939. The willingness of the Soviet delegation in the Moscow talks to accept Finnish suggestions for a treaty helped to dispel some of the worst suspicions, and the final draft signed on 6 April 1948 was in essence the work of Paasikivi, who remained in Helsinki during the negotiations.[2] In a broadcast to the nation on 9 April, Paasikivi was at pains to point out the limited commitments imposed on Finland by the treaty, and to stress that the treaty in no way infringed Finnish sovereignty. On the question of Finnish neutrality he was guarded, pointing out that the existence of a Soviet base at Porkkala was somewhat at variance with international concepts of neutrality. The return of the Porkkala base in 1955 removed this obvious hindrance to Finland's claim to be neutral, and the Kekkonen era has seen the evolution of what the Finns term a policy of active neutrality.

The starting-point of Finnish neutrality is the preamble to the 1948 treaty, which speaks of Finland's desire to remain outside the conflicting interests of the great powers; but as President Kekkonen admitted in 1965, the pact must be read in its entirety. In other words, 'Finland will defend her territory if Finland or the U.S.S.R. via Finnish territory becomes the object of an armed attack by Germany or states allied with her, and Finland may in precisely defined conditions undertake this with the military co-operation of the U.S.S.R.'[3] This has caused several commentators to speak of a peacetime neutrality which has regard to a military alliance in the event of war. Others, notably the Norwegian strategist Nils Ørvik, have claimed that Finnish neutrality is basically a fiction, since in the last instance it is subject to Soviet control. The view advanced in 1967 by Max Jakobson, then Finland's ambassador to the United Nations, that the Novosibirsk statement suggested that it was up to Finland to take the initiative for consultations under Article 2 of the 1948 treaty—an interpretation which 'further strengthened Finland's neutrality'—has since been challenged in a Soviet publication issued under the name of Yuri Komissarov. This writer maintained that the treaty must be read in its entirety, that the right to initiate consultations had not passed to Finland—a point made by Kekkonen in 1969—and that Finnish foreign policy was firmly founded on observance of the clauses, military or otherwise, of the 1948 treaty.[4] More recently, Jakobson has argued that the unqualified support given by the Soviet Union to Finnish neutrality in the 1960s has faded, and that there are circles in the Soviet Union that wish to forge some kind of closer military alliance with Finland. Jakobson has been criticised in Finland for seeing neutrality in the context of war, rather than as an instrument of peace. The fact remains, however, that the Soviet leadership—as Kekkonen observed in a statement in 1970—has spoken rather sparingly of neutrality since 1968. Whereas, for example, Khrushchev placed Finland among the neutral countries in 1956, Gromyko in 1969 spoke of Finland as a peace-loving neighbour of the Soviet Union. There are suggestions that the Finns tried to have the word 'neutrality' inserted in the protocol of the 1970 agreement to extend the friendship, co-operation and mutual assistance treaty, but when the Soviet side insisted on the removal of the clause in the preamble referring to Finland's desire to stay outside great power conflicts, the idea was dropped.

The Soviet view appears to be that there can be no question of Finland remaining neutral in the event of the security of northern Europe being threatened by Germany or her NATO allies; but, given stability in this area, Finland is free to pursue a 'peace-loving' neutrality. In that an active policy of peaceful neutrality can help to preserve the stability of northern Europe, there is no conflict between this view and Finland's own interests. But should this stability be threatened, a number of problems will arise, the most fundamental being that Finland might find herself in a military alliance with a country whose intentions are by no means trusted. The revelations in 1971 of the Czech defector General Šejna, who maintained that in a situation of conflict with the West the Soviet Union would take twenty-four hours to strike through Finland, and the continued interest of the Finnish army in training for guerrilla warfare are indications of this uncertainty.

Hostile or cynical observers have sometimes accused Finland of acting as the watchdog of Soviet interests in northern Europe. This accusation tends to gloss over the dilemma in which Finland, with her limited possibilities, finds herself. It also tends to assume that the Soviet Union harbours aggressive or expansionist designs in northern Europe, a suspicion which has surfaced sporadically in the West since the days of Palmerston. This assumption has been challenged by a number of Finnish writers. Törnudd has argued that the Soviet Union is concerned to prevent northern Europe from becoming drawn too closely into the anti-Soviet camp, while Jakobson has maintained that Soviet policy towards Finland and Scandinavia has been traditionally defensive, and that any alteration to the so-called Northern Balance which might increase Soviet suspicions can only be detrimental to Finland's interests. The essence of the Northern Balance for Finland is that there is a limited commitment both on the part of Norway and Denmark as members of NATO, and of Finland under the terms of the 1948 treaty, with neutral Sweden acting as a central pivot.

The Finnish nightmare is that increased tension might cause one or more of the Scandinavian countries to increase its commitment to NATO or, in the case of Sweden, to deviate from a policy of strict neutrality. It is for this reason that Finland has sought to advance the idea of a neutral northern Europe. As early as 1952, Kekkonen advocated the creation of a neutral alliance of the Scandinavian countries, which he maintained would constitute a logical conclusion to the 1948 treaty in that it would remove the theoretical threat of an attack on Soviet territory via Finnish territory. Kekkonen later claimed that this was an attempt to counter the efforts of the former Danish Prime Minister, H. C. Hedtoft, to draw Sweden away from its policy of neutrality, which would have had serious consequences for Finland. In 1965 he took up the idea that Norway might leave NATO and conclude a treaty with Britain and the United States similar to that concluded between Finland and the Soviet Union in 1948. Kekkonen has also mooted the idea of a north European nuclear-free zone, which has been seen by Norwegian politicians and strategists as denying their country the possibility of calling upon NATO to supply nuclear weapons in the event of conflict, while leaving the nuclear bases in the Kola peninsula unmolested. The Norwegians have reacted in a similar way to Finnish proposals for the neutralisation of the Norwegian-Finnish frontier, which would also restrict Norway's ability to utilise the full potential of her NATO membership. As Maude has pointed out, if Finland is seriously considering a stance of neutrality which includes defensive action against possible Soviet aggression, then it is not in her interests to weaken the NATO presence in Norway. The political initiatives aimed at neutralising northern Europe would thus seem to be at variance with an important aspect of Finnish military policy. This point has been made by Norwegians replying to Finnish initiatives, although the Finnish line seems to be that Finland wishes to maintain the Northern Balance by guarantees from the superpowers under the terms of the 1968 Security Council resolution on the non-proliferation treaty, which would offer assistance to non-nuclear states under threat of attack. But what sort of guarantee this would be and how it would work is open to question.

In the meantime, the possibility of a weakening of the stability of northern Europe continues to haunt the Finns, particularly in the wake of the energy crisis of the early 1970s. The development of the Norwegian maritime oilfields might well compel NATO to intensify its role in Norway, with the corresponding threat of a Soviet reaction. There is also the fear that Sweden might be compelled, through economic circumstances or political necessity, to abandon her neutrality, a possibility hinted at in a television broadcast by the Swedish Foreign Minister in May 1975. Most recently, considerable attention has been paid in Finland to the question of the exploitation of the resources of Svalbard and the Barents Sea by Norway and the Soviet Union, a further potential area of conflict.[5]

Finland's attempts to develop links with the Scandinavian countries have not been trouble-free. Although Finland welcomed the Danish proposal which led to the creation of the Nordic Council in 1952, the Finnish delegation at the inaugural negotiations made it clear that the country's delicate relationship with the Soviet Union precluded full membership of the Council. However, Finland did join the Nordic Council three years later, an indication that the Soviet Union no longer regarded the organisation as the cat's-paw of Western imperialism and indeed even saw a positive value in the presence of Finland in an organisation which had three NATO members.[6]

Membership of the Nordic Council was for Finland an important first step towards closer economic co-operation, though plans for a Nordic customs union in 1958–9 were strongly criticised in the Soviet press, and there is good reason to believe that the Soviet Union also adopted a negative attitude towards the attempts to form a Nordic customs union with certain common institutions such as a central investment bank in 1969–70. The earlier plan for a customs union gave way to Scandinavian membership of E.F.T.A., with Finland concluding a separate deal in 1961 after having assured the Soviet Union of the continuance of her most-favoured-nation status. The 1969 Nordek project for increased economic co-operation was partly overtaken by events, with the extension of the offer of membership in the E.E.C. to Norway and Denmark, which caused Finland to back out, though for reasons which are still not clear.[7]

Finland's desire to follow a policy consonant with her own interests and yet acceptable to the Soviet Union has thus not always succeeded— or rather, Finland has had to go to considerable lengths to assuage Soviet suspicions in order to obtain what she considers essential for her economic future (and, it might be added, as a demonstration of her determination to remain firmly in touch with the Western democracies). Furthermore, the Soviet Union is not the only stumbling-block in the way of Finland's declared policy of active neutrality, as the fate of the 'German package-deal' shows. Before 1971, Finland refused to recognise either German state. In September that year, however, the Finnish government suddenly offered recognition of both states in return for their recognition of Finnish neutrality, a promise not to use or threaten force against Finland, and the settlement of claims for compensation for the destruction wrought by the German army in Lapland in 1944–5. In the event, Finland was forced to 'untie' the package, after the West German government showed reluctance to go ahead with the deal; however, diplomatic relations with the two countries were established on 7 January 1973, with both states agreeing to 'respect' Finnish neutrality and to renounce the threat and use of force in their relations with Finland. The question of compensation has been shelved.

The German 'package-deal', although hastily concocted and not entirely successful in its aims, does represent something of a breakthrough for the Finnish policy of seeking greater security by a policy of active neutrality. Behind the stipulation concerning the renunciation of force lies Finland's desire for some sort of great power guarantee in the form of a renunciation of force by the allies of the two Germanies; and the whole initiative, in spite of Kekkonen's denials, was surely designed to make the implementation of the 1948 treaty less likely.

Willy Brandt's *Ostpolitik* and the general relaxation of tension in Europe formed the immediate background to the Finnish initiative on the two Germanies—and on the European Security Conference. A Finnish note of 5 May 1969 had sought to sound out Western opinion on such a conference, since the Finnish position adopted in reply to a Soviet proposal for a security conference in 1954 remained the same: i.e. Finland would only participate if all interested states were represented, irrespective of their political systems and diplomatic affiliation. The Finnish aim was to secure as much consensus as possible in advance, and to obtain not only the prestige of having been host of a successful and non-controversial conference but also a strengthening of the security of Europe which would *ipso facto* reduce the level of commitment under the 1948 treaty. It is still too early to say how successful these aims were, although it would appear that certain questions vital to Finland—such as that of Germany and the nuclear-free zone in northern Europe—were either by-passed or ignored, and that the vexatious issue of human rights became something of an embarrassment for the Finns, whose concept of détente is couched in more straightforward political–military terms.[8]

The staging of the Helsinki European Security Conference by Finland certainly served to focus attention on Finnish foreign policy, although not in the way which the Finns themselves might have hoped for. A number of foreign observers maintained that Finland was acting either to further Soviet interests or to appease her neighbour: the Security Conference was seen by the correspondent of the *Baltimore Sun* as a means of easing the U.S.A. out of Europe in preparation for Soviet dominance of the continent. The Stockholm correspondent of *Die Welt* noted in 1973 that Finnish attempts to pursue a more independent policy, as in the nomination of Max Jakobson for the post of Secretary-General of the United Nations, are doomed to failure without Soviet consent. Other foreign observers are markedly more optimistic. David Vital, for instance, sees the relationship between Finland and the Soviet Union as one of the successes of the post-war era, and characterises it as a 'paradigm for the future'; John Vloyantes, while consigning Finland to the 'soft sphere' of Soviet influence, has nevertheless argued that the relationship between the two states offers reciprocal advantages, in which Finland can and does exercise influence in Moscow. George Kennan has also weighed in with a vigorous condemnation of the proponents of the idea of 'Finlandisation', a term which has been bandied about rather freely in the wake of Brandt's *Ostpolitik*. Much of the debate concerning Finlandisation has been remarkably ill-informed, and the term has been used as much as a weapon in internal political debate as a means of characterising the Soviet-Finnish relationship.[9]

The most thorough argument on Finlandisation to date has been presented by the Norwegian Nils Ørvik, who maintains that Finland is subject to 'remote control' from Moscow, and lacks the ability or even the will to pursue an independent policy. Kekkonen is seen as a watchdog not only in the sphere of foreign policy, but also in internal politics: parties or individuals who are opposed to the official line of good relations with the Soviet Union are rigorously excluded from office. More recently, Walter Laqueur has distinguished four characteristics of Finland's subservience to the Soviet Union. First, Finland's neutrality is compromised by her binding special relationship with the Soviet Union; secondly, the size of her army is determined by the Soviet Union (in fact, by the Paris peace treaty, to which Great Britain was also a signatory); thirdly, only political parties approved by the Soviet Union can participate in government; and last, Finland is expected to have close commercial relations with the Communist bloc. Laqueur, in common with a number of other 'Finlandisers', fears that this Soviet model might well be extended further into a weak and divided Europe.[10]

Not surprisingly, the Finnish reaction to these comments has been sharp, although at times it has overshot the mark. The argument that Western observers condemn Finnish neutrality as pro-Soviet, whereas their real concern seems to be that it should be pro-West, is valid, but it tends to gloss over the somewhat special circumstances of Finnish neutrality, and ignores the differing views of that neutrality held within Finland itself. Finns have also stressed the positive side of the Soviet-Finnish relationship, and President Kekkonen has even proffered Finlandisation—in its positive sense—as a model for the rest of Europe. What is important for the success of Finnish foreign policy is precisely what its foreign critics fear Finlandisation is designed to erode: a strong and united Europe. Far from being a helpless tool of Soviet policy, Finland genuinely seeks to promote peace and a reduction of tension, since this is the best safeguard of her national security. It is the underlying reason for the Finnish initiatives of recent years, and was clearly voiced in 1965 by President Kekkonen during a visit to Moscow.

Kekkonen took up the question of the Western plan to establish a multilateral nuclear force, and voiced his country's concern, claiming that this did not conflict with Finland's neutral policy 'because peace in Europe is essential for the maintenance of our neutrality'.[11] Unfortunately for Finland, her desire for peace is all too frequently confused with what is taken to be a subtle Soviet plan to establish hegemony by stealth in Europe. The real nature of the Finnish dilemma is not fully understood, or is ignored by most foreign critics, who also tend to forget the other factors which play a part in shaping Finnish policy, notably the necessity of keeping in touch with Finland's important trading partners in the West.

The dilemma inherent in the relationship between democratic, 'capitalist' Finland and the Soviet Union is by no means new. The lines of Finnish foreign policy can be traced back to the period of autonomy, when Finnish liberals advanced the case for neutrality in the event of conflict between the great powers, and the nationalists stressed the importance of loyalty towards the Russian empire. Although the present official Finnish policy is one of peace-loving and active neutrality and friendly relations with the Soviet Union, there are distinct differences of emphasis. Those who incline to the right politically tend to stress the importance of neutrality, which even overshadows the 1948 treaty, while those on the left see the 1948 treaty as the safeguard for Finnish security in any conflict which might arise in northern Europe. These differences in interpretation have been carefully noted in the Soviet Union, even if they have escaped the attention of most Western commentators.[12]

The doubts and uncertainties of Finland's position are however masked by the dominant personality of Urho Kekkonen, five times Prime Minister between 1950 and 1956 and President of Finland from 1956, whose 'thinking about relations with the Soviet Union has become Finland's foreign policy'.[13] Kekkonen's conversion to the necessity of peaceful and friendly relations with the Soviet Union dates back to the Continuation War of 1941-4. He was closely associated with Paasikivi in the implementation of this new policy, which as President he has developed into something rather different. Paasikivi's *Realpolitik* was essentially cautious and conservative, coloured by the atmosphere of the Cold War and the restrictions placed on Finland by the victors. Paasikivi took little interest in changing Finnish society, or the attitudes of his fellow-countrymen towards the Soviet Union, other than by harsh warnings and exhortations. By contrast, Kekkonen was quick to sense that social change and the political liberation of the working class after 1944 could forge the basis for a new approach to Finland's position in the world. In a pamphlet published in September 1944, he argued the necessity of radical political and social changes, which corresponded with the demands of a new age and national interests in the changed post-war circumstances. For Paasikivi, the necessity of coming to terms with a powerful neighbour was dictated by history. Kekkonen too has drawn on the lessons of history, but he has seen the virtues of a more positive, 'bridge-building' approach towards not only the Soviet Union, but the rest of the world. Hence his declaration in 1960 that Finland could not be neutral in questions of war and peace, and his belief that neutrality cannot be an end in itself.

During Kekkonen's presidency, Finland has played an increasingly active part in the international community, whether sending troops as part of the United Nations peace-keeping force in the Suez Canal Zone or acting as host for the S.A.L.T. talks and the Helsinki Security Conference. The keynote of Kekkonen's policy is mutual trust. His personal role is of paramount importance. But his close personal relationships with world leaders, particularly those of the Soviet Union, have aroused criticism and fears that Finnish policy is being jeopardised in case a sudden and unforeseen change at the top should occur; and his more outspoken pronouncements have frequently provoked hostile replies, as in the case of his proposals for a Nordic nuclear-free zone. On the other hand, there can be little doubt that the present official foreign policy is wholeheartedly supported by the great majority of Finnish people. What was reluctantly accepted as a harsh necessity in the late 1940s has now become, in the words of a leading Finnish sociologist, the major integrating factor in Finnish society.[14]

The difference in the roles played by the Presidents of the Republic in foreign affairs before and after 1944 is particularly striking. The primary importance accorded to foreign policy in post-war Finnish politics has had a number of far-reaching consequences. The Paasikivi–Kekkonen line has become national policy, and has been accepted by all the major parties, who pushed through an enabling law in 1973 to allow the *Eduskunta* to prolong Kekkonen's period of office for four years, and who supported his candidature for a further six years of office in 1978. The desirability of continuity in foreign policy does, however, raise problems, not all of which are related to the personality and tactics of Urho Kekkonen. The President's role as guardian of national foreign policy may make it extremely difficult for the checks and balances provided for in the constitution to operate, since any attempt to challenge his authority might well be seen as an attempt to alter foreign policy. The President may also take advantage of this strong position to exceed the competence of his authority as specified in the constitution. In short, the primacy of foreign policy has led to what some observers see as an unwarrantable increase in President's power and authority. In 1974, socialist members of the constitutional revision committee appointed by the *Eduskunta* joined forces with right-wing members to present a majority proposal for the transfer of certain presidential powers in matters of foreign policy to the government and *Eduskunta*. This provoked a fierce reaction, and the Social Democratic Party quickly abandoned the idea, joining the other parties of the centre and left in reiterating their faith in the necessity of presidential control of foreign affairs.

What seems on the surface to be a willingness of all the major political parties to accept the Kekkonen line has led some commentators to suggest that acceptability in the eyes of Moscow is a prerequisite for entry into government. Ørvik has even suggested that, since Moscow can manipulate Finnish politics by compelling parties and individuals to acknowledge the necessity of good relations with the Soviet Union as a *sine qua non* for entry into government, there is correspondingly less need for a trustworthy President: in future, Moscow might even prefer to deal with a strong and friendly government than a personally unreliable President. In the meantime, however, Kekkonen fulfils a dual role as watchdog for Moscow: externally, and internally, making sure that the credibility of Finland in Soviet eyes is not endangered by 'unfriendly' press comments or political developments. To substantiate this argument, Ørvik cites a number of instances of official interference, such as the radio broadcast in 1971 by the then Foreign Minister, Väinö Leskinen (the most prominent individual to make a political conversion from an anti-Soviet attitude to full acceptance of the Kekkonen line), criticising the conservative newspaper *Uusi Suomi* for publishing an article which aroused Soviet ire. More recently, there have been a number of instances of self-censorship which substantiate the picture of Finlandisation although, as Laqueur remarks, Soviet complaints about Finnish transgressions continue 'almost without interruption'.[15] In 1960, Khrushchev declared that the Soviet Union, while naturally not wishing to interfere in the internal affairs of Finland, reserved the right to express criticism of those whom it considered hostile to good relations between the two countries. It is clear that the President, as head of state and the person responsible for the formation of governments, must also take heed of the necessity of maintaining good relations with Soviet Union; what is not clear is the extent to which Kekkonen has used the threat of Soviet displeasure to strengthen his own position, as in the run-up to the presidential election in 1961–2. Nor is it easy to determine precisely how much influence the Soviet Union has exercised in the past. What is certain is that while the Soviet Union has a variety of options which it can implement to ensure that a small state on its north-western borders remains within its sphere of influence, the options open to Finland are far fewer. It is for this reason that Finnish politicians have felt constrained to eschew controversy over foreign policy.

Nevertheless, although foreign policy has ceased to be a party political issue and has become a kind of symbol of national unity, there are nuances of interpretation and emphasis which often escape the foreign observer. In his study of party political attitudes on foreign policy during the years 1955–63, when the Kekkonen line was by no means accepted either by the parties or by the public at large, Dag Anckar has detected three categories of approach. Only the Finnish People's Democratic League fitted into the 'augmentative' category; in other words, it showed a willingness not only to accept friendly relations with the Soviet Union, but also to develop these relations. The Agrarians were in the second 'adaptive' category, showing a willingness to make friendly relations with the U.S.S.R. the basis of Finnish foreign policy. But the right-wing parties and the Social Democratic Party followed a 'limited' approach, placing more emphasis on the need to act independently and to pursue a 'national' policy. The Social Democrats under Tanner's leadership were particularly critical of Kekkonen's foreign policy and of his leadership generally, and were the moving force behind the candidature of Olavi Honka in the attempt to defeat Kekkonen in the 1962 presidential elections.

Even during the formation of the Honka front, a number of Social Democrats had voiced their dissent, and the centrist group around Fagerholm and Rafael Paasio (who succeeded Tanner as party chairman in 1963) began to sound out the way back to acceptability, as it became increasingly obvious that there could be no place in government for the party as long as it maintained its critical attitude towards official Finnish foreign policy as represented by Kekkonen. Kekkonen responded to conciliatory statements by Paasio and a younger party member, Pekka Kuusi, who declared in a speech in Turku in 1964 that if the party declared itself firmly behind the Kekkonen line, it would once more qualify for government; the electoral success of the Social Democratic Party in 1966 helped to bring the party back once more into government in a revival of the 'Big Three' governments of the immediate post-war years. Although doubts were expressed about the thoroughness of the conversion of the party, especially of some of Tanner's former henchmen, the party's left wing at least has now begun to enter Anckar's 'augmentative' category. The 'limited' approach is now taken only by the small splinter parties of the right, in which individual dissenters from the major parties have found a home. Although it is clear that there has been a significant shift of the parties towards unqualified acceptance of good relations with the Soviet Union, the right wing still lays emphasis on neutrality as the best safeguard for Finland, while the left wing looks for security in the development of trust between Finland and the Soviet Union, with the 1948 treaty as the ultimate safeguard. Hence the conservative candidate in the 1968 presidential campaign, while officially supporting the Kekkonen line, stressed the need to increase the defence budget—an indication of the right-wing belief that neutrality must be preserved even in the event of war. The left-wing socialist strategy of forging close ties with Eastern bloc countries and advocating the building of trust in the Soviet Union is in part motivated by the realisation that the Paasikivi–Kekkonen line is founded upon 'right-wing realism'; thus by virtue of acknowledging the necessity of close and friendly relations with the Soviet Union, the conservative Paasikivi and his Agrarian successor have succeeded in keeping Finland safe for capitalism —or put another way, Moscow is quite happy to allow Finland to remain in the capitalist world as long as her leaders take heed of Soviet security interests.[16] To what extent the left-wing parties can present themselves as a trustworthy and viable alternative to Kekkonen—and this is presumably the point of Ørvik's argument about the Soviet leadership preferring in future to put its faith in a strong and reliable government—will depend on the ability of the left to capture the majority of the popular vote in elections, and presumably on the implementation of constitutional revisions aimed at transfering power from the President to the government and *Eduskunta*. On the evidence of the past, neither seems very likely. The pole position is still held by President Urho Kekkonen, re-elected for a fifth term of office in January 1978 by 259 of the 300 members of the electoral college, elected on a popular poll of just over 69 per cent. Ørvik has commented: 'There is a sense of hubris which often overtakes men in key positions, namely that they are irreplaceable and must therefore occupy that position, as the situation requires those very properties which they alone possess. Such assumptions often end in tragedy. . . .' This may, in relation to Urho Kekkonen, seem excessively pessimistic, but there can be no denying the sense of uncertainty in Finland in the late 1970s about who or what is to succeed the man, born in 1900, who had become one of the world's longest-serving heads of state.[17]

Politics and society in the 1960s and 1970s

The collapse of the Fagerholm coalition government in January 1959 ushered in a seven-year period of minority Agrarian governments and majority centre-right coalitions, with a nine-month caretaker non-party government in 1964. Although President Kekkonen called on five separate occasions between 1957 and 1966 for the formation of a government of all parties to overcome the damaging effect upon the national economy of constantly changing ministries, the likelihood of his call being answered was extremely remote. In the first place, the gulf separating the National Coalition conservatives and the Communists was so wide as to make the idea of partnership in government between these two extremes 'utopian'.[18] Secondly, the Agrarians, as the standard-bearers of official Finnish foreign policy, had refused to enter into coalition with the Social Democrats as long as Tanner and his supporters remained in control of the party. The Social Democrats' gradual conversion to the Kekkonen line, and their electoral success in 1966, which made them the largest party in the *Eduskunta*, offered the possibility once more of coalition.

The moves begun in 1964 to reunite the trade union movement, which finally occurred in 1971, marked the beginnings of a *rapprochement* of the parties of the left. Within the People's Democratic League, dissatisfaction with the dominance of the old guard of Communist leaders resulted in the election of Ele Alenius, a non-Communist moderate, as general secretary in 1965 and as chairman two years later. The old guard was also replaced by trade unionist Communists in the leadership of the Communist Party in 1966. The declared willingness of the Communists to enter government, their new 'reformist' image and the urging of the trade unionists helped to forge the popular front government under the Social Democrat Rafael Paasio in May 1966. The popular front continued with one short break until 1971, when the Communists pulled out, partly over the question of association with the E.E.C., and partly because of the internal split within the party, but was revived, albeit with moderate success, in the mid-1970s.

The Agrarian Party continued to act as the pivot in the coalition-making system in Finland. In 1965, an extraordinary party conference voted to change the party name in an attempt to modernise the rural-agrarian image and to capture some of the growing urban vote. To date, the new Centre Party seems to have had far less success than its Swedish counterpart, which changed its name at the end of the 1950s. The party's share of the popular vote has fallen from 21 per cent in 1966 to around 16–17 per cent in the subsequent elections, and it has failed to make any substantial impact in the towns. In the late 1960s it had to face the challenge of the maverick Finnish Rural Party, led by the colourful and controversial Veikko Vennamo, which claimed to speak on behalf of the 'forgotten people'. In the 1970 elections, this party took 10 per cent of the popular vote, doing particularly well in those parts of eastern Finland with a high proportion of impoverished smallholder farmers. Although the Rural Party has since virtually disintegrated, riven by internal schism, and the Centre Party has managed to win back some of the votes lost in 1970, the continued problems of the impoverished peripheral regions and the rapid decline of the rural farming population poses a double dilemma for a party still rooted in the land and dependent on the rural vote, which is nevertheless anxious to break into the urban electorate. To this end the party has sought to present an attractive programme of social reforms, such as the payment of a mother's wage, cheaper housing, a better environment and a tougher regional policy designed to stem the drain of labour to the southern cities. Its overall strategy is to win over and possibly absorb the small Liberal People's Party and the Swedish People's Party, thereby further isolating the conservative National Coalition and strengthening its own claim to represent the centre of the political fulcrum.

The two major drawbacks to this strategy are, first, that the clash of policies in the economic sphere makes co-operation with the Social Democratic Party very difficult—and a left-wing group within the Centre Party has in fact pressed for coalition with the Communists in preference to the socialists—and secondly, that the National Coalition shows no sign of losing favour with the electorate, securing 18 per cent of the popular vote in the 1975 elections and thirty-five seats, as opposed to the thirty-nine seats of the Centre Party. The conservatives have made efforts in recent years to demonstrate their loyalty towards official foreign policy, but the occasional outbursts of some of the party's more intransigent right-wingers still tend to cast doubts upon the sincerity of the party's desire for good relations with Moscow. It is partly for this reason that the party's efforts to be considered worthy of a place in government in recent years have been frustrated. A coalition with the small People's parties is out of the question, as is a return to alliance it had in the 1950s with the Social Democrats. As Hakovirta suggests, the National Coalition seems destined to remain in opposition until the Centre Party tires of co-operation with the parties of the left. The party is still very much linked with big business, but its former dominance of the higher echelons of the civil service and the professions has been seriously eroded in the past decade or so, with the rise of a new generation with noticeable centre-left political affiliations.

At the other end of the political spectrum, the Finnish People's Democratic League has managed to retain the loyalties of one-fifth of the voters, in spite of setbacks in the elections of 1970 and 1972. The formation of a popular front government in 1966 was greeted with satisfaction by the Communist Party, but opposition soon began to mount towards that government's attempts to secure an incomes policy and its failure to implement a more socialist economic programme. The simmering crisis in the party came to a head in 1969, when the opposition walked out of the party conference and threatened to form a new party. A mediation committee managed to avoid formal rupture by distributing seats on the party's controlling bodies according to the relative strengths of the two wings. A precarious unity has been maintained ever since, although the party is virtually split between the pragmatic 'reformist' majority and the hard-line 'purist' minority. The minority draws much of its support from the industrial workers of the south and has a following also in the student body. A younger generation of hard-line Communists is well entrenched at local and central committee level, and it is unlikely that their 'opposition' will wither away very easily. At one level, the opposition has arisen in protest against the willingness of the party's pragmatic leadership to enter into government and thereby to abandon ideological principles; but the curious phenomenon of a divided Communist Party is certainly a good deal more complex and warrants further study.

The initial shift to a more pragmatic line in the mid-1960s began originally within the ranks of the non-Communists in the Finnish People's Democratic League, and was partly caused by growing dissatisfaction with the rigidity and isolation of the old guard leadership. The Soviet Union was prepared to tolerate this shift since the presence of Communists in government was a useful guarantee of the continuity of a friendly foreign policy and a model of left unity for the rest of Europe. It was not prepared to tolerate any condemnation of the invasion of Czechoslovakia, and the reformist Finnish Communist leadership soon retracted its initial condemnation. The opposition has sought to show its devoted loyalty to Moscow, although Moscow seems more concerned to preserve the unity of the party and has tried on a number of occasions to effect a reconciliation. On the other hand, the mysterious and hurried withdrawal of the Soviet ambassador in 1971, after complaints and rumours that he had been intriguing with the Communist opposition, and the continued attacks in the Soviet press on Alenius, the chairman of the People's Democratic League, suggest that Moscow is keeping its options open. In recent years, the Soviet Union has showed signs of discontinuing its line of support for the popular front experiment—which the opposition has already condemned as disastrous for the workers' interests. At a time of growing economic crisis for Finland, it may well be that the Soviet Union prefers to have a united Communist Party in watchful readiness rather than struggling with the hopeless task of steering the capitalist ship of state towards socialism.[19]

The formation of a centre-left government in 1966 occurred at a time of recession in Finland, with a corresponding fall in rates of production and a sharp decline of the foreign exchange reserves. Previous governments had been content to ride on the wave of economic growth stimulated by the devaluation of 1957 and the freeing of foreign markets through negotiated agreements, and had done little to curb inflation, or to tackle the trade deficit. The Paasio government attempted to overcome the crisis by reducing state expenditure and curbing consumer demand, but in the autumn of 1967 it was compelled to devalue the mark once again to restore the fortunes of the export industries. An export levy was also introduced as a means to accumulating an investment fund; the sluggishness of domestic investment in Finland

was and remains a hindrance to expansion. Devaluation further stimulated inflation, and in 1968 a new prices and incomes policy was accepted
by the government, unions and employers. This agreement, known by
the name of its architect, the national arbitrator Keijo Liinamaa, did
away with the principle of index-linked wage increases and substituted
that of productivity-linked increases, which would cover not only
wages but rents and agricultural food prices. The government was also
to ensure price controls until the end of 1969. A second similar agreement was made to cover 1970.

These agreements were concluded at a time of world economic
resurgence. Partly as a result of the 31 per cent devaluation of 1967,
Finland was able to promote a major export drive, not only in the
traditional wood-processing industries but also in the metal and
engineering industries which began to find new markets in Western
countries. The rapid growth in production on the one hand and tight
price controls on the other ensured a considerable rise in real earnings.
Nevertheless, in spite of the rapid expansion and diversification of the
national economy since 1950, many of its underlying structural
deficiencies remain unresolved. Attempts to remedy these deficiencies
have serious social and political repercussions. The Social Democrats'
policy in the late 1960s of favouring industrial expansion by a programme of tax reliefs and state investment was severely criticised
by the Centre Party and the left, who argued that the net result had
been a major shift of the tax burden from industry to the ordinary
taxpayer. On the other hand, the Centre Party compelled their social
democratic partners in government in 1974 to modify a proposal to
impose heavy export levies on the wood-processing industries in
order to create an investment fund to stimulate general industrial
growth by insisting on allowing these industries to channel profits into
their own investment fund. The Centre Party has also continued to
press for subsidies for agriculture, and advocates a strong regional
policy, neither of which is acceptable to the Social Democrats.

The transition from an agrarian to an industrial society which has
occurred in Finland over the past four decades has by no means been
easy. The country is still coping with the legacy of its rural-agrarian
past. Although the number of people actively engaged in farming and
forestry has steadily declined since the war—from 45 per cent of the
economically active population in 1950 to 20 per cent in 1970—the
figure is still very high by comparison with western European countries. In spite of the decline in the numbers of farms of less than 5
hectares and government measures designed to consolidate land-

holdings, the average size of the Finnish farm is still just a little above 10 hectares. Mechanisation and modern methods of husbandry and stockbreeding have advanced rapidly since the war, but the decline in labour input has been nearly matched by the rate of decline of the contribution of farming and forestry to the aggregate national output. Farming and forestry continue to provide employment for a greater proportion of people than can be justified by their contribution to the national economy. For a variety of social and political reasons, measures have been taken which have hindered efficacious structural changes in agriculture, such as the attempt between 1969 and 1974 to curb over-production by paying compensation to farmers who were willing to leave their fields untilled for a fixed period. This resulted in something like 9 per cent of the total arable land of the country being taken out of cultivation, but since farmers who sold their untilled land were liable to forfeit compensation, the measure did little to promote the consolidation of landholdings. The payment of special subsidies for social and economic reasons to farmers in remote areas has also hindered the overall process of agricultural rationalisation. Recent legislation such as the provision of pensions for aged farmers who agree to sell their land to the state for redistribution or to cede the entire holding to one of their heirs instead of dividing it may help speed up the diminution of the number of farms, especially as the proportion of persons over the age of fifty is considerably higher in agriculture than in any other sector of employment.

Although there has been considerable diversification in manufacturing industries in Finland since the war, the wood-processing industries still dominate the vital export trade. A slump in world market demand for pulp and paper therefore has serious repercussions across the whole spectrum of economic activity. Such was the case in the early seventies, with the consequent fall in the volume of exports and increased unemployment. The sharp increase in the imports bill caused by the rise in world prices of raw materials on which Finnish industry is dependent and the steep increase in oil prices led to a massive trade deficit and renewed inflation. In November 1975, to tackle the crisis, President Kekkonen appointed a government of national emergency of the centre-left. A programme of price controls, unemployment relief schemes, increased taxation and an import deposit scheme designed to curb imports was introduced, and the unions were persuaded to accept a 7 per cent threshold for wage increases. These measures, together with a slight improvement in the economic situation, reduced the trade deficit from the record 8,000 million marks of 1975 to around 4,000 million marks a year later. The annual inflation rate also fell from 18 per cent in 1975 to around 11 per cent in 1976 and there was a slight fall in the numbers of unemployed. The continuing recession and the collapse of the government in September 1976 after disagreement among its members over general economic policy did not however hold out any immediate prospect of a return to better times for the country.

Finland's commitment to economic growth has in the past three decades resulted in remarkable advances in the living standards of its people; but it has also created a new range of problems. The social consequences of this transformation will be examined later, but here a number of economic aspects may be pointed out.

Industrial expansion in Finland has been hampered by, among other things, the sluggish rate of domestic investment, the shortage of skilled manpower, in some instances by uncompetitive prices, and by the vulnerability of the national economy to fluctuations in world markets. Efforts to remedy these deficiencies have not always been successful. The state has financed a number of new enterprises, such as the Pekema petrochemical firm and the iron and steel complex at Raahe, and has sought through investment funds and other measures to redirect the flow of investment. This, as we have seen, has frequently been opposed by powerful interests which have close ties with political parties. Attempts have been made to overcome the shortage of skilled labour by vocational training schemes and by seeking to induce the return of skilled workers who have migrated to Sweden, but the chronic shortage of dwellings in the urban areas, less attractive wages than can be earned in Sweden, and currently, the high unemployment rate in Finnish industry have tended to work against such efforts.

The loss of potential labour through emigration is a serious blow to Finland. It is thought that something like 300,000 Finns have emigrated to Sweden since the war. In 1970 alone, net emigration was around 42,000, and although by 1973 there were signs that the level of return migration exceeded that of emigration, the latter had once more risen by 1975, although the recession had also reduced job opportunities in Sweden. Furthermore, many of those who emigrate are skilled or semi-skilled workers seeking higher wages and better prospects. In normal times, therefore, Finland has a shortage of skilled labour, but in the peripheral regions and in certain occupations there is persistent under-employment.

In his widely influential blueprint for social planning in the 1960s in Finland, the Social Democrat Pekka Kuusi characterised the problem of how to find ancillary earnings for the smallholder population in Finland as 'virtually the pivot of Finnish manpower policy'.[20] Having pointed out that the risk of unemployment in the rural north was something like twenty times greater than in the Helsinki area, Kuusi went on to criticise the 'northern orientation' of employment and agricultural policies, which were diametrically opposed to the requirements of economic growth. The Employment Act of 1956 had merely hampered social mobility by providing for unemployment relief through public works, which had become a kind of fall-back for the local population. Kuusi advocated a national unemployment insurance scheme, which would transfer the onus of providing for those out of work from the local authority to the state, would end short-term public relief works, and guarantee security for the smallholder. The key to Kuusi's plan was rapid economic growth: to this end, he advocated the creation of some 50,000 new jobs each year in the secondary and tertiary sectors, with an annual rate of growth in production *per capita* of 3·5–4 per cent. This was to be the foundation whereby an increase of 3·5 per cent in the ratio of the social income transfer to the national income could take place during the decade.

The economic growth of the 1960s—with a total increase of 243,000 workers in commerce and services and 82,000 in manufacturing industry, an annual average growth rate of industrial production of about 2 per cent more in volume terms than the growth rate of total production, and a tripling in the gross value of industrial production—laid the foundation for a considerable programme of social legislation, even though Finland still lags behind the other Nordic countries in terms of the proportion of social services expenditure to the net national income.

To maintain and develop her system of social security and standards of living, Finland is dependent on foreign trade, which constitutes over a quarter of her gross national product. Nearly three-quarters of Finland's foreign trade is with the O.E.C.D. countries, and over one-third is with members of the E.E.C. The ratification of a free-trade treaty with the E.E.C. in 1973 was therefore of paramount importance to Finland's export industries, but it also had political implications. During the 1960s, Finland's trade with the Soviet Union steadily declined in proportion, despite the safeguards built into the 1961 Finn/EFTA treaty. It was therefore considered expedient to enter into an agreement with Comecon, followed by individual agreements on tariffs with Eastern bloc countries, modelled on the agreement made with the E.E.C. Bilateral trading agreements with the Communist countries have brought benefits to Finland. The use of the clearing system precludes any balance of payments crises at the cost of flexibility. The Soviet Union agreed to accept a greater volume of Finnish products to offset the increased cost of oil (of which Finland imports 75 per cent from the Soviet Union), and by means of a number of agreements on technical, scientific and economic co-operation has helped to relieve unemployment and stimulate production. On the other hand, political as well as commercial reasons have probably influenced certain decisions of the Finnish government, such as the dropping of a British offer to build a nuclear power station at Loviisa in favour of a contract with the Soviet Union—which made an initial tender that was less competitive than the tenders of the Western countries. It has also been suggested that Finland's heavy dependence on the Soviet Union for her energy supplies may prove crucial in the event of a political crisis in Europe, although, given Finland's geographical location, it is hard to see what immediate alternative she has, other than to exploit her own limited energy resources.

On balance, it would seem that Finland's trade with the Comecon countries (of whom the Soviet Union is by far the biggest customer, with around 17 per cent of the total volume of Finnish trade) offers trading stability by virtue of the bilateral agreements, employment in labour-intensive industries which produce the bulk of Finnish exports to the Communist world (i.e. engineering, textile and furniture industries), and the possibility of mutually advantageous economic co-operation whereby the Finnish labour market reaps the benefits of projects (e.g. the construction of a mining complex at Kostamus, which has provided employment for many Finns in the economically impoverished Kainuu district). Not least, also, it relieves the Finns of the necessity to increase still further their imports from the Western countries. At a time of record trade deficits, this is no mean advantage. Moreover, there are limits to the expansion of trade between Finland and her eastern neighbour. The volume of its trade with Finland is relatively insignificant for the Soviet Union, which is also a major world producer of pulp, paper and sawn timber, and is therefore highly unlikely to import these commodities in any quantity from Finland. As long as the wood processing industries continue to dominate the Finnish economic scene, Finland will remain at the mercy of fluctuations in demand in the Western world, and must therefore regulate her economy accordingly. This is a point well made by Maude in reference to the obligations placed upon the Finnish government in 1975 by the I.M.F., which granted a loan of 735 million marks to help tide Finland over a balance of payments crisis. Finland is very tightly bound to the Western economic system, something which the pundits of Finlandisation often forget.[21]

Two Finlands?

Of the 4·6 million inhabitants of Finland in 1970, more than half live in the four southern provinces of the country. The province of Uusimaa, in which the capital is situated, has experienced a spectacular increase in population since the war. One Finn in five now lives in this province, as against one in ten at the turn of the century. The population of Helsinki has more than quintupled in seventy years, and there has been a rapid development of commuter suburbs since the war: the western suburb of Espoo, given urban status in 1963, is now the fourth largest town in the country in terms of population.

In the remaining provinces, which cover four-fifths of the total land area, the population has steadily declined since the 1960s as a result of migration to the south or to Sweden. There is thus a distinct contrast between a dynamic urban and industrialised society in the south and a dying rural, agrarian society, in what has been characterised by the geographer Ilmari Hustich as 'marginal' Finland.[22] This distinction is not a new one: the vicious circle of poverty, too many children, ignorance and isolation of the smallholder in the remoter areas of eastern Finland was brilliantly portrayed by the novelists Lehtonen and Kianto in the early years of Finnish independence. But the plight of Ryysyrannan Jooseppi and his descendants is now highlighted by the rapid advances towards the affluent society and the welfare state. Jooseppi may no longer have to fight off the cockroaches and eat birch-bark bread, but his standard of living still lags far behind that of his more affluent brothers in the southern cities. Mechanisation has robbed him of work in the forests; the best he can hope for is a state pension in return for surrendering his small farm for redistribution (assuming that Jooseppi had been sufficiently fortunate to acquire land of his own in the intervening period), and a state-financed holiday for his hard-worked wife.[23] His poverty is now relieved by the state, but his children leave home to find work in the cities. As a result, local authorities in 'marginal' Finland are more and more hard pressed to provide adequate services for a shrinking and ageing population, which has been led to expect such services. It is often difficult to attract qualified professional staff to such remote areas. The *per capita* cost of maintaining social services in these areas is tremendous and could not be supported but for large capital grants from the central government. Inevitably, there is a lack of facilities, particularly in vocational and higher education, which means that those seeking higher qualifications are trained elsewhere and usually find jobs outside the area. The quality of life suffers in other respects, as rural bus services are curtailed, shops go out of business and youth and sports clubs close for lack of support. The extension of the road network and electricity grid system into rural areas since the war has in a way tolled the death-knell of the old rural way of life. The city and the countryside have been brought closer together through the medium of television, the telephone and the motor-car; but it has been an unequal relationship, and the thousands of summer-cottagers who return to the land every year are no compensation for the sons and daughters who leave for the cities and Sweden, never to return.

Urbanisation in Finland is costly. The old wooden dwellings with their wood-burning stoves, kerosene lamps and earth closets have been replaced by high-rise brick and concrete flats, heated from a large centrally-sited oil-burning plant. Because of the climate, construction costs in Finland are extremely high. The 'bill for winter' paid by Finland is, as Hustich remarks, greater than the costs borne by some states as a result of earthquakes or other natural disasters—and it is moreover an annual bill. The establishment of a government housing production committee (*Arava*) after the war has done a great deal to reduce over-crowding and increase the production of dwellings, although Finland still has a higher habitation density than its Scandinavian neighbours. This is particularly true in the remote rural areas. Over 40 per cent of the dwellings in the provinces of Lapland and North Karelia in 1960 had more than two persons per room, while the corresponding percentage in the southern provinces was only 17 per cent. The proportion of dwellings with bathroom, hot running water, W.C. and central heating was markedly higher in the towns than in country districts.

The contrast between 'marginal' and 'industrial' Finland can be illustrated in a number of other ways. A. S. Härö's study of mortality rates in northern Europe (1966) revealed that not only was the mortality rate for middle-aged and old men twice as high in Finland as in other Nordic countries, but that within Finland itself, adult mortality rates were appreciably higher in eastern Finland. Later studies have reinforced Härö's suggestion that a reluctance to seek treatment was a major cause of premature death in rural areas in the years before the introduction of a compulsory health insurance scheme in the mid-1960s, although the high incidence of premature deaths among middle-aged men in eastern Finland is still a subject of intense research. The declining proportion of the 'average family' budget spent on necessities and the growing expenditure on leisure activities and luxury goods conceals the growing gap between the affluent consumer society of the south and those whose low level of earnings, lack of job opportunities and large families cause real deprivation. Those who live in the remote and isolated settlements of Lapland, Kainuu and eastern Finland 'are economically and in regard to their large families in relatively the same situation as the poor peoples of the underdeveloped countries of the world, with their ever-growing and unplanned families.'[24] A newspaper report on a sharp rise in the number of suicides in the commune of Kittilä in Lapland (February 1978) indicated that 25 per cent of the workforce was unemployed, more than 1,000 others were receiving old age or disability pensions, and 1,000 of the total registered population of 7,600 were working in Sweden. Even in times of 'full' employment (unemployment in the first quarter of 1978 in Finland was almost 7 per cent), there are not enough jobs for all in such places. Not surprisingly, suicide rates are higher and the flow of emigration is greater than elsewhere. Fundamentalist religious movements and 'protest' political parties also find ready recruits and regular support.

The gulf between centre and periphery already evident in the early phases of industrialisation still exists and threatens to grow greater as the flight from the land accelerates. In other respects however the divisions and cleavages of Finnish society have undergone considerable change. The language question is no longer a serious political issue, although the absolute decline in the number of people speaking Swedish as a first language—from 348,286 in 1950 to 303,406 (6·6 per cent of the population) in 1970—has raised doubts about the future of Finnish-Swedish culture. The replacement of Swedish by English as the first foreign language in Finnish-language schools is perhaps symptomatic of the declining influence of the Finnish-Swedish élite, who were still able to exercise considerable political pressure to protect their cultural interests up to the war.

Economic growth has meant the demise of the small entrepreneur. The number of industrial firms employing fewer than ten workers fell from 45 per cent of the total in 1957 to 28 per cent in 1969, a process considerably accelerated by the continuing recession of the 1970s, in which a record number of bankruptcies occurred. By the end of the 1960s, 60 per cent of the industrial workforce were employed by 100 major concerns, responsible for four-fifths of all industrial investment and controlling 90 per cent of the export market.

Economic growth has also seen the rapid development of the service industries, which now provide employment for nearly half the economically active population (especially working women). This means of course that there is now a sizeable middle class of urban white-collar workers whose attitudes, background and aspirations are very different from those of the much smaller urban middle class of fifty years ago. In the first place, the range of jobs available to the white-collar worker is far greater. Social and cultural background is far less important than it was at the turn of the century, when the Swedish-speaking élite still dominated the upper echelons of the public service, commerce and industry. The distinctions which formerly marked off the middle class from the workers are also much less evident. Many skilled workers earn far more than office-workers, clerks and typists—more even than clergymen and schoolteachers. Many office jobs are as undemanding and alienating as any production-line job in a factory.

The education explosion of recent years, which has produced an enormous increase in the number of highly-qualified job seekers, has not been met by a concomitant expansion in the job market; with the result that frustration has built up and has led to a marked increase in trade union activity among the professional and salaried classes. It also partly explains the radical agitation for university reform in the late 1960s. The number of students enrolled in institutions of higher education rose from 23,552 in 1960-1 to 58,615 ten years later, giving Finland the highest ratio of students to the overall population in western Europe. Not unnaturally, this placed a severe strain upon the antiquated and inadequate administrative structure of these institutions, especially the University of Helsinki, where nearly half the students were enrolled. The clash over university reform was also very much a conflict between political and cultural values. In the 1960s, for the first time in the history of independent Finland, significant numbers of university students began to take up left-wing and Marxist ideas. The first signs of this change had occurred at the end of the 1950s, when the student newspaper *Ylioppilaslehti* took on a more radical tone under its socialist editor Arvo Salo. In 1967 the traditional *osakunnat* or 'nations' suffered losses to openly political organisations in student elections, and demands for root-and-branch reform became the order of the day. The highpoint came in 1968, with the student occupation of the Old Student House in Helsinki, which forced President Kekkonen and his audience to celebrate the centenary of the University of Helsinki student union elsewhere.

Fresh winds were blowing in other quarters. Under the direction of the 'cultural liberal' Eino Repo, the Finnish broadcasting corporation delighted some but incensed many more with provocative and controversial programmes which challenged a number of conservative and nationalist shibboleths. The Finnish theatre discovered Brecht, and the film industry, as the film critic of the *Sunday Times* in London observed, discovered sex. Poets and novelists turned their attention to the problems and seamier side of modern Finnish society, which in one famous instance led to a conviction on a charge of blasphemy. Historians began a fundamental reassessment of their country's immediate past, and were joined in this task by President Kekkonen, as always the barometer of change. There was considerable public discussion of a number of social issues, such as the neglect of Finland's gypsies and Lapps, and a plethora of new pressure groups sprang up.

The last two decades have in fact witnessed considerable and far-reaching changes in Finnish society, and this has led some commentators to speak of a post-war 'second republic'. In the view of three close supporters of the so-called 'K-line':

The first republic was built upon the principles of classical liberalism. The role of the state in regard to the welfare of the nation as a whole was passive and aimless . . .
The second republic was based on a train of thought peculiar to the K-line. This entailed shifting the emphasis from the individual to the community in political terms. This shift came to have decisive importance in the conduct both of foreign and domestic policy.[25]

It might, however, be argued that a similar change occurred in most of the Western democracies after the Second World War. A more plausible argument is advanced by the Swede Krister Wahlbäck, who sees not only a fundamental change in foreign policy since the war, but also a change in the balance of power on the internal political front, with the legalisation of the Communist Party. The Finnish labour movement, after three decades of virtual political and economic impotence, now occupies a central position on the domestic stage. The parties of the left, though divided, take half the popular vote in national elections. The trade unions play a leading role not only in industrial relations, but in the planning of social and economic policy. Left-wingers now occupy important positions in the institutions of their country—although Communists are still carefully excluded from the higher echelons of the army and security forces. This has also taken place, *mutatis mutandis*, in the Western democracies. It is thus rather difficult to see how the redressing of the political balance after 1944 and the increasingly active role of the state can be taken to mark an entirely new phase in the history of the Finnish republic.

The nationalist 'peasant' republic was destroyed in the defeat of 1944 and the rapid industrialisation and urbanisation of the last three decades has ensured that it will not rise again. The political ideals of inter-war Finnish nationalism are irrelevant in the world of nuclear weapons, supersonic travel, superpowers and the export drive. Finland has changed as the world has changed. Her economy is highly vulnerable to fluctuations in world markets. Her citizens strive for the same material benefits of the affluent society as are enjoyed in other advanced countries. Her politicians must take heed of world events and seek to implement official Finnish foreign policy in the light of developments.

But in one very important respect Finland has not changed, and indeed cannot change. For a nation of less than 5 million people, isolated not only physically and linguistically but also placed in a permanent dilemma by the need to live in harmony with a powerful neighbour, the question of national identity is vitally important. The history of modern Finland is essentially moulded around this very issue. What do the Finns themselves think about the future of their country?

A survey carried out in 1977 revealed that an overwhelming majority regarded Finland as a safe country to live in, though a clear majority also felt that the general world situation had deteriorated in the 1970s. A series of opinion surveys carried out between 1964 and 1974 revealed, among other things, that over three-quarters of those polled believed that Finland stood a good chance of remaining independent over the coming half-century, with the younger respondents markedly more optimistic than those over fifty. The great majority (90 per cent in 1964, 96 per cent in 1971, though only 85 per cent in 1974) believed Finland's foreign policy had been well conducted in recent years; two-thirds believed Finland should resist aggression in any circumstances, and one in five believed that Finland should offer armed resistance even if threatened with a nuclear attack. Though few denied the existence of differences between various interests and sections of the community, a sizeable number felt that these differences were diminishing. A majority of the respondents felt a strong sense of identification with family (82 per cent), language (70 per cent) and nation (64 per cent); only 22 per cent felt a strong sense of identification with a political party. When asked which values or things were worth defending if Finland should be attacked, the respondents' clear favourite was national independence and the right to self-determination.[26]

The picture presented by these surveys is one of the high degree of national unanimity (*yksimielisyys*) on the need to defend Finland's independence, on the value of the 1948 treaty with the Soviet Union, and on the efficacy of official foreign policy. This may be interpreted as evidence of powerful persuasion from the highest levels, which has convinced the Finnish people that the Kekkonen line is the right and only one; but it may also be seen as a genuine recognition of the benefits as well as the necessity of Finland's relationship with the Soviet Union. In terms of national identity, however, *yksimielisyys* over an issue as vital as foreign policy is very important.

However, there is a price to pay, which outside observers are quick to see and Finns are reluctant to recognise. First, the necessity of a fixed doctrine or idea which will serve to rally and integrate the nation tends to discourage heterodoxy. The flowering of the thousand flowers during the cultural breakthrough of the 1960s was short-lived. Today the old high priests of Finnish peasant nationalism have been replaced by the new presbyters of the Kekkonen orthodoxy. Those who dissent are on the fringe—a few lone wolves of the New Left (which found Finnish soil somewhat infertile), right-wing political mavericks such as Tuure Junnila and Georg Ehrnrooth, and the 'forgotten people' who make up the discontented supporters of right-wing and fundamentalist Christian parties. Secondly, the doctrine needs disciples. The young man of burning ideals before the war joined the Academic Karelia Society in order to further the cause of Greater Finland. The young man of today who has ambitions will find a party card a distinct advantage, as long as the party supports the K-line.

Yksimielisyys also leads to self-censorship. It is obvious that heedless provocation of the Soviet Union through hostile statements, press articles and films is likely to endanger good relations, and as such is undesirable. But the real danger of self-censorship, as Carl-Gustaf Lilius has pointed out, is that it is a way of hiding from reality, of trying to forget that the Soviet Union exists. Although the firm and friendly relations between Finland and the Soviet Union have been praised countless times by the top politicians and cemented with countless agreements, there is still very little knowlelge of the Soviet Union and its people within Finland itself, in spite of the growth of tourism, the number of scientific and technical exchanges, and the increase in Russian language tuition in the schools—where the vast majority of pupils choose English as their first foreign language. The point Lilius is making is that unless self-censorship is replaced by mutual frankness, sincerity and candour, in conformity with the terms of Basket Three of the European Security Conference, it will in the long run lead to the under-mining of self-respect; 'and when a country begins to lose its self-respect, it runs the risk of undermining its right to exist.'[27]

The sixtieth anniversary of Finnish independence provoked a number of Finns to ask how much the Finnish people's view of themselves and their identity had altered. Their answers probably reflected the then current gloom caused by a lengthy economic recession, but they did reveal certain anxieties. The chairman of the Education Council, for example, maintained that his countrymen tended to belittle all national achievements outside the field of sport. Opening the 1978 session of the Eduskunta on 2 February, President Kekkonen reiterated that national integration had been the central goal of his entire political career, and warned of the dangers of discord on the issue of economic powers which might be granted to the government, and which might become a source of controversy, dividing the nation in two. The fear of such division in a nation which began its independent existence with a bitter civil war is a powerful force, but it does have a tendency to weaken genuine debate and dissension.

The future of Finland, beset by economic problems and a growing political impasse, did not seem as rosy in 1978 as it had done when the fiftieth anniversary of independence was celebrated. In a lengthy discussion on the eve of the sixtieth anniversary, President Kekkonen regretted the seeming loss of identity of his fellow-countrymen. Whereas the older generation had found an identity in the image of the heroic and hardy Finnish peasant as portrayed by the nineteenth-century poet J. L. Runeberg, this image was no longer valid for the younger generation. This theme was taken up by Väinö Linna, the one man who through his novels has done more than any other Finn to change his fellow-countrymen's attitudes and image of the past, and it is perhaps fitting that Linna's words should end this survey:

I would start by saying that we cannot think of the future identity of the [Finnish] youth in the same terms as we used to think of it before the war—and even then there was no all-embracing image, since society was divided into many sub-groups, and each group had fragments of an identity which differed from the others. Now however it might be said that internationalism will of necessity be part of the Finnish identity in the future; it can no longer be introspective as it was earlier. And maybe the spirit of the European Security Conference is one positive feature in the creation of this identity.

Where then will [the Finn] find his own national identity. I have no real doubts but that the ordinary man will find it in the concrete circumstances of the life which he lives, since we are surely tied to this earth and our environment in our everyday lives. And we will still feel ourselves to be Finns even though we have become internationally conscious. But it is very hard to define those values which are related to identity, because the workings of this society are such that this identity and its values are constantly being broken up. . . .

One difference there must be with regard to the old Finnish identity. The old Finnish identity contained a lot of aggressive elements, and there was a great deal of aggressiveness in its values, which were almost always directed against something. But now the world situation makes it absolutely essential that the negative elements are humanist and humanitarian. And this in turn means that a greater degree of equality must be achieved in society in order to bring about greater peace, so that crises and conflicts diminish and we can then share a greater degree of common values than now or previously. It may be said that these are pious hopes, but it is only on this basis that a common sense of identity can be found.[28]

GOVERNMENTS IN FINLAND 1917–1978

(a) Heads of state

1. P. E. Svinhufvud, 'possessor of supreme authority', 18 May 1918–12 Dec. 1918
2. C. G. E. Mannerheim, Regent, 12 Dec. 1918–25 July 1919
3. K. J. Ståhlberg, President of the Republic, 25 July 1919–1 Mar. 1925
4. L. K. Relander, President of the Republic, 1 Mar. 1925–1 Mar. 1931
5. P. E. Svinhufvud, President of the Republic, 1 Mar. 1931–1 Mar. 1937
6. K. Kallio, President of the Republic, 1 Mar. 1937–19 Dec. 1940
7. R. Ryti, President of the Republic, 19 Dec. 1940–1 Aug. 1944
8. C. G. E. Mannerheim, President of the Republic, 4 Aug. 1944–4 Mar. 1946
9. J. K. Paasikivi, President of the Republic, 11 Mar. 1946–1 Mar. 1956
10. U. K. Kekkonen, President of the Republic since 1 Mar. 1956

(b) Governments and their composition

Key to parties

IKL—People's Patriotic Movement (1932–1944)
Cons.—*Kansallinen Kokoomus* (1918–) (Conservative)
Swed.—Swedish People's Party (1906–)
Prog.—National Progressive Party (1918–1951)
Finn.—Finnish People's Party (1951–1965)
Lib.—Liberal People's Party (1965–)
Agr.—Agrarian Union (1906–1965)
Centre—Centre Party (1965–)
Soc.—Social Democratic Party (1899–)
Comm.—Finnish People's Democratic Union (1944–) (Communist)

Prime Minister	*Composition of government*	*Duration*
1. P. E. Svinhufvud	Old Finn, Young Finn, Swed., Agr.	Nov. 1917–May 1918
2. J. K. Paasikivi	Old Finn, Young Finn, Swed., Agr.	May 1918–Nov. 1918
3. L. Ingman	Cons., Prog., Swed.	Nov. 1918–Apr. 1919
4. K. Castrén	Prog., Swed., Agr.	Apr. 1919–Aug. 1919
5. J. H. Vennola	Prog. Agr.,	Aug. 1919–Mar. 1920
6. R. Erich	Cons., Prog., Swed., Agr.	Mar. 1920–Apr. 1921
7. J. H. Vennola	Prog., Agr.	Apr. 1921–June 1922
8. A. K. Cajander	Non-party	June 1922–Nov. 1922
9. K. Kallio	Agr., Prog.	Nov. 1922–Jan. 1924
10. A. K. Cajander	Non-party	Jan. 1924–May 1924
11. L. Ingman	Cons., Prog., Swed., Agr.	May 1924–Mar. 1925
12. A. Tulenheimo	Cons., Prog., Agr.	Mar. 1925–Dec. 1925
13. K. Kallio	Agr., Cons.	Dec. 1925–Dec. 1926
14. V. Tanner	Soc.	Dec. 1926–Dec. 1927
15. J. E. Sunila	Agr.	Dec. 1927–Dec. 1928
16. O. Mantere	Prog., Cons.	Dec. 1928–Aug. 1929
17. K. Kallio	Agr., Prog.	Aug. 1929–Jul. 1930
18. P. E. Svinhufvud	Cons., Prog., Swed., Agr.	Jul. 1930–Mar. 1931
19. J. E. Sunila	Agr., Cons., Prog., Swed.	Mar. 1931–Dec. 1932
20. T. M. Kivimäki	Prog., Cons., Swed., Agr.	Dec. 1932–Oct. 1936
21. K. Kallio	Agr., Cons., Prog.	Oct. 1936–Mar. 1937
22. A. K. Cajander	Progr., Agr., Soc.	Mar. 1937–Dec. 1939
23. R. Ryti	Prog., Agr., Swed., Soc.	Dec. 1939–Mar. 1940
24. R. Ryti	Prog., Cons., Swed., Agr., Soc.	Mar. 1940–Jan. 1941
25. J. W. Rangell	Prog., Cons., Swed., Agr., Soc., IKL	Jan. 1941–Mar. 1943
26. E. Linkomies	Cons., Prog., Swed., Agr., Soc.	Mar. 1943–Aug. 1944
27. A. Hackzell	Cons., Prog., Swed., Agr., Soc.	Aug. 1944–Sept. 1944

Prime Minister	*Composition of government*	*Duration*
28. U. J. Castrén	Cons., Prog., Swed., Agr., Soc.	Sept. 1944–Nov. 1944
29. J. K. Paasikivi	Cons., Prog., Swed., Agr., Soc., Comm.	Nov. 1944–Apr. 1945
30. J. K. Paasikivi	Cons., Prog., Swed., Agr., Soc., Comm.	Apr. 1945–Mar. 1946
31. M. Pekkala	Comm., Swed., Agr., Soc.	Mar. 1946–July 1948
32. K.-A. Fagerholm	Soc.	Jul. 1948–Mar. 1950
33. U. K. Kekkonen	Agr., Prog., Swed.	Mar. 1950–Jan. 1951
34. U. K. Kekkonen	Agr., Finn., Swed., Soc.	Jan. 1951–Sep. 1951
35. U. K. Kekkonen	Agr., Finn., Swed., Soc.	Sep. 1951–Jul. 1953
36. U. K. Kekkonen	Agr., Swed.	Jul. 1953–Nov. 1953
37. S. Tuomioja	Non-party	Nov. 1953–May 1954
38. R. Törngren	Swed., Agr., Soc.	May 1954–Oct. 1954
39. U. K. Kekkonen	Agr., Soc.	Oct. 1954–Mar. 1956
40. K.-A. Fagerholm	Soc., Finn., Swed., Agr.	Mar. 1956–May 1957
41. V. J. Sukselainen	Agr., Finn., Swed.	May 1957–Jul. 1957
	Agr., Finn.	Jul. 1957–Sep. 1957
	Agr., Finn., Soc. opposition	Sep. 1957–Nov. 1957
42. R. von Fieandt	Non-party	Nov. 1957–Apr. 1958
43. R. Kuuskoski	Non-party	Apr. 1958–Aug. 1958
44. K.-A. Fagerholm	Soc., Cons., Finn., Swed., Agr.	Aug. 1958–Jan. 1959
45. V. J. Sukselainen	Agr.	Jan. 1959–Jul. 1961
46. M. Miettunen	Agr.	Jul. 1961–Apr. 1962
47. A. Karjalainen	Agr., Cons., Finn., Swed.	Apr. 1962–Dec. 1963
48. R. Lehto	Non-party	Dec. 1963–Sep. 1964
49. J. Virolainen	Agr., Cons., Finn., Swed.	Sep. 1964–May 1966
50. R. Paasio	Soc., Centre, Comm., Soc. opposition	May 1966–Mar. 1968
51. M. Koivisto	Soc., Centre, Swed., Comm., Soc. opp.	Mar. 1968–May 1970
52. T. Aura	Non-party	May 1970–Jul. 1970

Prime Minister	Composition of government	Duration
53. A. Karjalainen	Centre, Lib., Swed., Soc., Comm.	Jul. 1970–Oct. 1971
54. T. Aura	Non-party	Oct. 1971–Feb. 1972
55. R. Paasio	Soc.	Feb. 1972–Sep. 1972
56. K. Sorsa	Soc., Lib., Swed., Centre	Sep. 1972–Jun. 1975
57. K. Liinamaa	Non-party	Jun. 1975–Nov. 1975
58. M. Miettunen	Centre, Lib., Swed., Soc., Comm.	Nov. 1975–Sep. 1976
59. M. Miettunen	Centre, Lib., Swed.	Sep. 1976–May 1977
60. K. Sorsa	Soc., Centre, Lib., Swed., Comm.	May 1977–

THE PATTERN OF FINNISH GOVERNMENT 1917–1978

1. The Presidency

The 1919 Finnish constitution decrees that the President of the Republic shall be elected every six years. Three hundred electors are first elected by the people to constitute the electoral college, which meets a month after the elections, on 15 February, to choose a President. This procedure has been followed eight times. In 1940 and 1943, presidential elections were carried out by the electoral college chosen in 1937. In 1919, 1944, 1946 and 1974 the elections were carried out by the *Eduskunta*, after the necessary legislation had been enacted. The election has been decided by the first ballot in the electoral college (ignoring the 'unanimity' voting for Ryti in 1940 and 1943) on four occasions: 1950, 1962, 1968 and 1978. In 1931 and 1956, the outcome was decided on the third ballot by the narrowest possible margin (1931: Svinhufvud 151: Ståhlberg 149. 1956: Kekkonen 151: Fagerholm 149). Finland has never elected a socialist President, though the parties of the left have supported Urho Kekkonen's candidature since 1968.

2. Government

The President appoints and dismisses governments, which must however enjoy the confidence of the *Eduskunta*. The government, or State Council (*Valtioneuvosto*) consists of a Prime Minister and not more than fifteen other ministers. There have been sixty governments in the sixty years of Finnish independence; the longest period of office was that of T. M. Kivimäki's minority Progressive-Agrarian ministry (1932–6), which was however supported by the other two non-socialist parties. A substantial number of politicians have, however, served for long periods in a variety of ministerial capacities: such men provide the core of experience and a degree of continuity in government.

The pattern of government in Finland can conveniently be divided into seven periods. The presidencies of K. J. Ståhlberg and L. K. Relander (1919–31) were distinguished by a series of short-lived minority coalitions of the centre, or centre-right. The National Progressive Party played a leading role in government, although its parliamentary base dwindled from twenty-six seats in 1919 to seven ten years later. The 'crisis' of weak minority governments was brought to an end with the formation of Svinhufvud's centre-right majority coalition in July 1930, and the parties of the centre and right dominated the political scene during Svinhufvud's presidency (1931–7). The electoral gains made by the Social Democratic Party in 1936 marked the beginning of a revival of the left. Svinhufvud refused to admit the party into government, but his defeat in the 1937 presidential elections inaugurated a period of centre-left co-operation (the 'Red Earth' coalition) which lasted until the war, when the need for an all-party government was realised.

The fourth period saw Communist participation in government for the first time in Finnish history (1944–8). The Communist-led Finnish People's Democratic League withdrew into opposition in July 1948, and remained out of government for the next eighteen years. The period 1948–58 was dominated by Urho Kekkonen, who formed five ministries before his election as President in 1956. The always uneasy collaboration in government between Agrarians and Social Democrats ended with the collapse of the Fagerholm majority government in January 1959; the Social Democrats then remained outside government for the next seven years, as a result of their 'untrustworthiness' in foreign affairs. The intervening period of non-socialist government (1959–66) witnessed the return to government of the National Coalition conservatives, who, apart from the brief episode of the Fagerholm government in 1958–9, had been out of office since the war. The main burden of government was, however, borne by the Agrarian-Centre Party.

The re-emergence of the Social Democratic Party as the largest party in the 1966 elections marked the return of the 'popular front' centre-left coalition, headed first by Rafael Paasio and from 1968 by Mauno Koivisto, both Social Democrats. The popular front pattern of government has continued, with interruptions, ever since. The Communists, after a three-year period in opposition, were prevailed upon by President Kekkonen to join Martti Miettunen's government of national emergency in the autumn of 1975, and after a brief interlude of centrist minority government in 1976–7, the popular front was restored under the premiership of Kalevi Sorsa, a Social Democrat.

(On the structure and functions of government in Finland, see chapter 7 in J. Nousiainen, *The Finnish political system*, Cambridge, Mass., 1971.)

ELECTIONS IN FINLAND 1907–1975

The Finnish parliament (*Eduskunta*) has 200 members, returned by direct, proportional (d'Hondt system) and secret election by all citizens over the age of eighteen. Elections are conducted by electoral districts, which at present number fifteen. The division of seats among these districts is made by the State Council before each election on the basis of the population census. The Åland islands, which also have their own local assembly, or *Landsting*, return one member. Since 1954, the statutory term for an elected *Eduskunta* has been four years, although the President can order premature elections, as in 1972 and 1975.

Analysis of the regional basis of party support shows that:

1. The three parties traditionally to the right of centre (National Coalition, Swedish People's Party and the present Liberal People's Party) take a higher share of the vote in the south-western corner of the country than in eastern and northern Finland.

2. The Centre Party, formerly the Agrarian Party, is much stronger in its traditional eastern and northern strongholds than in the south, and has so far failed to capture more than 8 per cent of the total urban vote. In the 1975 elections, two-thirds of its popular vote came from the seven electoral districts of northern and eastern Finland.

3. The Social Democratic Party polls well in all four provinces of 'industrial' Finland, but is particularly strong in the traditional 'red' areas of Häme province. The party is weakest in northern Savo, Ostrobothnia and the north.

4. The Communist vote is proportionately greatest in northern Savo and northern Finland, although there is a fairly equal division of votes between the parties of the left in Turku-Pori province in southern Finland.

5. The Finnish Rural Party, a 'protest' party which enjoyed the support of 10 per cent of the Finnish electorate in the 1970 elections, drew its main support from eastern and northern Finland, but it also performed surprisingly well in the Cities. In Helsinki, for example, it

secured double the number of votes cast for the Centre Party in 1970 and 1972.

Parliamentary elections in Finland fall into three distinct periods. The voter turnout since 1945 has been considerably higher than during the inter-war period or the first decade of parliamentary elections. The period 1907–17 was characterised by the steady increases in the socialist vote, culminating in the winning of an absolute parliamentary majority of 103 seats with 47·3 per cent of a low poll in 1916. The party lost its majority in the 1917 elections, which marked the first real breakthrough for the Agrarian Party, whose share of the poll exceeded 20 per cent in the inter-war years, making it the largest non-socialist party. The Social Democratic Party, in spite of the competition of the Communist 'front' parties in the 1920s, remained by far the largest single party, although, apart from a brief period of minority government in 1926–7, it was to remain in opposition until 1937. The combined vote of the left-wing parties (including the dissident Social Democrats of the Workers' and Smallholders' Socialist League from 1958 to 1972) in the post-war era has always been above 40 per cent, reaching a peak of 51 per cent in 1966. However, with the notable exception of the sharp decline in the popular vote of the Social Democratic Party in 1958–62 when the Finnish People's Democratic League emerged as the senior left-wing party, the profile of support for the parties in postwar elections is very even, showing the slow decline of the vote for the Progressive Party (Finnish People's Party 1951–65; Liberal People's Party 1965–) and the Swedish People's Party, with the Centre Party falling below a 20 per cent share of the poll for the first time since independence in 1970, an election in which the Communist vote also fell heavily. The conservative vote has remained buoyant, in spite of the exclusion of the National Coalition from government. Of the three major parties in the popular front governments which have existed since 1966, the Social Democratic Party seems to have held its own best, although all three have suffered a loss of popularity with the electorate since the 1966 elections.

EDUSKUNTA SEATS BY PARTY 1907–1975[1]

Election Year	Conservative	Liberal	Swedish	Centre	Social Democrat	Communist	Others
1907	59	26	24	9	80		2
1908	54	27	25	9	83		2
1909	48	29	25	13	84		1
1910	42	28	26	17	86		1
1911	43	28	26	16	86		1
1913	38	29	25	18	90		—
1916	33	23	21	19	103		1
1917	32	24	21	26	92		5
1919	28	26	22	42	80		2
1922	35	15	25	45	53	27	—
1924	38	17	23	44	60	18	—
1927	34	10	24	52	60	20	—
1929	28	7	23	60	59	23	—
1930	42	11	20	59	66	—	2
1933	18	11	21	53	78	—	19[2]
1936	20	7	21	53	83	—	16[2]
1939	25	6	18	56	85	—	10[2]
1945	28	9	14	49	50	49	1
1948	33	5	14	56	54	38	—
1951	28	10	15	51	53	43	—
1954	24	13	13	53	54	43	—
1958	29	8	14	48	48	50	3[3]
1962	32	13	14	53	38	47	3[3]
1966	26	9	12	49	55	41	8[3]
1970	37	8	12	36	52	36	19[4]
1972	34	7	10	35	55	37	22[4]
1975	34	8	10	41	54	40	13[5]

NOTES
1. For changes in party names, see above.
2. People's Patriotic Movement (Fascist): 1933, 14; 1936, 14; 1939, 8.
3. Workers' and Smallholders' League (socialist opposition) 1958, 3; 1962, 2; 1966, 7.
4. Rural Party (right-wing 'protest' party): 1970, 18; 1972, 18; 1975, 2.
5. Christian League (right-wing 'protest' party): 1972, 4; 1976, 9.

THE NATIONAL ECONOMY

1. THE POPULATION OF FINLAND, 1900–1970

Year	Total population	Urban areas No.	%	Rural areas No.	%
1900	2,655,900	333,300	12·5	2,322,600	87·5
1910	2,943,400	432,200	14·7	2,511,200	85·3
1920	3,147,600	507,400	16·1	2,640,200	83·9
1930	3,462,700	715,000	20·6	2,747,700	79·4
1940	3,695,600	991,700	26·8	2,703,900	73·2
1950	4,029,800	1,302,400	32·3	2,727,400	67·7
1960	4,446,200	1,707,000	38·4	2,739,200	61·6
1970	4,598,300	2,340,300	50·9	2,258,000	49·1

2. THE ECONOMICALLY ACTIVE POPULATION OF FINLAND BY OCCUPATION 1950–1970

Occupation	1950 No.	%	1960 No.	%	1970 No.	%
Agriculture and forestry	909,332	45·8	720,817	35·5	428,999	20·3
Industry	413,553	20·8	439,282	21·6	549,506	25·9
Construction	125,384	6·3	176,157	8·7	176,786	8·3
Commerce	187,483	9·5	276,400	13·6	399,853	18·9
Transport and communications	106,785	5·4	128,844	6·3	150,190	7·1
Services	213,392	10·8	285,539	14·0	383,906	18·1
Unknown	28,353	1·4	6,299	0·3	29,017	1·4
Total	1,984,282	100·0	2,033,268	100·0	2,118,257	100·0

Source: Suomen tilastollinen vuosikirja—Statistical yearbook of Finland 1972, Helsinki 1973, tables 8 and 16.

3. DISTRIBUTION OF POPULATION ACCORDING TO OCCUPATION IN THE NORDIC COUNTRIES 1910–1970 (%)

(D=Denmark; S=Sweden; N=Norway; F=Finland)

Year	Agriculture, forestry				Manufacturing				Other sectors			
	D	S	N	F	D	S	N	F	D	S	N	F
1910	36	49	39	80	28	32	25	12	36	19	36	8
1930	30	39	36	71	29	36	27	16	41	25	37	13
1950	24	20	26	47	35	41	37	28	41	39	47	25
1970	11	8	11	20	37	40	38	34	52	52	51	46

Note: The figures for Norway, Finland, Denmark for 1970, and those for Sweden for 1950–70 refer to the actively employed population; otherwise the total population referred to.

Source: C. Cipolla (ed.), *The Fontana Economic History of Europe*, Contemporary Economies, Part 2, London 1976, p. 384.

4. GROSS DOMESTIC PRODUCT AT FACTOR COST 1954–76

Industry	1954 Mill. marks	%	1964 Mill. marks	%	1976 Mill. marks	%
Agriculture and forestry	1,902	23·9	3,913	18·6	10,997	11·0
Mining and Industry	2,202	27·7	5,595	26·5	31,509	31·0
Construction	791	9·9	1,960	9·3	9,233	9·0
Public utilities	199	2·5	594	2·8	10,849	11·0
Transport and communications	534	6·7	1,533	7·2		
Commerce, banking, insurance	968	12·2	2,734	12·9	13,585	14·0
Ownership of dwellings	324	4·1	1,446	6·8	3,639	4·0
Public administration and defence	284	3·6	843	4·0	5,264	5·0
Services	747	9·4	2,522	11·9	15,581	15·0
G.D.P.	7,951	100·0	21,140	100·0	101,017	100·0

Sources: Kansallis-Osake-Pankki, *Economic Review*, 1971 : 4, Helsinki 1971, table 2; *Bank of Finland Monthly Bulletin*, March 1978, p. 19.

5. INDUSTRIAL PRODUCTION 1931–1969
GROSS VALUE OF PRODUCTION

Branch	Million marks			% of total industrial production			Output growth (Total= 100) 1913 1938		Exports as % of production	
	1913	1938	1969	1913	1938	1969	-38	-69	1962	1969
Timber	171	3,476	1,764	25	16	6	66	35	66	65
Paper	101	4,955	5,227	15	23	17	159	73	66	66
Metallurgical	84	3,627	7,256	12	17	24	140	138	20	27
Textiles	94	2,248	1,280	14	11	4	77	39	5	22
Foodstuffs	135	3,614	6,772	20	17	22	87	129	2	2
Chemical	—	—	1,430	—	—	5		190	8	15
Other	97	3,172	6,947	14	15	23	106	180	—	—
Total	683	21,092	30,676	100	100	100	100	100	—	—

Sources: P. Virrankoski, *Suomen taloushistoria*, Helsinki 1975, pp. 155, 205, 251: Kansallis-Osake-Pankki, *Economic Review*, 1971 : 3, Helsinki 1971, p. 102.

6. FOREIGN TRADE

(a) *Principal exports 1909–1972* (in terms of value, % of total)

Commodity	1909–13	1923–5	1935–7	1956–8	1970–2
Farm produce	15	9	7	4	3
Uncut timber	10	9	7	8	1
Timber (boards, deals, etc.)	44	49	36	23	16
Pulp and paper	18	28	40	46	37
Textiles	3	—	2	—	—
Metallurgical	2	1	3	14	25
Other industrial commodities	—	—	4	4	16
Others	8	5	2	—	2

Source: P. Virrankoski, *Suomen taloushistoria*, Helsinki 1975, pp. 212, 267.

(b) Principal trading partners, 1936–1977

(i) Value of imports at current prices, averaged annually, and principal importers

Period	Average annual value (1,000 marks)	% of total trade	U.K.	Germany*	Sweden	U.S.S.R.
1936–40	82,039	53·5	18·3	20·2	15·7	1·5
1941–5	101,104	62·1	2·2	55·9	18·3	4·1
1946–50	586,078	51·7	22·3	1·9	6·2	11·4
1951–5	1,577,215	49·2	19·1	9·2	5·1	14·3
1956–60	2,544,776	51·0	17·1	15·9	8·1	16·4
1961–5	4,313,671	52·8	15·2	19·0	12·5	15·3
1966–70	7,521,187	51·8	15·7	16·4	15·9	14·8
1977	30,712,000	49·8	9·0	15·3	16·0	19·3

The header for the "Principal importing countries / Share of total imports, %" spans U.K., Germany*, Sweden, U.S.S.R.

(ii) Value of exports at current prices, averaged annually, and principal export markets

Period	Average annual value (1,000 marks)	% of total trade	U.K.	Germany*	Sweden	U.S.S.R.
1936–40	71,171	46·5	40·0	16·9	5·7	0·5
1941–5	61,169	37·9	7·0	51·3	7·7	6·2
1946–50	543,736	48·3	26·7	2·7	5·1	12·7
1951–5	1,626,290	50·8	24·9	8·0	2·9	17·5
1956–60	2,444,203	49·8	22·8	10·4	3·5	17·1
1961–65	3,856,615	47·2	21·5	11·8	6·3	14·8
1966–60	6,990,758	48·2	19·6	10·2	11·8	14·6
1977	30,945,000	50·2	12·1	10·5	16·5	9·0₁

The header for the "Principal export countries / Share of total exports, %" spans U.K., Germany*, Sweden, U.S.S.R.

*From 1950, the German Federal Republic

Sources: Suomen tilastollinen vuosikiria 1972, pp. 135, 165; and Bank of Finland Monthly Report, Match 1978, p. 11.

THE TREATY OF FRIENDSHIP, CO-OPERATION AND MUTUAL ASSISTANCE BETWEEN THE REPUBLIC OF FINLAND AND THE UNION OF SOVIET SOCIALIST REPUBLICS*

The President of the Republic of Finland and the Presidium of the Supreme Soviet of the U.S.S.R.; desiring further to develop friendly relations between the Republic of Finland and the U.S.S.R;

Being convinced that the strengthening of good neighbourly relations and co-operation between the Republic of Finland and the U.S.S.R. lies in the interest of both countries;

Considering Finland's desire to remain outside the conflicting interests of the Great Powers; and expressing their firm endeavour to collaborate towards the maintenance of international peace and security in accordance with the aims and principles of the United Nations Organisation;

Have for this purpose agreed to conclude the present treaty and have appointed as their plenipotentiaries:

The President of the Republic of Finland: Mauno Pekkala, Prime Minister of the Republic of Finland; the Presidium of the Supreme Soviet of the U.S.S.R.: Vyacheslav Mikhailovich Molotov, Vice-Chairman of the Council of Ministers of the U.S.S.R., and Minister for Foreign Affairs,

who, after exchange of their full powers, found in good and due form, have agreed on the following provisions:

ARTICLE 1

In the eventuality of Finland, or the Soviet Union through Finnish territory, becoming the object of an armed attack by Germany or any stated allied with the latter, Finland will, true to its obligations as an independent state, fight to repel the attack. Finland will in such cases use all of its available forces for defending its territorial integrity by land, sea and air, and will do so within the frontiers of Finland in accordance with obligations defined in the present treaty and, if necessary, with the assistance of, or jointly with, the Soviet Union.

In the cases aforementioned the Soviet Union will give Finland the help required, the giving of which will be subject to mutual agreement between the Contracting Parties.

ARTICLE 2

The High Contracting Parties shall confer with each other if it is established that the threat of an armed attack as described in Article 1 is present.

ARTICLE 3

The High Contracting Parties give assurance of their intention loyally to participate in all measures towards the maintenance of international peace and security in conformity with the aims and principles of the United Nations Organisation.

ARTICLE 4

The High Contracting Parties confirm their pledge, given under Article 3 of the Peace Treaty signed in Paris on 10 February 1947, not to conclude any alliance or join any coalition directed against the other High Contracting Party.

ARTICLE 5

The High Contracting Parties give assurance of the decision to act in a spirit of co-operation and friendship towards the further economic development and consolidation of economic and cultural relations between Finland and the Soviet Union.

ARTICLE 6

The High Contracting Parties pledge themselves to observe the principle of the mutual respect of sovereignty and integrity and that of non-interference in the internal affairs of the other state.

ARTICLE 7

The execution of the present treaty shall take place in accordance with the principles of the United Nations Organisation.

ARTICLE 8

The present treaty shall be ratified and remain in force ten years after the date of its coming into force. The treaty shall come into force upon the exchange of the instruments of ratification, the exchange taking place in the shortest possible time in Helsinki.

Provided neither of the High Contracting Parties has denounced it one year before the expiration of the said ten-year period, the treaty shall remain in force for subsequent five-year periods until either High Contracting Party one year before the expiration of such five-year periods in writing notifies its intention of terminating the validity of the treaty.

In witness hereof the Plenipotentiaries have signed the present treaty and affixed their seals.

Done in the City of Moscow on the sixth day of April 1948 in two copies, in the Finnish and the Russian languages, both texts being authentic.

NOTES

Chapter 1. THE BACKGROUND: FINLAND IN 1900

1. Cited in W. Mead and H. Smeds, *Winter in Finland*, London 1967, pp. 15–16. This useful book also contains a survey of impressions of the Finnish winter by foreign visitors.
2. Figures from *Foreign Office Handbook No. 98: Finland*, London 1919, p. 88.
3. Linna's superb trilogy, which spans the period from the 1880s to the early 1950s, has unfortunately not been translated into English. There is a brief survey of Linna's works by Y. Varpio in *Books from Finland*, vol. 11, no. 3, 1977, pp. 192–7.
4. R. Forsman, *Mistä syystä sosialismi levisi Suoman maalaisväestön keskuuteen?*, Helsinki 1912, p. 33.
5. M. Engman, 'Migration from Finland to Russia during the nineteenth century', *Scandinavian Journal of History*, vol. 3, no. 2, 1978, p. 164.
6. D. Kirby, ed., *Finland and Russia 1808–1920: From autonomy to independence. A selection of documents*, London 1975, p. 25. The Emperor goes on to to enumerate six of the privileges he has granted his new subjects.
7. M. Klinge, *Bernadotten ja Leninin välissä*, Helsinki 1975, p. 12. Much of my subsequent argument rests heavily upon this excellent collection of essays, and on O. Jussila's *Suomen perustuslait 1808–1863*, Helsinki 1969 (English summary: 'Finnish fundamental laws as interpreted by Russia and Finland 1808–1963').
8. *Herratko ne vaan turhia hätäilevät?*, Kajaani, 1899.
9. C. St.-Julien, *Impressions et souvenirs de Finlande*, St. Petersburg 1834, p. 5.
10. Mrs. Alec Tweedie, *Through Finland in Carts*, London 1897.
11. The phrase 'embryonic state' was used by a Finnish official in a graphic portrayal of increasing Russian suspicion of Finland's special status in the 1880s. Kirby, op. cit., pp. 70–1.

Chapter 2. OPPRESSION AND RESISTANCE: THE LAST YEARS OF AUTHORITY

1. For the functions of the Senate, see Kirby, *Finland and Russia 1808–1920*, pp. 16–18, and pp. 28–33, 71–4, 124–5 for extracts from the debate on Finland's status.

2. J. Gripenberg to Y. Yrjö-Koskinen in 1889, cited in Kirby, op cit., p. 71. On citizenship in Finland and Russia, see O. Jussila, 'Från ryska undersåtare till finska medborgare—om medborgarskapsbegreppets utveckling under första hälften av 1800-talet', *Historisk Tidskrift för Finland*, no. 1, 1978, pp. 5–20, and M. Engman, 'Borgare och skenborgare i Finland och Ryssland under första hälften av 1800-talet', *Historisk Tidskrift för Finland*, no. 2, 1978, pp. 189–207.

3. T. Torvinen, J. R. *Danielson-Kalmari Suomen autonomian puolustajana*, Helsinki 1965, and R. Schweitzer, *Autonomie und Autokratie. Die Stellung des Grossfürstentums Finnland im russischen Reich in der zweiten Hälfte des 19. Jahrhunderts (1863–1899)*, Giessen 1978, deal extensively with the question of Finland's status in the empire. See also J. R. Danielson, *Finland's union with the Russian Empire*, Borgå 1891 and L. Mechelin, *A precis of the public law of Finland*, London 1889.

4. Bobrikov's 1898 programme in Kirby, op. cit., pp. 77–8. See also A. Pogorelskin, 'The politics of frustration: the Governor-Generalship of N. I. Bobrikov in Finland, 1898–1904'. *Journal of Baltic Studies*, vol. 7, no. 3, 1976, pp. 231–46.

5. A *Kagal* is an assembly of Jewish elders; the epithet was adopted by the passive resistance.

6. For documents illustrating the course of the strike see Kirby, op. cit., pp. 104–117.

7. V. Pohlebkin, *Suomi vihollisena ja ystävänä 1714–1967*, Porvoo-Helsinki 1969, pp. 153–8.

8. Kirby, op. cit., pp. 83–90, 102–3, has selections of documents relating to the passive resistance campaign, and pp. 93–5, 132–4 offers examples of Zilliacus' writings.

9. Letter from A. Rissanen, 10 May 1907, in the Halonen papers, Finnish Labour Archives (*Työväenarkisto*) Helsinki.

10. Quoted in E. Kuusi, *Talvityöttömyys*, Tampere 1914, p. 4.

11. J. Lehtonen, *Sorron lapset*, Helsinki, 1962 edn, pp. 35–7. The two novels were originally published in the early 1920s.

Chapter 3. A HARD-WON INDEPENDENCE

1. Kirby, *Finland and Russia 1808–1920*, pp. 161–7.

2. Letter from Yrjö Sirola to Karl Wiik, 8 September 1918, in the Finnish Labour Archives (*Työväenarkisto*), Helsinki. See also D. Kirby, 'Stockholm —Petrograd—Berlin: International social democracy and Finnish independence 1917', *Slavonic and East European Review*, January 1974, pp. 63–84.

3. Kirby, *Finland and Russia 1808–1920*, pp. 175–8, gives a translation of the law, and selected Russian and Finnish opinions.

4. J. Hannula, *Finland's war of independence*, London 1939, offers a comprehensive survey of the events of the war. It should be noted that the White

Guards were an amalgam of vigilante groups and units (*Suojeluskunnat*) set up to fight for Finnish independence in the summer and autumn of 1917.

5. V. Rasila, 'The Finnish civil war and landlease problems', *Scandinavian Economic History Review*, 1, 1969, pp. 134–5. L. Puntila, 'Vapaussota— kapina—kansalaissota', in *Neljän vuosikymmenen takaa*, Porvoo-Helsinki 1958, pp. 19–20.

6. The quotations are from the Senate's proclamation to the Finnish people of 28 January 1918, printed in Kirby, op. cit., pp. 225–6. On the socialists' misgivings about making revolution, see J. Hodgson, *Communism in Finland. A history and an interpretation*, Princeton 1967, pp. 58–9, and Karl Wilk's diary for 1917–18, relevant extracts of which are published in H. Soikkanen (ed.), *Kansalaissota dokumentteina*, vol. 2, Helsinki 1969, pp. 27–32.

7. M. Jääskeläinen, *Die ostkarelische Frage*, Helsinki 1965, pp. 112–13. V. Kholodkovsky, *Finlyandiya i Sovetskaya Rossiya 1918–1920*, Moscow 1975, p. 46, mistakenly seems to suggest that the new draft treaty emanated from the German side, and was an aspect of the 'double game' Germany was playing with Finland and Soviet Russia.

8. C. Enckell, *Politiska minnen*, Vol. 1, Helsingfors 1956, p. 389.

9. On German economic penetration of the Baltic area, see J. Hiden, 'German policy towards the Baltic states of Estonia and Latvia, 1920– 1926', unpublished Ph.D. thesis, London University, 1970.

10. Quoted in K. Hovi, *Cordon sanitaire or barrière de l'est? The emergence of the new French eastern European alliance policy 1917–1919*, Turku 1975, p. 162, n. 101.

11. The Karelian Workers' Commune became an autonomous republic in 1923, and was to develop into a centre of Red Finnish nationalism: as such it was suppressed by Stalin in the 1930s. See Hodgson, op. cit., and S. Churchill, *Itä-Karjalan kohtalo*, Porvoo-Helsinki 1970.

Chapter 4. THE FIRST DECADE OF INDEPENDENCE 1918–1928

1. The figures are given in H. Soikkanen, *Kohti kansanvaltaa*, vol. 1: 1899–1937, Helsinki 1975, pp. 301–2.

2. Matti Kurjensaari's essays, 'Tie Helsinkiin' and 'Musta lippu' in his *Taistelu huomispäivästä*, Helsinki 1948, give good impressionistic pictures of student life and politics in the nineteen-twenties. On the student membership of the A.K.S., see R. Alapuro, *Akateeminen Karjala-Seura*, Porvoo-Helsinki 1973, pp. 58–87.

3. The quote is taken from P. Virkkunen, *Itsenäisen Suomen alkuvuosikymmeniltä*, Helsinki 1954, pp. 223–4, cited in M. Rintala, 'Generational conflict in the Finnish army', paper presented to the Finnish Research Seminar, London 16 October 1969, p. 21.

4. J. Nurmi, 'Sosiaalidemokraattien tie hallitukseen 1920-luvulla', *Historial-linen Aikakauskirja* 2/1974, pp. 139–50. See also L. Haataja, S. Hentilä *et al.* (eds), *Suomen työväenliikkeen historia*, Helsinki-Joensuu 1977, pp. 105ff.

5. *SKP puoluekokousten, konferenssien ja keskuskomitean plenuumien päätöksiä. Ensimmäinen kokoelma*, Leningrad 1935, p. 36.

6. E. Jutikkala, 'Torppariksymys' in E. Jutikkala (ed.), *Suomen talous—ja sosiaalihistorian kehityslinjoja*, Porvoo-Helsinki 1968, p. 203.

7. Kurjensaari, op. cit., p. 54.

8. O. Tudeer, *The Bank of Finland 1912–1936*, Helsinki 1940, p. 130.

9. Quoted in M. Klinge, *Vihan velijstä valtiososialismiin*, Porvoo-Helsinki 1972, p. 110.

10. A. Kuusinen, *Before and after Stalin*, London 1974, pp. 149–80.

11. Quoted in T. Helelä, *Työnseisaukset ja teolliset suhteet Suomessa vv. 1919–1939*, vol. 2 (Suomen Pankin taloustieteellinen tutkimuslaitos. Sarja D:21), Helsinki 1969, p. 212n.

Chapter 5. CRISIS AND RECOVERY 1929–1939

1. *Presidentin päiväkirja II. Lauri Kristian Relanderin muistiinpanot vuosilta 1928–1931*, ed. E. Jutikkala, Helsinki 1968, pp. 350–1.

2. On the alienation of the Italian nationalists, see S. Saladino's chapter on Italy in H. Rogger and E. Weber (eds.), *The European Right*, London 1965, pp. 208–60. See also M. Rintala's contribution on Finland in the same volume, pp. 408–42.

3. The political unrest of 1921–2 still awaits detailed investigation. Tuomo Silenti has recently suggested that Ritavuori's murder might have been part of a rightist conspiracy, but the evidence is circumstantial. T. Silenti, 'Toimiko ampuja yksin vai oliko hänen takanaan salaliitto kun Suomessa vuonna 1922 tehtiin ministerin murha', *Helsingin Sanomat*, 10 July 1977.

4. J. Hampden Jackson, *Finland*, London 1940 (revised edn.) p. 160.

5. Ibid., p. 185. The 1939 election results were (gain or loss since 1936 elections in parentheses): IKL 8 (−6): National Coalition 25 (+5): Swedish People's Party 18 (−3): National Progressives 6 (−1): Agrarians 56 (+3): Social Democrats 85 (+2): Others 2.

6. J. Nousiainen, *The Finnish political system*, Cambridge, Mass. 1971, p. 227. The most detailed and lucid account in English.

7. The term seems to have been first coined by the writer Matti Kurjensaari in his book *Taistelu huomispäivästä*, Helsinki 1948, p. 204. More recently, it has been used as a means of chronological, if not political division in a university textbook, V. Rasila, E. Jutikkala, K. Kulha (eds.), *Suomen poliittinen historia 1809–1975*, Vol. 2 (1905–1975), Porvoo-Helsinki 1977. This provoked some discussion in the Finnish press.

8. L. Haataja, S. Hentilä, J. Kalela, J. Turtola (eds.), *Suomen työväenliikkeen historia*, Helsinki-Joensuu 1977, p. 221.

9. Cited in R. Alapuro, *Akateeminen Karjala-Seura*, Porvoo-Helsinki 1973, p.52.

10. It is interesting to note that Ruutu, in his *Uusi suunta* (1920), used the term *keskisääty*, for which the German *Mittelstand* is the best translation. A leading Finnish sociologist, H. Waris, has remarked in his *Muuttuva suomalaisen yhteiskunta*, Porvoo-Helsinki 1968, that the aristocratic attitudes of the society of rank are still alive in present-day Finnish society (p. 41). See also U. Rauhala, *Suomalaisen yhteiskunnan kerrostuneisuus*, Helsinki 1966.

11. It is certainly not unusual, however: politicians are moulded by the world in which they grew to maturity, and not by that in which they live. The *laissez-faire* orthodoxy of all major Western governments in the 1920s is an excellent example. Alapuro, op. cit., goes into Tönnies' *Gemeinschaft* and *Gesellschaft* concepts with regard to Finnish society.

12. Quoted in P. Hemanus, *Reporadion nousu ja tuho*, Helsinki 1972, p. 34. The 'Kalevalan spirit' refers to the inspiration provided by the epic folkpoem, the *Kalevala*.

13. L. Jörberg, O. Krantz, 'Scandinavia 1914–1970' in C. Cipolla (ed.), *The Fontana Economic History of Europe*, vol. 6, pt. 2, London 1976, p. 386.

Chapter 6. FINLAND AND HER NEIGHBOURS 1920–1948

1. J. Paasivirta, 'Itsenäisen Suomen ulkopolitiikka suuntaa etsimässä' in I. Hakalehto (ed.), *Suomen ulkopolitiikan kehityslinjat 1809–1966*, Porvoo-Helsinki 1966, pp. 71–2. I. Seppinen, *Ulkopolitiikan puolustuspoliittiset tavoitteet. Tutkielma sotilaallisista näkökohdista Suomen ulkopolitiikassa 1919–1939*, Research Reports, Institute of Political History, University of Helsinki, no. 1, 1974, pp. 3–20.

2. See S. Zetterberg, *Suomi ja Viro 1917–1919*, HT 102, Helsinki 1977. O. Hovi and T. Joutsamo, 'Suomalaiset heimosoturit Viron vapaussodassa ja Itä-Karjalan heimosodissa vuosina 1918–1922', *Turun Historiallinen Arkisto*, Vol. 24, Turku 1971, analyses the motives of the Finnish volunteers.

3. K. Korhonen, *Naapurit vastoin tahtoaan. Suomi neuvostodiplomatiassa Tartosta talvisotaan. 1. 1920–1932*, Helsinki 1966, p. 130, for details of the Finnish conditions.

4. *Neutrality. The Finnish position. Speeches by Dr. Urho Kekkonen, President of Finland*, London 1970, p. 111. Seppinen, op. cit. pp. 81–2. J. Kalela, 'Näkökohtia pohjoismaisesta yhteistyösta Suomen ulkopolitiikassa maailmansotien välisenä aikana', *Historiallinen Aikakauskirja*, No. 3, 1971. M. Jakobson, *Finnish neutrality*, London 1968, p. 7.

5. K. Korhonen, *Turvallisuuden pettäessä. Suomi neuvostodiplomatiassa Tartosta talvisotaan. 2. 1933–1939*, Helsinki 1971, p. 136.

6. Korhonen, op. cit., p. 174. J. Suomi, *Talvisodan tausta. Neuvostoliitto Suomen ulkopolitiikassa 1937–1939. 1. Holstista Erkkoon*, Helsinki 1973, p. 204. According to Suomi, an industrial and commercial lobby in Finland was anxious to take up the Soviet offer of improved trade. Finnish trade with the U.S.S.R. in 1938 was minimal.

234

234 Notes

7. E. L. Woodward and R. Butler (eds.), *Documents of British Foreign Policy*, Third Series, vol. VI, London 1952, pp. 227–8. Details of the negotiations are to be found in E. L. Woodward, *British foreign policy in the second world war*, vol. 1, London 1970.

8. K. Wahlbäck, *Veljeys veitsenterällä*. *Suomen kysymys Ruotsin politiikassa 1937–1940*, Porvoo-Helsinki 1968, p. 241. On the Åland plan, see T. Munch-Petersen, 'Great Britain and the revision of the Åland convention 1938–1939', *Scandia*, No. 1, 1975, pp. 68–71.

9. Ling had spoken of between 20,000 and 22,000 men; Vereker spoke of between 12,000 and 13,000. M. Häikiö, *Maaliskuusta maaliskuuhun. Suomi Englannin politiikassa 1938–1940*, Porvoo-Helsinki 1976, pp. 147–52. J. Nevakivi, *The appeal that was never made*, London 1976, pp. 122–4.

10. E. Jutikkala, 'Ensimmäinen tasavalta (1919–1945)' in V. Rasila, E. Jutikkala, K. Kulha (eds.), *Suomen poliittinen historia 1809–1975*, 2. *1905–1975*. Porvoo-Helsinki 1976, p. 224. A. Upton, *Finland in crisis 1940–1941*, London 1964, pp. 37–8, 244ff. For the debate on Upton's book, see the contributions by Upton, O. Manninen and Jutikkala in the 1970 volumes of the periodical *Aika*.

11. Details in Upton, op. cit., pp. 86–132.

12. P. Talvela, *Sotilaan elämä. Muistelmat 1*, Helsinki 1976, p. 235.

13. The nickel question has been studied in H. Peter Krosby, *Finland, Germany and the Soviet Union 1940–1941: The Petsamo dispute*, Madison 1968

14. O. Manninen, 'Saksa tyrmää Ruotsin-Suomen unioniin', *Historiallinen Aikakauskirja*, No. 3, 1975, pp. 233ff; Upton, op. cit., pp. 190, 207–8; Krosby, op. cit., p. 125.

15. Krosby, op. cit., p. 170. For details of Operation Silver Fox, see Krosby, op. cit., pp. 123–4, and Upton, op. cit., pp. 209–10.

16. The term 'Continuation War' (*Jatkosota*) is the one in general use in Finland, though the wartime term 'war of compensation' does occasionally surface, e.g. in Jutikkala, op. cit., p. 225. Both terms imply that the Peace of Moscow was regarded merely as a truce in Finland. The wartime leadership and the opposition are dealt with more fully in the next chapter.

17. T. Polvinen, *Suomi suurvaltojen politiikassa 1941–1944*, Porvoo-Helsinki 1964, pp. 51ff. At a meeting of top-ranking officers at the Führer's headquarters on 16 July, Finland had been assigned East Karelia and the site of Leningrad in the future division of Russia, though not the Kola peninsula, which was to be reserved for German exploitation of its mineral wealth.

18. *Foreign Relations of the United States 1942*, Vol. 2, Washington 1962, pp. 82–3. The claim made by Edvin Linkomies, Prime Minister from March 1943 to August 1944, while on a visit to Hungary in the winter of 1943, that there could be no doubt of Finland's status as a great power would seem to be the most foolish public utterance made by any leading

Finn, though there is ample evidence of privately expressed *folies de grandeur*. General Talvela appears to have believed in a German victory well into 1943, for instance, and many others continued to hope for it.

19. For the terms, see *Foreign Relations of the United States 1943*, Vol. 3, Washington 1963, p. 256.

20. For example, the communiqué issued by the Social Democratic Party council on 19 February 1943, and the publication in the Swedish newspaper *Dagens Nyheter* on 29 August 1943 of an address to President Ryti by thirty-three leading 'peace opposition' activitists. Polvinen, op. cit., pp. 186–211.

21. Polvinen, op. cit., p. 248. V. Tanner, *Suomen tie rauhaan 1943–1944*, Helsinki 1952, pp. 165, 177–8.

22. Polvinen, op. cit., p. 271.

23. M. Djilas, *Conversations with Stalin*, Harmondsworth 1963, p. 120. P. Winterton, 'The aims of the U.S.S.R. in Europe', *International Affairs*, No. 1, 1946, p. 19.

24. *Foreign Relations of the United States 1945*, Vol. 4, Washington 1968, pp. 613–14. J. K. Paasikivi, *Paasikiven linja*. *Puheita vuosilta 1944–1956*, Porvoo-Helsinki 1966, pp. 50–1. The internal repercussions of the presence of the Allied Control Commission are dealt with in the next chapter.

Chapter 7. RECASTING THE MOULD 1940–1960

1. O. Paavolainen, *Synkkä yksinpuhelu*, Helsinki 1963 (paperback), pp. 183–4.

2. M. Favorin, J. Heinonen (eds), *Kotirintama 1941–1944*, Helsinki 1972, p. 15. Hitler's speech of 22 June 1941, in which he spoke of Finland standing '*im Bunde*' with Germany, further confused the issue. One Finnish national newspaper issued a supplement the same day, announcing that Finland had already entered the war. The issue was confiscated by the authorities.

3. Paavolainen, op. cit., p. 77. E. Salminen, *Propaganda rintamajoukoissa 1941–1944*, Helsinki 1976, pp. 79–9. There were 23,371 recorded cases of desertion or being absent without leave during the Continuation War (op. cit., p. 99).

4. L. Puntila, 'Valtasuhteet Suomessa toisen maailman sodan aikana', in T. Joutsamo, T. Perko (eds), *Suomi toisessa maailmansodassa*, Turku 1973, p. 5. Puntila himself played a leading role during the war as the private secretary to Prime Minister Rangell and subsequently in the information centre of the State Council.

5. C. Frietsch, *Finlands ödesår 1939–1943*, Helsingfors 1945, pp. 479–81. A. Paasonen, *Marsalkan tiedustelupäällikkönä ja hallituksen asiamiehenä*, Helsinki 1974, p. 136. Paasonen's own comment is: 'To tell the truth, the *Eduskunta* was not prepared to listen to such a realistic review.'

6. See the speech made in December 1943 in Stockholm by Kekkonen in *Neutrality. The Finnish position. Speeches by Dr Urho Kekkonen, President of*

Finland, London 1970, pp. 18–31. See also J. Nevakavi, 'Urho Kekkonen and postwar Finnish foreign policy' in *Yearbook of Finnish Foreign Policy 1975*, Helsinki 1976, pp. 6ff. Kekkonen was not one of the thirty-three signatories of the address urging Ryti to renew peace initiatives; instead, he preferred to voice his views in private to the President.

7. V. Tanner, *Suomen tie rauhaan 1943–1944*, Helsinki 1952, p. 400.

8. The eight accused were: Risto Ryti, President of Finland 1940–4; two wartime Prime Ministers, Jukka Rangell and Edvin Linkomies; two Finance Ministers, Väinö Tanner and Tykö Reinikka; a Foreign Minister, Henrik Ramsay; an Education Minister, Antti Kukkonen; and the Finnish minister in Berlin throughout the war, Toivo Kivimäki.

9. A. Wirtanen (ed.), *Salaiset keskustelut. Eduskunnen suljettujen istuntojen pöytäkirjat 1939–1944*. Lahti, 1967 p. 230.

10. J. K. Paasikivi, *Paasikven linja. Puheita vuosilta 1944–1956*, Porvoo–Helsinki 1966, p. 33.

11. V. Voionmaa, *Kuriiripostia 1941–1946*, Helsinki 1971, p. 406.

12. This view was voiced at the November 1944 party conference. The term 'comrade-in-arms socialist' originated in the wartime Finnish Comrades-in-Arms Union (*Suomen aseveljien liitto*), in which a number of right-wing socialists were involved.

13. J. K. Paasikivi, op. cit., p. 46.

14. J. O. Söderhjelm, *Tre resor till Moskva*, Helsingfors 1970, p. 110. Söderhjelm was one of the delegates sent to Moscow. For further discussion of the nature of the 1948 treaty, see the next chapter.

15. In 1948, the Soviet Union cancelled half of the remaining payments, or roughly one-quarter of the original sum. Ships, machinery and telecommunications equipment comprised some 72 per cent of the total value of reparations. In addition Finland had to transfer, under the Potsdam agreement, a sum equivalent to the aid given by Germany during the war. This was achieved by the transfer of territory on the frontier, the battleship *Väinämöinen* and state property in Tallinn and Leningrad. Finland also agreed to build a new Soviet embassy in Helsinki, and transferred 460 million marks in the form of foreign currency.

16. O. Apunen, *Paasikiven-Kekkosen linja*, Helsinki 1977, p. 148.

17. M. Kurjensaari, *Jäähyväiset 50-luvulle*, Helsinki 1960, pp. 149ff.

18. P. Hemanus, *Reporadion nousu ja tuho*, Helsinki 1972, p. 38.

Chapter 8. THE KEKKONEN ERA

1. For the full text of the treaty, see Appendix E. It was renewed for a further period of twenty years in 1955, and again in 1970. For a brief survey of some of the foreign-language literature on Finnish foreign policy, see *The Yearbook of Finnish Foreign Policy 1974*, Helsinki 1975, pp. 63–6.

2. A detailed account of these negotiations by one of the members of the Finnish delegation is J. Söderhjelm, *Tre resor till Moskva*, Helsingfors 1970, pp. 80–178. See also M. Jakobson, *Finnish neutrality*, London 1968, pp. 35–41.

3. *Neutrality: the Finnish position.* Speeches by Dr Urho Kekkonen, President of Finland, London 1970, p. 176.

4. Jakobsen, op. cit., p. 79. J. Komissarov, *Suomi löytää linjansa*, Helsinki 1973, pp. 143–56.

5. G. Maude, *The Finnish dilemma. Neutrality in the shadow of power*, London 1976, pp. 70–7. For the text of Kekkonen's 1952 and 1965 speeches, see *Neutrality: the Finnish position*, pp. 53–6 and 180–90. On Finland and the Nordic balance, see the chapters by Wahlbäck, Pajunen and Brundtland in *Urho Kekkonen: A statesman for peace*, London 1975, pp. 68–119; O. Apunen, 'A Nordic nuclear-free zone—the old proposal or a new one?' *Yearbook of Finnish Foreign Policy 1974*, Helsinki 1975, pp. 42–9; J. Blomberg, 'The security policy of the northern sea-areas from the Finnish point of view'; and P. Väyrynen, 'Economic cooperation in the North Cap areas', in *Yearbook of Finnish Foreign Policy 1976*, Helsinki 1977, pp. 4–9.

6. On Finland and the Nordic Council, see J. Vloyantes, *Silk glove hegemony. Finnish-Soviet relations 1944–1971*, Kent, Ohio 1975, pp. 166–170, and the articles therein cited.

7. C. Wiklund, 'The zig-zag course of the Nordek negotiations', *Scandinavian Political Studies*, Vol. 5, 1970, pp. 307–36; Maude, op. cit., pp. 115–17.

8. Maude, op. cit., pp. 77–91. On the Finnish view of the European Security Conference, see the section devoted to this in *Yearbook of Finnish Foreign Policy 1975*, Helsinki 1976, pp. 32–65.

9. As for instance in the *Bundesrepublik*, where the C.S.U. chairman Franz-Josef Strauss used the term in the 1970 electoral campaign as a warning of the consequences for Germany of the *Ostpolitik* of Willy Brandt. H. Hakovirta, *Suomettuminen*, Jyväskylä 1975, pp. 24ff.

10. W. Laqueur, 'Europe: the specter of Finlandization', *Commentary*, vol. 64, no. 6, 1977, pp. 37–41. See also R. Aron, 'Vers un nouvel ordre européen', *Le Figaro*, 6 October 1971.

11. *Neutrality, the Finnish position*, p. 177.

12. Maude, op. cit., pp. 68–9. O. Apunen, 'Some conclusions about the Komissarov debate', *Yearbook of Finnish Foreign Policy 1976*, Helsinki 1977, pp. 14–19. A. Rosas, *Sodanaikainen puolueettomuus ja puolueettomuuspolitiikka*, Turku 1978, provides interesting information on the reports of the Defence Committees of the *Eduskunta* (1971 and 1976) and the 1963 Neutrality Statute, all of which seem to reinforce the desire to remain outside conflict at all costs.

13. R. Hyvärinen, 'Urho Kekkonen's Eastern Policy' in *Urho Kekkonen. A statesman for peace*, London 1975, p. 61.

14. Lecture given by Erik Allardt in London, 5 December 1977.
15. Laqueur, op. cit., p. 39. For a detailed analysis of incidents of self-censorship, see A. Küng, *Mitä Suomessa tapahtuu*, Helsinki 1976, pp. 216–74.
16. For a recent left-wing critique of the Paasikivi-Kekkonen line, see the interview with Antero Jyränki, 'Presidentin vallanraamit', *Helsingin Sanomat*, 12 February 1978. Maude, op cit., pp. 116–17, 141.
17. N. Örvik, *Sicherheit auf finnisch*, Stuttgart 1972, p. 136.
18. H. Hartovirta, 'Suomalaisen parlamentarismin kriisi' in *Suomen*. H. Hartovirta, T. Koskiaho (eds), *Suomen hallitukset ja hallitusohjelmat 1945–1973*. Helsinki 1973, p. 128. In recent years, cautious advances towards the idea of co-operation with the Communists in government have been made by the conservatives, but with little success. Both parties remain 'prisoners' of the system, dependent on the Agrarian-social democratic axis for inclusion in government.
19. P. Hynynen, 'Popular Front in Finland', *New Left Review*, no. 57, 1969, pp. 3–20, J. Hodgson, 'Finnish communism and electoral politics', *Problems of Communism*, no. 23, 1974, pp. 34–45.
20. P. Kuusi, *Social policy for the sixties*, Kuppio 1964, p. 139.
21. On the problems of Finland's foreign trade, see Maude, op. cit., pp. 95–104; P. Laitinen, 'Finland's international economic relations 1956–1975' in *Urho Kekkonen. A statesman for peace*, pp. 162–86. See also Appendix D for details of foreign trade.
22. I. Hustich, *Finland förvandlas*, Helsingfors 1967, pp. 49–56.
23. See Kuusi, op. cit. pp. 79–82 for extracts from Lehtonen's *Putkinotko*, (1918) and Kianto's *Ryysyrannan Jooseppi* (1923).
24. H. Waris, *Muuttuva suomalainen yhteiskunta*, Porvoo-Helsinki 1968, p. 78.
25. P. Kähkölä, T. Pihlajaniemi, S. Pyyluoma, *Toinen tasavalta*, Helsinki 1976, pp. 170–1.
26. 'Turvallisuuspolitiikkaan liittyviä mielipiteitä 1964–1974', *Henkinen maanpuolustus. Katsauksia*, no. 1, Helsinki 1975, 28 pp.
27. C.-G. Lilius, 'Self-censorship in Finland', *Index on Censorship*, Vol. 4, No. 1, 1975, p. 25. Lilius is himself a Finnish artist and writer.
28. 'Keskustelu Tamminiemessä', *Helsingin Sanomat*, 9 October 1977.

SELECT BIBLIOGRAPHY

Authors whose works are referred to in the text are indicated by an asterisk.

General

M. Klinge, *Bernadotten ja Leninin välissä*, Porvoo–Helsinki 1975. General essays on the theme of national identity.

E. Jutikkala (ed.)*, *Suomen talous—ja sosiaalihistorian kehityslinjoja*, Porvoo–Helsinki 1968. A general textbook on aspects of social and economic history.

E. Jutikkala, *Suomen talonpojan historia*, Helsinki 1958. A history of the Finnish peasantry.

J. Nousiainen, *The Finnish political system*, Cambridge, Mass., 1971.

L. Puntila, *The political history of Finland 1809–1966*, London 1975.

K. Wahlbäck*, *Från Mannerheim till Kekkonen. Huvudlinjer i finländsk politik, 1917–1967*, Stockholm 1967.

Chapter 1. THE BACKGROUND: FINLAND IN 1900

A. Kollontay*, *Zhizn' finlyandskikh rabochikh*, St. Petersburg 1903.

V. Rasila, *Suomen torpparikysmys vuoteen 1909*, Helsinki 1961, with English summary: 'Finland's crofter question up to 1909'.

R. Schweitzer, *Autonomie und Autokratie. Die Stellung des Grossfürstentums Finnland im russischen Reich in der zweiten Hälfte des 19. Jahrhunderts (1863–1899)*, Giessen 1978.

J. Screen, *The entry of Finnish officers into Russian military service 1809–1917*. London 1976 (duplicated).

J. Snellman*, *Samlade arbeten*, 10 vols., Helsingfors 1894–8.

A. Soininen, *Vanha maataloutemme*, Helsinki 1974, with English summary: 'Old traditional agriculture in Finland in the eighteenth and nineteenth centuries'.

H. Waris, *Työläisyhteiskunnan syntyminen Helsingen Pitkänsillan pohjoispuolella*, Helsinki 1973, second revised edition. A sociological study of a working-class community in Helsinki from the 1870s to the 1930s.

Chapter 2. OPPRESSION AND RESISTANCE: THE LAST YEARS OF AUTONOMY 1900–1917

W. Copeland, *The uneasy alliance. Collaboration between the Finnish opposition and the Russian underground 1899–1904*, Helsinki 1973.

L. Harmaja, *The effects of the war on economic and social life in Finland*, New Haven 1933.

G. Maude★, 'The Finnish question in British political life, 1899–1914', *Turun Historiallinen Arkisto*, no. 28, Turku 1973.

V. Rasila, *Torpparikysmyksen ratkaisuvaihe*, Helsinki 1970, with English summary: 'The solution of the Finnish crofter problem'.

H. Soikkanen, *Sosialismin tulo Suomeen*, Porvoo–Helsinki 1961. The early history of the labour movement and the Social Democratic Party.

J. Teljo, *Suomen valtioelämän murros 1905–1908*, Porvoo–Helsinki 1949. Parliamentary reform, and the first *Eduskunta*.

P. Tommila (ed.), *Venäläinen sortokausi Suomessa*, Porvoo–Helsinki 1960. Essays on the period 1899–1916.

Chapter 3. A HARD-WON INDEPENDENCE 1917–1920

K. Hovi★, 'The winning of Finnish independence as an issue in international relations', *Scandinavian Journal of History*, vol. 3, no. 1, 1978.

M. Jääskeläinen, *Die Ostkarelische Frage*, Helsinki 1965.

V. Kholodkovsky, *Revolyutsiya v Finlyandii i germanskaya interventsiya*, Moscow 1967.

E. Lyytinen★, 'Finland in British politics in world war one and its aftermath', unpublished D.Phil. thesis, University of Oxford 1973.

J. Paasivirta, *Suomen itsenäisyyskysymys vuonna 1917*, 2 vols., Porvoo–Helsinki 1947, 1949.

J. Paasivirta, *Suomi vuonna 1918*, Porvoo–Helsinki 1957. Paasivirta's three books cover the winning of independence, the civil war and the aftermath.

T. Polvinen, *Venäjän vallankumous ja Suomi*, 2 vols., Porvoo–Helsinki 1967, 1961. Finland and the Russian revolution, 1917–1920.

V. Rasila, *Kansalaissodan sosiaalinen tausta*, Helsinki 1968. A study of the 'social background' of the civil war, using factor analysis.

R. Ullman, *Anglo-Soviet relations 1917–1921*, 3 vols., Princeton N.J., 1961, 1968, 1974.

Chapter 4. THE FIRST DECADE OF INDEPENDENCE 1918–1928

R. Alapuro★, *Akateeminen Karjala-Seura*, Porvoo–Helsinki 1973.

D. Arter★, *Bumpkin against bigwig. The emergence of a green movement in Finnish politics*, University of Tampere Institute of Political Science Research Reports 1978 (duplicated).

J. Hodgson, *Communism in Finland. A history and an interpretation*, Princeton, N.J. 1967.

L. Hyvämäki, *Sinistä ia mustaa*, Helsinki 1971. Essays on aspects of right-wing radicalism.

M. Klinge*, *Vihan veljistä valtiososialismiin*, Porvoo-Helsinki 1972. Essays on Finnish nationalism and russophobia.

S. Lindman, *Parlamentarismens tillämpning i Finland 1919–1926*, Åbo 1937.

Y. Ruutu*, *Uusi suunta. Suomalaisen yhteiskuntaohjelman ääriviivoja*, Helsinki 1920. A blueprint for Finnish society.

G. Schauman, *Kampen om statsskicket i Finland 1918*, Helsingfors 1924.

Chapter 5. CRISIS AND RECOVERY 1929–1939

P. Hirvikallio, *Tasavallan presidentin vaalit Suomessa 1919–1950*, Helsinki 1958. Presidential elections in Finland 1919–1950.

P.-K. Hämäläinen*, *Kielitaistelu Suomessa 1917–1939*, Porvoo-Helsinki 1968. The language conflict in Finland during the interwar years.

J. Hampden Jackson*, *Finland*, London 1938.

M. Jääskeläinen, *Itsenäisyyden ajan eduskunta 1919–1938*, Helsinki 1973. The seventh volume of the history of popular representation in Finland.

J. Kalela*, 'Right-wing radicalism in Finland during the interwar period', *Scandinavian Journal of History*, vol. 1, nos. 1–2, 1976.

M. Rintala*, *Three generations: the extreme right in Finnish politics*, Bloomington 1962.

H. Soikkanen, *Kohti kansanvaltaa*, vol. 1: 1899–1937, Helsinki 1975. A history of the Social Democratic Party.

Chapter 6. FINLAND AND HER NEIGHBOURS 1920–1948

W. Carlgren*, *Swedish foreign policy during the Second World War*, London 1977.

M. Jakobson, *The diplomacy of the Winter War*, Cambridge, Mass., 1961.

K. Korhonen, *Suomi neuvostodiplomatiassa Tartosta talvisotaan*, 2 vols., Helsinki 1966, 1971. Finland in Soviet foreign policy 1920–39.

H. Krosby*, *Finland, Germany and the Soviet Union 1940–1941: The Petsamo dispute*, Madison 1968.

J. Nevakivi, *The appeal that was never made*, London 1976.

J. Nevakivi, *Ystävistä vihollisiksi. Suomi Englannin politiikassa*, Helsinki 1976. Anglo-Finnish relations, 1941–4.

T. Polvinen*, *Suomi suurvaltojen politiikassa 1941–1944*, Porvoo-Helsinki 1964. Finnish policy during the Continuation War.

H. Seppälä, *Itsenäisen Suomen puolustuspolitiikka ja strategia*, Porvoo-Helsinki 1974. Defence policy and strategic thinking in independent Finland.

J. Suomi, *Talvisodan tausta. Neuvostoliitto Suomen ulkopolitiikassa*, vol. 1, Helsinki 1973. Soviet-Finnish relations 1938–9.

J. Söderhjelm, *Tre resor till Moskva*, Helsingfors 1970.

A. Upton*, *Finland in crisis 1940–1941*, London 1964.

A. Upton, *Finland 1939–1940*, London 1974.

Chapter 7. RECASTING THE MOULD 1940–1960

E. Allardt*, 'Social sources of Finnish communism', *International Journal of Comparative Sociology*, no. 1, 1964.

A. Eskola*, *Maalaiset ja kaupunkilaiset*, Helsinki 1963. A sociological study of attitudes and prejudices of rural and city dwellers in Finland.

H. Hakovirta, T. Koskiaho (eds.)*, *Suomen hallitukset ja hallitusohjelmat 1945–1973*, Helsinki 1973. Essays on the formation and cohesion of governments in Finland.

T. Heikkilä, *Paasikivi peräsimessä*, Helsinki 1965. A political biography of Paasikivi in office after 1944.

L. Hyvämäki*, *Vaaran vuodet 1944–1948*, Helsinki 1954. An account of the postwar years in Finland.

S. Klockare, *Yleislakosta kansanrintamaan*, Helsinki 1972. The trade union movement from the mid-fifties to the mid-sixties.

E. Linkomies*, *Vaikea aika. Suomen pääministerinä sotavuosina 1943–1944*, Helsinki 1970. A prime minister remembers.

J. Nousiainen*, *Kommunismi Kuopion läänissä*, Joensuu 1956. A study of backwoods communism in eastern Finland.

T. Perko, *Aseveljen kuva. Suhtautuminen Saksaan jatkosodan Suomessa 1941–1944*, Porvoo–Helsinki 1971. The German image in Finland during the Continuation War.

P. Sorvali, *Niukkasesta Kekkoseen*, Helsinki 1975. Agrarian Party politics in the decade following 1944.

A. Upton*, *Communism in Scandinavia and Finland*, London 1973.

Chapter 8. THE KEKKONEN ERA

D. Anckar*, *Partiopinioner och utrikespolitik*, Åbo 1971.

O. Apunen, *Paasikiven-Kekkosen linja*, Helsinki 1977. A broad survey of postwar Finnish foreign policy.

H. Hakovirta, *Suomettuminen*, Jyväskylä 1975. A survey of the debate on Finlandisation.

H. Hakovirta, R. Väyrynen (eds.), *Suomen ulkopolitiikka*, Helsinki 1975. Essays on aspects of foreign policy.

M. Jakobson*, *Finnish neutrality*, London 1968.

J. Komissarov*, *Suomi löytää linjansa*, Helsinki 1974. A Soviet view of Finnish foreign policy.

P. Kuusi*, *Social policy for the sixties*, Kuopio 1964.

G. Maude*, *The Finnish dilemma. Neutrality in the shadow of power*, London 1976.

N. Örvik*, *Sicherheit auf finnisch*, Stuttgart 1972.

K. Törnudd*, *Soviet attitudes towards non-military regional co-operation*, Helsinki 1961.

D. Vital*, *The survival of small states*, London 1971.

J. Vloyantes*, *Silk glove hegemony. Finnish-Soviet relations 1944–1974*, Kent, Ohio 1975.

U. Wagner, *Finnlands Neutralität*, Hamburg 1974.

H. Waris, *Muuttuva suomalainen yhteiskunta*, Porvoo–Helsinki 1968. A general survey of changing Finnish society.

INDEX